International Organizations

D0166180

Now in its third edition, this leading undergraduate textbook has been revised and updated throughout to take account of recent developments in world politics. Concise and engagingly written, the book is core reading for courses on international organizations, international law and politics, and global governance. Unlike other textbooks in the field, it takes readers behind the scenes of the world's most important international institutions to explore their legal authority and the political controversies that they generate. It presents chapter-length case studies of the world's leading international organizations with attention to the legal, political, and practical aspects. The new edition features new case material on Brexit, the Argentine sovereign debt, the Syrian war, the cholera in Haiti, and more, and adds depth to the discussion of international relations theory.

Ian Hurd is Associate Professor of Political Science and Director of the International Studies program at Northwestern University. He is an award-winning teacher and researcher on international law, politics, and international relations. He has written several books on the UN Security Council and is the co-editor of *The Oxford Handbook of International Organizations*. His latest book is *How to do Things with International Law*.

International Organizations

POLITICS, LAW, PRACTICE

Third Edition

Ian Hurd

CAMBRIDGE
UNIVERSITY PRESS

University Printing House, Cambridge CB2 8BS, United Kingdom

One Liberty Plaza, 20th Floor, New York, NY 10006, USA

477 Williamstown Road, Port Melbourne, VIC 3207, Australia

314–321, 3rd Floor, Plot 3, Splendor Forum, Jasola District Centre, New Delhi – 110025, India

79 Anson Road, #06–04/06, Singapore 079906

Cambridge University Press is part of the University of Cambridge.

It furthers the University's mission by disseminating knowledge in the pursuit of education, learning, and research at the highest international levels of excellence.

www.cambridge.org
Information on this title: www.cambridge.org/9781107183308
DOI: 10.1017/9781316869604

First edition published 2011
Second edition published 2016
Third edition published 2018
3rd printing 2018

Printed in the United Kingdom by TJ International Ltd. Padstow Cornwall

A catalogue record for this publication is available from the British Library.

Library of Congress Cataloging-in-Publication Data
Names: Hurd, Ian, author.
Title: International organizations : politics, law, practice / Ian Hurd.
Description: Third edition. | New York, NY : Cambridge University Press, 2017.
Identifiers: LCCN 2017014552| ISBN 9781107183308 (Hardback) | ISBN 9781316634455 (Paperback)
Subjects: LCSH: International agencies. | International organization. | BISAC: POLITICAL SCIENCE / International Relations / General.
Classification: LCC JZ4850 .H87 2017 | DDC 341.2 LC record available at https://lccn.loc.gov/2017014552

ISBN 978-1-107-18330-8 Hardback
ISBN 978-1-316-63445-5 Paperback

Contents

Preface

This book examines each of the main global international organizations. It looks at the legal rules that constitute the United Nations, the World Trade Organization and other institutions and then considers how these rules are used in practice to shape international politics. It is unique among textbooks on international organizations with its emphasis on the interaction between international politics and international law.

The book begins from the twin assumptions that international politics cannot be understood without thinking about international organizations, and that international organizations cannot be understood without thinking about their legal and their political features. From this starting point we get a clearer view into these organizations as power players in world politics and also how governments and others try to use them to advance their own interests. It also gives a window into deeper questions in international relations about the dynamics among power, interests, institutions, and actors.

Thinking about international organizations requires paying attention to power, law, politics, and more all at once. It needs practical as well as theoretical thinking. The chapters in this book look at the world of global governance with an eye on these big issues.

To see the big picture we must first see the details. And so each chapter tells stories from the daily life of the institution. For instance, we see how the government of Burma has manipulated the International Labor Organization around the problem of forced labor in that country. We also see how Japanese whale hunting got it in trouble with the International Court of Justice and how it tried to escape that trouble by claims its whaling is really about 'scientific research.' These and other stories provide the raw materials that we can use to construct our understanding of international organizations and from there to understand the bigger questions about international relations.

This third edition of the book brings it up to date with the rapidly changing world of international politics and law.

- The dramatic developments of Brexit are covered in Chapter 10 on the EU.
- A new case study in Chapter 3 looks at how the United Nations accidentally sparked a cholera epidemic in Haiti in 2010, and how its legal immunities make it impossible for the victims to get compensation from the organization.
- The ongoing Syrian war involves international organizations on both the security and the humanitarian fronts, and it is discussed at length in a new case in Chapter 4.
- The debt crisis has reshaped the landscape for international financial institutions in recent years and Chapter 6 includes a new section that details the Argentine default and restructuring. This helps understand the politics of financial flows as well as the role of international institutions in shaping the movement of money.
- The International Court of Justice was asked to rule on whether Japan was illegally hunting whales in the Southern Ocean. Chapter 8 includes a new case study of the dispute that ensued, pitting Australia and NGOs against Japan and its whaling industry.
- Chapter 1 directly challenges the common assumption that international organizations are naturally good and progressive. I call this the 'enchanted' attitude toward global governance and argue that it is important that we can get beyond it.

All of today's global issues are linked to the international organizations in this book. From human rights to financial flows to overfishing, a broad range of government decisions are influenced by the rules, decisions, and powers of international organizations: a government that wishes to subsidize a steel factory must consider how this fits with the rules of the World Trade Organization; Iceland's decision to allow whale hunting is causing problems in its application to join the European Union; the International Court of Justice has some say over the legal implications of Israel's wall inside the Palestinian territories; the International Criminal Court may have jurisdiction over US soldiers in Afghanistan.

The goal of the book is to understand the power and limits of these and other international organizations. Some institutions make major contributions, as when the International Criminal Court convicted Thomas Lubanga in 2012 for using children as soldiers in the Democratic Republic of Congo. Some are paralyzed by internal disagreement, as when the UN Security Council failed to either endorse or condemn the US invasion of Iraq in 2003. Some, such as the

International Labor Organization, survive by making relatively few demands on their member states.

Both the failures and the successes of international organizations stem from the rules and competencies set out in their legal charters, and from the interaction between these rules and the wider world of states and other kinds of actors. It is as important to understand why these organizations sometimes fail to take collective action as it is to understand when they act. For instance, the international response to the Libyan uprising in 2011 was very different than to the Syrian uprising a year later, and the reason for this has much to do with the internal rules of the UN Security Council: the permanent members of the Council were much more divided over what to do about Syria than they were about Libya. The Syrian civil war continues, while the Libyan civil war was ended by UN and NATO intervention and the conflict reopened soon after in new ways.

Despite the changes, the main goal and overall structure of the book remains the same: to understand the international organizations that operate in the most important areas of international policy-making, including trade, finance, courts, and international peace and security. Throughout, it strives for a realistic view of these organizations, one that neither overstates nor understates their power and influence.

To that end, each chapter first presents the legal foundation of the organization and then explores how it operates. The controversies that surround the organizations come out of the interaction between their legal powers and the political context in which they find themselves, the push and pull of motivated actors seeking to use the organization in the pursuit of some goals. What comes out of this interaction may be judged to be good or bad, or somewhere in between, but it is clear that one cannot make sense of contemporary global politics without understanding the network of inter-state institutions.

Acknowledgments

This book is a snapshot of a continuing conversation about international organizations that I have been lucky to have had with colleagues, students, and friends. I am particularly grateful to Michael Barnett, Martha Finnemore, José Alvarez, Ken Abbott, Karen Alter, Philippe Sands, Terry Halliday, Greg Shaffer, John Hagan, Bruce Carruthers, Bruce Russett, Alexander Wendt, Alexandre Grigorescu, Stephen Nelson, James Sutterlin, Jean Krasno, Roland Paris, M.J. Peterson, David Malone, Frédéric Mégret, and Hendrik Spruyt. In preparing the book I also wish to thank Sidra Hamidi for her excellent contribution to the new edition and Mitch Troup for assistance on the earlier editions.

1 Introduction to International Organizations

All international organizations exist in the conceptual and legal space between state sovereignty and legal obligation. They are created by the commitments made by sovereign states, and their purpose is to bind those states to their commitments. This chapter examines three forces in world politics: the commitments states make to international organizations, the choices states make regarding compliance and non-compliance with those commitments, and the powers of enforcement held by each international organization.

Some international organizations are able to coerce their member states into complying with their commitments; for instance, the UN Security Council has a military component and the IMF has coercive leverage over its borrowers. But far more commonly they are left to find ways to cajole or induce compliance from their members. In each organization, the particular relationship between obligation, compliance, and enforcement is different which in turn creates interesting patterns of politics between states and organizations.

The main problems of international economics and international politics are at some level also problems of international organization. As interdependence between states increases, the importance of international organizations increases with it. International organizations in one form or another are found at the heart of all of the political and economic challenges of the twenty-first century. From international credit markets to endangered species to war crimes and torture, today's leading controversies all involve some measure of international cooperation and commitment managed through formalized international organizations (IOs). Some IOs work well and some work hardly at all; some need reform, some need abolishing, and some need strengthening. To understand how the world works requires understanding the politics, powers, and limits of international organizations.

The book introduces eleven of the most important international organizations, including those most central to international economics, international security, and international law. It considers their legal powers, their practical effects, and their political controversies. The organizations are:

- the United Nations (UN),
- the World Trade Organization (WTO),
- the International Monetary Fund (IMF),
- the World Bank (WB),
- the European Union (EU),
- the International Court of Justice (ICJ),
- the International Criminal Court (ICC),
- the International Labor Organization (ILO),
- the Organization of American States (OAS),
- the African Union (AU), and
- the Association of Southeast Asian Nations (ASEAN).

Each chapter is structured around three key questions:

(1) What are the obligations that countries consent to when they join the organization?
(2) Do states in practice comply with these obligations?
(3) What powers of enforcement does the organization have when member states fail to comply?

This approach allows us to look at both the law and the politics of these organizations. It begins with an examination of the obligations that states take on when they become members of the organization. The details of these obligations come from the legal treaties and charters that found the organizations. These obligations are usually presented in clear language (for instance, the UN Charter says members must "refrain from the threat or use of force" to settle their disputes) but they inevitably leave a good deal of room for arguments over interpretation – for the Charter, we need to know much more about what counts as a "threat of force" and how self-defense should fit with this obligation.

Despite the ambiguity that exists in all these commitments, it is still useful to begin the study of international organizations by looking at what states have committed to doing or not doing. It is only through a familiarity with the legal terms of IO treaties that one can evaluate the competing claims put forward by states regarding those obligations. States show a strong inclination to present their own behavior as fully compliant with their legal obligations, and they equally often suggest that their counterparts in a dispute are breaking the law. Most IOs are not equipped with a legal body that has the authority to make authoritative judgments in disputes over compliance (the EU and the WTO stand out as exceptions to this rule). Most often, contestation over compliance spills over from the organization to the wider worlds of international law and international politics. International organizations are also usually given only very weak instruments of enforcement, and they rely on more subtle tools that work through persuasion, reputation, and status in order to induce compliance. As a result, the politics of compliance with international organizations are complicated and represent the fusion of legal interpretation and political practice.

Obligations

The treaties that provide the foundation to each of these international organizations set the starting point for studying their powers and effects. The UN Charter, the IMF Articles of Agreement, the Rome Statute of the ICC, and others spell out the commitments that member states are taking on and the powers that are being granted to the organizations themselves. Once in place, the activities of the organization are governed by the terms of the treaty, and the obligations of the members are defined by the commitments they made there. As a result, any examination of the powers and problems of international organizations must begin with the rules included in the treaties. These rules range from the commitment in the UN Charter to "accept and carry out the decisions of the Security Council" (Art. 25), to the commitments that states make with the International Monetary Fund that require policy changes in exchange for loans, to the promise to bring new labor conventions proposed by the International Labor Organization to one's national legislature for consideration (Art. 19 of the ILO Constitution).

The IOs in this book were all founded by inter-state treaties. These treaties spell out in explicit, "black-letter" law the goals and powers of the organization and the obligations and rules that member states must take on. When governments join international organizations, they promise to accept the rules and obligations that are in these treaties. These may include rules that are explicitly set out in the treaty, as when the Statute of the International Court of Justice says that decisions of the Court are final and binding on the states in the dispute

(Arts. 59 and 60), and they may as well include indirect obligations that arise in the course of the operation of the organization, as when the UN Charter gives the Security Council the authority to create new legal obligations on UN members (Arts. 25, 39, 49). The former are known in advance by states when they join the organization, while the latter are more open-ended and involve some risk that future practice might create obligations on states that they were not expecting. In both cases, however, it is imperative to any understanding of the role and power of the organization that one pay close attention to its founding treaty. The legal terms in each treaty are the authoritative source of the obligations that states owe to each other and will be finely parsed long into the future by diplomats, activists, and states who look to use them to serve their own purposes.

When assessing the impact of international organizations, it is important to be realistic about these obligations. It is easy to criticize the UN General Assembly, for instance, on the grounds that it passes many resolutions that governments then fail to implement. However, this complaint makes little sense when we remember that the UN Charter gives the General Assembly (GA) only the power to "make recommendations" to states, and does not give it the power to take decisions or impose new obligations (Art. 10). UN members are not legally obligated to carry out General Assembly resolutions. As we shall see in Chapter 3, many of the UN's member states would likely not have joined the organization if the General Assembly had been given the power to compel them through binding resolutions. The existence of the GA with its majority-rule voting system is premised on it being a body that makes recommendations rather than one that takes binding decisions. The Assembly's influence therefore cannot realistically be assessed by measuring compliance and non-compliance with its resolutions – it should instead be assessed in light of the more subtle power it has to define legitimate and illegitimate behavior, and the contribution that this makes to the broader political environment of state behavior.

For example, it is difficult to understand US behavior toward the International Criminal Court without close attention to the how the Rome Statute defines the powers of the Court relative to the states that are its members.[1] The US helped create the Court, signed (but didn't ratify and subsequently withdrew from) the Rome Statute, and professes a strong affinity with the goals of

---

[1] William A. Schabas, *An Introduction to the International Criminal Court.* Cambridge University Press, 2007.

the organization. It has used it via the UN Security Council with respect to Sudan, Darfur, and Libya. And yet it is highly ambivalent toward the organization itself, and we can expect more hostility to it throughout the Trump presidency. The US has refused to become a member and for several years it actively sought to punish governments that did choose to become members. These apparently contradictory positions toward the ICC can be reconciled by looking at the particular obligations of members set out in the Rome Statute in light of the official American view that the Rome Statute gives too much autonomy to the ICC's prosecutor and judges. A complex balance between state power and prosecutor's power is defined deep in the fine print of the treaty. The technical language in the Statute where states' obligations are defined has political implications in international relations that go beyond the formal bounds of the organization.

Compliance

With a well-grounded understanding of the legal obligations of states, we can then consider why, when, and how well states comply with those obligations. Compliance is almost always looked at as a choice of states, but this book also looks at how IOs might shape world politics in ways that are not understood by the imagery of "choice." There are two moments where state consent is explicit in and around international organizations: at the moment of joining the organization, and at the point where states see the opportunity to follow or to violate its rules. There are also many moments where governments find themselves operating on an international political terrain that is shaped by international organizations, where IO effects are structural and constitutive and thus inescapable for states.

It is common to think about international organization at those moments where a state is faced with strong incentives to go against some rule of an international organization. This is often in the context of an international crisis where a country wants to violate the rules. This was the case, for instance, with the American decision to invade Iraq in 2003 in the face of the UN Security Council's refusal to grant it the necessary authorization. These are often dramatic moments as they pit state choices directly against international rules. Not surprisingly, the record of state compliance with IOs at such moments is mixed: given sufficient incentive, states are often willing to ignore their legal obligations – though we should not ignore those very interesting (and probably equally frequent) instances where states choose to comply despite the incentive to violate. The chapters which follow examine these moments of choice, where states are faced with a choice between compliance and violation. However, they also do more by examining how international organizations influence the resources with which states conduct their disputes and therefore how state behavior is understood.

The focus on these moments of explicit consent or choice by states does not account for everything of interest that passes in the relationship between states and international organizations. Therefore, each chapter of this book also looks at more subtle ways that international organizations influence the behavior of states and other actors in world politics. Many of the interesting effects that IOs have on states occur in a different register than that of conscious strategic choice – the organizations in this book all operate in part by shaping the environment in which states exist, the interests and goals states have, and the background sense of what is reasonable and normal in international politics. For instance, the decisions of the UN Security Council over the years have helped construct the idea of humanitarian intervention and as a result the international response to new crises is heavily conditioned by this idea and by its limits.[2] Similarly, the ICJ advisory opinion on the legality of the Israeli wall was not legally binding on Israel but it has made it more politically costly for the government of Israel to continue with policies that were criticized by the Court. These effects can sometimes be subtle, but they are an important component of the practical life of modern international relations and they must be taken into account as we consider the effects of IOs in the world. To understand the power of international organizations, as well as the controversies around them, it is important to be attentive to these more subtle effects as well as the more dramatic moments where states choose to violate or comply with their obligations.

Enforcement

It is rare that international organizations are constituted in such a way that they can take effective enforcement action against states who fail to live up to their

---

[2] See Martha Finnemore, *The Purpose of Intervention.* Cornell University Press, 2003.

obligations. A few do have robust means of enforcing the rules against violators: for instance, the IMF can withhold further loans from a state that fails to fulfill the terms of previous loans; the UN Security Council can authorize military action against a state that threatens international peace and security (such a threat is by itself a violation of the Charter); and the WTO can authorize trade sanctions against members who violate their commitments. But the more normal condition is that members face at most a very indirect threat of punishment for their violations – for instance, the loss of reputation that might come from being publicly branded as a rule-breaker.[3] IO enforcement often involves playing on the apparent desire of states to be seen in a positive light, as good international citizens. This may be very powerful indeed, but it follows a different logic than more direct kinds of enforcement threats.

The absence of direct enforcement power is often held up as evidence of the irrelevance, or at least the marginal importance, of international organizations and as a justification for paying little attention to their rules and decisions. Without the threat of enforcement, why would states ever concede to international organizations when their interests point in the direction of violation? It is easy to dispense with this objection on empirical grounds – that is, it is easy to show that states do indeed often comply with international organizations despite the lack of enforcement. The examples in this book show this in action.

What is harder to explain is *why* they do it. For example, most countries that lose a case at the International Court of Justice end up changing their policies as required by the Court despite the fact that the ICJ's powers of enforcement are essentially nil.[4] Why this result obtains is hard to know. It may be that states feel highly committed to the idea of the rule of law and so they are naturally motivated to follow through with Court rulings. It may be that states fear that other countries will be less inclined to enter into agreements with them if they are thought to have reneged on commitments in the past. It is easy to hypothesize plausible reasons but impossible to test among them. It may be that the only cases that make it all the way through the ICJ process are ones that the parties are comfortable having resolved by the Court, in which case the compliance rate is merely an artifact of the selection process that filters its cases. Any of these mechanisms might produce the high rate of "compliance without enforcement" that we observe around the ICJ. They differ greatly, though, in what they mean

---

[3] On the force of reputation, see Andrew Guzman, *How International Law Works: A Rational Choice Theory.* Oxford University Press, 2008.

[4] Nagendra Singh, *The Role and Record of the International Court of Justice.* Springer, 1989.

for the power and authority of the Court. And to figure out which one is the correct explanation for any particular case requires a close look at the working of the ICJ and at the details of the case and its parties. This kind of examination is done in Chapter 8 of this book.

Sovereignty and Consent

The tensions between state obligations and state sovereignty provide the fuel that drives world politics in and around international organizations. State sovereignty is defined by the legal and normative framework that constitutes states as the final authority over their territory and the people within it. States are sovereign in the sense that they are not subject to any higher political or legal authority. As a result, they have the exclusive right to make decisions over all domestic matters without interference from the outside. Attempts by other states to apply their laws or policies across the border are usually seen as illegal and possibly aggressive moves of extra-territoriality.

The laws and practices of state sovereignty lead to a clear distinction between domestic and foreign affairs. This is as clear (in concept, at least) as the borders on the map that delineate physical territory into separate countries.

Sovereignty is an international institution in the broadest sense of the word "institution": it is a set of rules that organizes social and political practice. It is not, however, a formal organization as I use the term in this book. The institution of sovereignty demarcates a domestic realm in which states have absolute authority and an international realm in which the problems of interdependence get worked out. In practice, of course, there is always some room for argument about the limits of the domestic sphere and of the absoluteness of sovereignty over domestic affairs themselves. The following chapters show that a good deal of the work of international organizations arises because of such arguments. For instance, since changes in one state's domestic monetary policy (such as the interest rate) can have large and immediate effects on the economic conditions in other states, it is not self-evident how to draw the line between the rights of one state to set its own policies and the rights of others to be independent from outside influence. Indeed, its not clear what autonomy can possibly mean in circumstances of interdependence. The inability to control one's own internal conditions is the premise of international interdependence in the first place.

The principle of non-intervention is a logical corollary of state sovereignty. It is clear what non-intervention means when it comes to military invasion from the outside, but its implications are less clear when it comes to the more complex forms of cross-border influence that arise under conditions of "complex interdependence" as they exist today.[5] Where cross-border flows exist – formal and informal, licit and illicit, of goods, people, ideas, and money – non-intervention across borders in any strict sense is inconceivable. The demand for international organizations arises due to the unavoidable interdependencies between states, and their utility is measured by their contribution to managing them.

Because states are understood to be the highest political and legal authorities in the modern states system, the rules of international law and of international organizations are always subordinate to the rights of states. This creates many of the tensions that animate world politics. To the extent that international laws exist, they exist because states have consented to them, and (for the most part) international laws apply only to those states that have consented to them. State consent is therefore the crucial element that brings international obligations into existence.

Exceptions to this generalization are revealing: for instance, the UN Charter includes a clause that requires that members of the organization "shall ensure that states which are not Members of the United Nations act in accordance with" the principles of the UN Charter (Art. 2(6)). This article is written carefully so that it creates a legal obligation on members rather than non-members, and is therefore consistent with the traditional interpretation of sovereignty, but its effect is to set some standards of behavior on non-members. Its status is provocatively ambiguous. As a general rule, however, international organizations create obligations on states only because the states have agreed to be bound by them.

Under the system of state sovereignty, states are free to withhold or to withdraw their consent to these rules as they see fit. This leads to the familiar problem of international organization (and of international law more generally) of figuring out how an IO can enforce its rules against a member state whose subordination under the rules rests on its consent to them. State sovereignty both empowers international law (when states consent to be bound by the rules of an international organization) and undermines it (when states withdraw or withhold that consent so that the rule ceases to apply to them). All of the

---

[5] Robert O. Keohane and Joseph S. Nye, *Power and Interdependence*, 3rd edn. Longman, 2000.

politics, practice, and law of international organizations take place in the puzzling shadow of state consent.

Consent is evident in the choice to join or not join an international organization. This is presumably based on a national-level assessment of the state's interests. Switzerland, for instance, for many years declined to join the United Nations, and it changed its position only in 2002. The organization and its existing members may set rules on which states they will accept as members, and when a state refuses to join an organization, it generally has no legal obligation to pay any attention to what it says. Interests and choices are evident again in a more micro-fashion each time a member state is confronted with the need to comply or not comply with the rules or decisions of an organization. The choice to join and the choice to comply lead to distinct conversations about violation and compliance: states are violating their international obligations when they break rules that they have consented to, but it cannot be said that they are breaking the rules if they have chosen not to join the organization in the first place. The need to consent means that states can choose to violate international rules, and they can also choose to make the rules not apply to them. The second form probably should not be counted as a violation of international law.

The difference is interesting in the practice of world politics. For instance, Canada has long accepted that the International Court of Justice has automatic jurisdiction over its legal disputes with governments that have similarly accepted this automatic jurisdiction. This is known as an "optional clause" declaration under the ICJ Statute and is described in Chapter 8. Canada's commitment dates back to at least 1930, when it made this commitment to the ICJ's precursor: the Permanent Court of International Justice. In the early 1990s, however, Canada developed an interest in reducing fishing in the North Atlantic, including by foreign fishing vessels on the high seas. Extending its governance of fishing beyond Canadian waters was legally suspicious, and so in anticipation of legal challenges Canada sent a memo to the ICJ that excluded from its promise any "disputes arising out of or concerning conservation and management measures taken by Canada with respect to vessels fishing in" the area of the North Atlantic.[6] This was in 1994. The following year a brouhaha arose when Canada seized a Spanish trawler and arrested its crew for fishing on

---

[6] See American Society of International Law Insights, December 1998, www.asil.org/insigh28.cfm. Accessed March 24, 2009.

the high seas. When Spain complained to the ICJ that this was illegal, the judges there refused to consider the case because of the Canadian memo.[7] The Canadian move was entirely unilateral and entirely legal, and it had the effect of eliminating the legal obligation on Canada to accept that the case could be heard by the ICJ. Where Canada previously had a legal obligation to accept ICJ jurisdiction, by this move it no longer had any such obligation.

North Korea similarly redefined its legal obligations when it withdrew from the Non-Proliferation Treaty in 1993. It went from having a legal obligation not to develop a nuclear weapon (an obligation which it was violating at the time) to having no such legal obligation. It could therefore no longer be accused of breaking international law with respect to nuclear proliferation, even though its policies on nuclear development remained the same. Consider also that the US cannot be accused of violating the Rome Statute of the International Criminal Court, since it is neither a party to nor even a signatory of that treaty.[8] While other states have obligations to the Court, the US has none. These illustrations show a more general fact about international law and politics: state sovereignty is such that governments can withdraw their consent from some international obligations and thereby eliminate obligations that they find unacceptable.

International organizations are thus fraught with conceptual and practical problems. They exist only because states have created them, and their powers apply only to the extent that states consent to them. They remain forever legally subordinate to the states. At the same time, their reason for being is to regulate those same states and to require (or to encourage) them to behave differently than they would in the absence of the organization. When states choose to ignore the commitments they have made to international organizations, IOs are expected to find some way to force them to change their policies and comply. Failing to do that is generally seen as a sign of weakness or even of failure in the organization. IOs are stuck in the position of trying to influence actors that have the legal right and perhaps also the political power to resist that influence. One goal of this book, therefore, is to explore how and why international

---

[7] Fisheries Jurisdiction (*Spain v. Canada*) 1995.

[8] The US under President B. Clinton signed the ICC Statute in 2000 and in 2002 the Bush administration attempted to withdraw that signature. This "unsigning" has few precedents in international law and it is not clear whether the US should be counted among its signatories or not.

organizations have succeeded in having as much influence as they have, given their inherent structural disadvantage vis-à-vis sovereign states.

"Enchanted" International Organizations

I do not assume that international organizations are any better than governments or any other entity or process at managing global issues. Instead, this book asks what IOs do, how they work, and where they come from. It does not presume that they are necessarily *good* in moral, political, or other terms. Whether IOs contribute to desirable outcomes is in this book treated as an empirical question – that is, as a matter for research and inquiry in specific cases – not a starting assumption.

It is surprising how often scholars adopt *a priori* a position *in favor* of IOs and global governance. They frequently follow a chain of reasoning that says since cooperation is better than conflict, and since IOs exist due to international cooperation, they must therefore be an improvement over whatever existed before the IO was invented. This leads to what I call the "enchanted" view of international law and global governance that celebrates IOs as the manifestation of international cooperation and promotes compliance with their rules as an inherently desirable policy choice.[9] This is evident whenever writers take it for granted that existing international organizations represent a progressive development toward desirable global order, without actually considering their real-world effects. If international law is seen as the foundation to a civilized world order and international organizations as the embodiment of cooperation, then compliance with them seems like the only sensible choice and anything that undercuts them is a danger.[10] This attitude was widely displayed around the British referendum on EU membership in 2016, which commentators with an enchanted view took as evidence of a step away from "peace in Europe . . . and global political order"[11] and as "politics" getting in the way of globalization.[12]

Instead, this book advances a "disenchanted" approach to international organizations, neither assuming that IOs represent progress nor that they only serve to limit state behavior. Instead, I suggest that international organizations

[9] Ian Hurd, "Enchanted and Disenchanted International Law," *Global Policy*, **7**(1), 2016.
[10] Hedley Bull.   [11] Roger Cohen, *New York Times*, June 24, 2016.
[12] Kevin Carmichael, *CIGI Online*, August 2016.

should be seen in the same way that one approaches other political institutions or instruments: they can be used for a wide range of purposes and their political effects depend on who is using them and for what ends. Their political outcomes depend on the political purposes to which they are put, which are presumably neither unambiguously good or bad. International organizations shape conflict as much as they shape cooperation. All substantive political decisions have their winners and losers and there is no reason to assume that the decisions of international organizations are any different. Together, these two features mean that it is not possible to conclude that international cooperation through existing international organizations is better than any other form of decision making until one looks at the specific substance of the organization in question as well as the interests it pursues and the distribution of benefits and costs that it imposes on the world. These are empirical questions that are worth investigating. The answers should not be assumed in advance.

Global Governance and International Organizations

The useful distinction is often made between global governance and international organization. Global governance refers to the broad range of rules and actors that make up the international regime on an issue. This is a capacious category with uncertain boundaries, and it could include many important international forces, actors, and rules. These might be formal and informal, explicit and implicit, regulative and constitutive, states and non-state, etc. The study of global governance is therefore often seen as a more comprehensive endeavor than is required to understand merely the official and formal international laws on an issue.[13] Formal international organization scholarship, by contrast, focuses on the particular rules that define or issue from a specific legal body such as the United Nations or the ICJ.

Each approach can have worthwhile results and the utility of each often depends on what question one is looking to answer. For instance, if the question

---

[13] Compare for instance the content of two scholarly journals *Global Governance* and the *Journal of International Organization Studies* (http://acuns.org/category/publications/global-governance-journal and www.journal-iostudies.org). The former generally aims at broader themes than the latter. See also Thomas Weiss and Ramesh Thakur, Global Governance and the UN: An Unfinished Journey. Indiana University Press, 2010.

is why did the United Nations fail to respond more effectively to the Rwandan genocide in 1994, the answer lies mainly in the legal rules that delimit the authority of the Security Council: the UN Charter assigns to the Security Council the authority to decide on military interventions on behalf of the United Nations, and then gives a veto over resolutions to all five permanent members. With the US and other strong states unwilling to support a forceful intervention in Rwanda as the genocide progressed, the only formal legal path to stop the genocidaires was closed and little could be done. For other questions, such as the globalization of labor standards, it makes little sense to focus on any particular international organization since most of the field is defined by the interests and actions of activist groups, firms, governments, and others. For still a third set of questions, both approaches may be necessary. For instance, to understand the development of international criminal law as it has evolved in the past fifty years, it is useful to understand both the formal rules of the new International Criminal Court as well as how domestic courts can play a role, and also the web of lawyers, laws, and advocacy groups that cross easily between the national and the international levels and between the formal and the informal domains. The rules on immunity for government officials, which play a large role in the Yerodia case study in Chapter 8, are customary international laws that are evident only by watching the long-term trends of behavior by specific states. They are not well suited to a formal approach to studying international organizations, though their effects were decisive in this case because they combined in a particular way with Article 38 of the ICJ Statute.

This book begins with a legalist's approach to the treaties and laws that frame the main international organizations, but it opens up with a political scientist's ambition to see how these formal devices shape the political environment and outcomes that make up international relations. The former rests in the traditional domain of the study of formal international organizations while the latter is the concern of "global governance." The book therefore seeks to show the importance of transcending the distinction between the "global government" as formal institutions and "governance" as a practice of power; to get to that point, however, it also makes the case that a close reading for the formal language of international legal agreements is a necessary step in the process.

Conclusion

The key questions about international organizations arise from the interaction between the obligations that states take on and the compliance and enforcement that may or may not follow from them. These questions apply to the full range of substantive problems in modern international relations. To understand (for instance) modern trade disputes, or the laws on the use of force, or the politics of conditionality in IMF loans, we must understand what commitments states make to international organizations as well as the ways these commitments shape their decisions, both toward compliance and non-compliance.

The treaties that establish international organizations are like partial constitutions of the international order. They set the basic rules for inter-state relations and they therefore define the obligations of states and also their general operating environment. Each is limited to its particular issue area, such as trade for the WTO, individual criminal behavior for the ICC, and inter-state legal disputes for the ICJ, and not all areas of world politics are covered by an international organization. This is a patchwork constitution with some topics largely ungoverned by formal international organizations because states have not been able to agree on a common set of commitments. That the treaties of international organizations are also the creation of states themselves, and that states remain sovereign both within and without the organizations, make the relationship between states and IOs interestingly complex. This book examines both the rules of IOs and the complexities of international law and politics that arise from them.

Further Reading

The design and administration of international organizations is covered at length in the essays in the exhaustive *Oxford Handbook of International Organizations* (Oxford University Press, 2016).

José Alvarez provides an excellent introduction to the tangled relationships among international organizations, international law, and international politics in *International Organizations as Law Makers* (Oxford University Press, 2006). The best overview of the legal powers of specific international organizations is Philippe Sands and Pierre Klein, *Bowett's Law of International Institutions* (Sweet & Maxwell, 6th edn.), 2009. Even more detailed is the ultra-complete reference book *Principles of the Institutional Law of International Organizations* by C. F. Amerasinghe (Cambridge University Press, 2nd edn., 2005).

For serious scholarship on international organizations by academics and practitioners, see the academic journals *Global Governance*, the *Journal of International Organization Studies*, and *Review of International Organizations*, among others. On current developments, the excellent blog opiniojuris.org hosts well-informed and timely discussions on international law which often involve aspects of organizations.

The international organizations of the nineteenth century, known as "public international unions," are extremely interesting and are discussed in Craig N. Murphy, *International Organization and Industrial Change: Global Governance since 1850* (Oxford University Press, 1994) and in the classic *Swords into Plowshares: The Problems and Progress of International Organization* by Inis L. Claude Jr. (Random House, 4th edn., 1988). Even earlier ideas of international cooperation and international society are discussed in Ian Clark, *Legitimacy in International Society* (Oxford University Press, 2005).

2 Theory, Methods, and International Organizations

International organizations shape the politics and controversies that arise among countries in a number of ways. They are sometimes powerful forces in their own right, as when an international court decides that a state is violating its legal obligations or when the UN sends peacekeepers to intervene in a conflict. They can also be centers where diplomacy and negotiation among states take place – this "forum" role accounts for part of the importance of the World Trade Organization and of the UN General Assembly. In still other situations, international organizations provide the tools or resources by which countries try to advance their interests in world politics. These diverse functions mean that the relations between states and international organizations can be studied from very different perspectives, with different emphases that produce different insights.

International organizations are diverse and sophisticated entities, with legal, political, and social dimensions that overlap and conflict in interesting ways. They vary widely in their substantive areas of authority, their internal structures, and their political salience. Their complexity allows for an equally complex field of study in which contrasting perspectives offer distinct emphases and tools of analysis, and which therefore come to very different interpretations of the same real-world patterns.

For all their differences, these organizations also all share some basic features. This leads on from the basic paradox of consent and obligation that was noted in Chapter 1: all the organizations in this book were (1) founded by states with an explicit inter-state treaty; (2) have states as their members; and (3) have independent corporate personalities. Taken together these mean that they exist as autonomous legal actors distinct from their members.

Jan Klabbers uses these three features to organize his excellent book on the law of international organizations.[1]

These features mean that formal international organizations are stuck in an eternal dilemma as their powers and existence are derivative of precisely those actors (i.e. states) that they are supposed to regulate (or govern, or influence). The existence of international organizations therefore raises deep conceptual questions about the nature of international politics and the capacity for international rules to bind or even coexist with sovereign states. Their powers are in principle devolved to them from nation-states but in practice are much more complex than that and may be either more or less than they appear on paper.

This chapter provides two ways for thinking about this complexity. First, it presents the leading theoretical approaches from the field of International Relations and considers what insight they provide into the world of international organizations. These theories (realism, liberalism, constructivism, and Marxism) should not be taken to provide competing accounts of the work of international organization. Rather, they are better seen as alternative attitudes regarding how to think about world politics more broadly. I draw out of these approaches implications for research on international organizations. On this question, the chapter shows how the diversity and complexity of IOs lead to a range of distinct methods and conceptual approaches to their study, and how these approaches in turn produce competing interpretations of the organizations' power, behavior, and impact. The chapter introduces the jargon and debates of academic studies of international organizations that are motivated by realist, liberal, constructivist, and Marxist premises and attitudes. In various manifestations, these represent the main currents of contemporary scholarship on international organizations. They help you guide your thinking about the role and power of international organizations.

The second half of the chapter gives three ways for answering the question "what *is* an international organization?" This is a question about the ontology of IOs, that is: what kind of a thing it is. The three answers I discuss are that IOs can be actors in their own right, or tools in the hands of other actors, or places where states come to hold meetings with other states. I call these three the *actor, resource,* and *forum* views of international organizations. The three are not necessarily mutually exclusive but they are often seen as alternatives in the interpretive lenses of scholars and also sometimes in the political strategies of states. For instance, at the inception of the International Criminal Court the US wanted it to be more of

---

[1] Jan Klabbers, *An Introduction to International Institutional Law.* Cambridge University Press, 2002.

a resource to be used by the UN Security Council and less of an actor with independent investigative and prosecutorial power, while the majority of states insisted it be an actor with the capacity to launch cases on its own initiative. It is inevitable that one take some position on this tripartite ontological starting point in order to study international organizations, even if only provisionally. It nevertheless has implications for research methods, concept formation, and even the empirical findings of scholarship.

IOs and International Theory

In social science, a theory is a set of ideas that simplifies the complexity of the world and gives suggestions for how to identify the key forces and actors within it. Different theories give different ideas about how the world can be understood and what to look for to make sense of it. These are sometimes in competition with each other – for instance, when Benedict Anderson presents nationalism as an "imagined community" in contrast to the linguistic nationalism of Johan Herder – but more often they direct us to ask different questions about an issue, and their distinct conclusions are a product of different assumptions about what is worth asking. Competing theories therefore might not generate competing answers. They may instead differ on what is an interesting question.

This section takes up some of the most familiar schools of thought from International Relations theory and examines their contribution to the study of international organizations. These are realism, liberalism, constructivism, and Marxism. Each of these is contested and none of them is entirely self-contained – defining them and drawing boundaries around them is somewhat controversial and arbitrary.[2] Nevertheless, this chapter makes an effort to organize each approach into a coherent set of ideas so that some key differences among them can be made clear.

Realism

The realist school of thought begins from a premise that states are motivated by a sense of their own insecurity to continually look for ways to increase their power. This is a claim that realism shares with most other approaches to international

---

[2] On the difficulty in defining IR theories, see Ian Hurd, "Constructivism," in Christian Reus-Smit and Duncan Snidal (eds.), *Oxford Handbook of International Organizations*. Oxford University Press, 2009, pp. 298–316.

politics and so it does not do much to help differentiate a realist approach to international organizations; more is needed. The distinctive feature of realism comes when realists offer a definition of what they mean by "power" in this formulation. For realists, power is understood in terms of material, military resources such as tanks and bombs, and in the contribution of these to the power or security of a country.

At this point, a distinctive perspective to international relations emerges: it suggests that international politics should be understood as the pursuit of military dominance by states in an effort to reduce their intrinsic sense of insecurity in relation to other countries. It is from this view of power that we can derive the central realist prediction: "that great powers will develop and mobilize military capabilities to constrain the most powerful among them."[3]

For the study of international organizations, this framing leads to two paths of research, one empirical and one normative. The empirical strand asks whether and how international organizations might influence the decisions of states as they pursue their military objectives relative to one another. Because of their interest in the material hierarchy of international politics, realists are particularly intrigued by the interests of the Great Powers (as opposed to small states or other kinds of actors).[4] International organizations are important in the realist perspective to the extent that they have implications for Great Powers' pursuit of material, military advantage over rivals. There is a great deal of debate over how much this exists, and it is basically an empirical question: do strong states defer to international organizations? To answer this question requires looking carefully to see how world politics is affected by the existence of international organizations.

The best realist scholarship aims to explore the nature and degree of this influence. Lloyd Gruber, for instance, finds that the existence of the Canada-US Free Trade Agreement gave the US more power in its negotiations with Mexico over NAFTA.[5] Robert Gilpin saw post-World War II international institutions as important investments in systemic stability made possible by, and in the interest of, American military power.[6] John Mearsheimer, relying more on logical deduction than on empirical evidence, comes to the general conclusion that "[international] institutions have a minimal influence on state behavior, and

---

[3] Stephen G. Brooks and William C. Wohlforth, *World out of Balance: International Relations and the Challenge of American Primacy*. Princeton University Press, 2008, p. 22.

[4] Barry Buzan, "Great Powers," in Alexandra Gheciu and William C. Wohlforth (eds.), *The Oxford Handbook of International Security*. Oxford University Press, 2018.

[5] Lloyd Gruber, *Ruling the World: Power Politics and the Rise of Supranational Institutions*. Princeton University Press, 2000.

[6] Robert Gilpin, *War and Change in World Politics*. Cambridge University Press, 1981.

thus hold little promise for promoting stability in the post-Cold War world."[7] This has produced a good deal of debate over the proper interpretation of the relationship between military power and international organizations.

The normative strand of realism promotes the view that international organizations should not be allowed to interfere with the military pursuit of great powers. This is essentially a nationalist position, and is represented in the US by the "new sovereigntist" group of neo-conservatives.[8] In this view, promoted by John Bolton in the policy world and Jack Goldsmith and Eric Posner in the academic world (among others), the entanglements of international organizations and international law should be resisted by the US, and international law should be used instrumentally to advance American interests.[9] This is a normative position in the sense that it advocates how the US should behave in the world. (There is an empirical version of this claim as well, which asks whether countries really do behave instrumentally toward international organizations – this scholarship is not very productive since it leads very quickly to a tautology: assuming that states take decisions based on perceptions of their interests, then anything they do toward international organizations must presumably be because they saw some interest in doing it, and it is conceptually impossible that they would act other than in their interests.[10])

The realist approach to international politics involves an ontological claim (that states are the starting point), a theory of their motivations (power-seeking due to insecurity) and a theory of what constitutes power (materiality). It is mainly the last of these that separates realism from other approaches, since state-centrism and a desire for power can feature equally in the other perspectives as well.

Liberalism

The liberal approach to world politics begins with an emphasis on the choices that actors make in the pursuit of their interests, in relation to the choices and interests of other actors. This generally means the choices of states but it can also refer to

---

[7] John J. Mearsheimer, "The False Promise of International Institutions," *International Security*, Winter 1994/95, **19**(3): 7.

[8] Peter Spiro, "What Happened to the 'New Sovereigntism'?" *Foreign Affairs*, July 28, 2004.

[9] See John Bolton, *How Barack Obama is Endangering Our National Sovereignty*, Encounter Broadside, no. 11. Encounter Books, 2010; Jack L. Goldsmith and Eric A. Posner, *The Limits of International Law*. Oxford University Press, 2005.

[10] See Andrew T. Guzman, *How International Law Works: A Rational Choice Theory*. Oxford University Press, 2008.

how domestic actors such as firms, leaders, and political parties make choices that shape the "national interest" at the international level. As with realism, this general focus is not enough to differentiate this approach from others, since any of the theories in this chapter could also be compatible with this starting point.

The distinctiveness of the liberal approach is in how this idea is put into practice in research: liberalism suggests that IOs can be seen as a series of agreements which states enter into expecting to receive a gain. The focus of scholarship is therefore on what kinds of international coordination might produce these mutual benefits for their members and what unintended consequences might follow from the arrangements that they make. These research questions lead many scholars in the liberal tradition to see IOs in contractual terms: as bargains struck among self-interested states. From this beginning, it is characteristic of the liberal approach to see international organizations in terms of the costs and benefits that they offer various actors. It takes as axiomatic that the participants in the organization are there because they believe there is some advantage for them from their participation, and the liberal tradition of research seeks to understand what those gains are, when they do or do not exist, and what are the side effects or unintended implications of these inter-state bargains. The purpose of international organizations, in this view, is to reduce transaction costs and find more optimal outcomes among interdependent but autonomous units.

The imagery of IOs as contracts has been popular among IR scholars in the liberal tradition. The diplomacy over the Rome Statute of the International Criminal Court in the 1990s (for instance) looks a lot like negotiating the terms of a contract among the states. The parties to the negotiation are expected to advance options that suit the interests of their governments, and a deal can be struck if there is sufficient overlap among these interests. Those who find the terms acceptable have the option of joining the "contract" and taking on the legal obligations it contains. From the liberal perspective, in this case the US and a few others did not like the terms of the final document and so refused to endorse it at the close of the Rome Conference in 1998 (see Chapter 9).

A similar story can be told about the World Trade Organization (Chapter 5 of this book). The General Agreement on Tariffs and Trade (GATT) of the WTO represents the promise by the contracting parties to manage their trade policies within the limits set by rules on most-favored nation, national treatment, and bound tariffs. The architecture of the dispute-settlement mechanism of the WTO exists as recourse for contracting parties who believe others have reneged on their promises. The UN Charter might also be seen in the same way (though at the risk of misrepresenting the breadth of the UN's authority): the Charter sets up its members to commit to respect the borders of other members and to resolve their inter-state disputes peacefully.

Contractualism, when applied to international organizations, takes as its starting point the states that make up the organization, and it studies their choices, options, and behaviors. States are the active agents, and even though they may agree to certain limits on their freedom as they consent to international rules, they remain legally and conceptually free to renounce those limits and revoke their consent at any time. States choose the terms on which they delegate powers to international organizations, and remain in control of the delegation throughout. It tends to minimize the organizations themselves, seeing them instead as by-products of the inter-state promises in the treaty. By making states the center of attention, international organizations in the contractualist view take on the status of dependents, descendants, or servants. To the extent that international organizations have the capacity to act as independent actors in this approach, it is generally seen as a problem. That is, it is an unfortunate consequence of the limits of contract-writing, as the parties cannot foresee all future circumstances and cannot fully control how their acts of delegation might be used by others. Following these themes, the contractual approach has generated a substantial literature which seeks to understand how the unavoidable incompleteness of all contracts might create room for IO autonomy, and how states (i.e. "principals") monitor and enforce the performance of the organization (i.e. their "agent") relative to the terms of the contract.[11]

The sparest version of contractualism treats international organizations as nothing more than contracts made between states. In this view, the founding treaty is important because it codifies promises made between states to which they are expected to adhere, but the key commitments are among the signatory states and the organization itself is as a consequence essentially epiphenomenal. It doesn't add anything beyond what states bring to it. Jan Klabbers has described it as akin to imagining "a zero-sum game between the organization and its members, where powers exercised by the members on Monday may be transferred to the organization on Tuesday only to flow back to the members on Wednesday."[12] Despite being empirically unrealistic, it may nonetheless be

---

[11] On incomplete contracts see Alexander Cooley and Hendrik Spruyt, *Contracting States: Sovereignty Transfers in International Relations*. Princeton University Press, 2009, ch. 2. On delegation and "principal-agent relations" see Darren G. Hawkins et al. (eds.), *Delegation and Agency in International Organizations*. Cambridge University Press, 2006.

[12] Jan Klabbers, *An Introduction to International Institutional Law*. Cambridge University Press, 2002, p. 336.

useful sometimes to adopt this extreme perspective on international organizations in order to see more clearly its contrast with other approaches.

Work that begins from a liberal, contractual premise tends to produce research
that emphasizes the terms of the bargains made between states. It de-emphasizes
factors that other approaches make more central, including the agency of the
international organization itself, the effects of differences in power among the
parties, and the feedback process by which the organization might reshape states,
their beliefs about their interests, and their understanding of the problems they
confront in international politics. These themes are more central in the other
approaches. To the extent that these things are dominant in the case one wants to
study, the liberal approach reaches the limits of its usefulness.

Two subsets of liberalism are worth highlighting, dealing with domestic institutions and international regimes respectively. On domestic institutions, Andrew
Moravscik has argued for disaggregating the state in international liberal theory.[13]
He suggests focusing instead on how domestic actors come together to produce the
policy positions that the state pursues through international organizations. For
trade negotiations, this might mean examining what powerful industrial companies want, whether other groups are contesting those demands, how politicians
respond to them based on the incentives they face in domestic political institutions,
and more. Rather than take states as unitary international actors making choices,
this "interest-group liberalism" looks at the interests, position, and relative power
of substate actors that contribute to making the collective "national interest."

"Regime theory" is a subset of the liberal approach that goes in the opposite
direction – it is interested in the web of international rules and norms that
govern an issue. It arose among political scientists in the 1980s looking to
identify the formal and informal rules of the international system and to assess
their impact on the choices that states make.[14] This approach is characterized by
the tendency to first ask the question "what are the rules?" and then consider
how (or indeed whether) they affect the choices of states. The rules form the
basis of the regime. This might be allied with a kind of legal formalism (that is,
the emphasis on the formal rules and laws that govern states), and yet it need
not carry the necessary assumption that states will actually follow the rules, or
that states will not be strategic manipulators of those rules.

---

[13] Andrew Moravscik, "The New Liberalism," in Christian Reus-Smit and Duncan Snidal (eds.),
Oxford Handbook of International Organizations. Oxford University Press, 2009, pp. 234–254.

[14] For a good statement of the approach, see Oran R. Young, *International Governance: Protecting
the Environment in a Stateless Society*. Cornell University Press, 1994.

The study of international organizations as regimes is often augmented by the recognition that the relevant rules for any particular question do not end with formal international organizations. Informal rules, soft law, and practices matter too. The international regime on refugees, for instance, includes not only the powers of the International Migration Organization but also of the 1951 Convention on the Status of Refugees and other treaties and of the United Nations High Commissioner for Refugees, as well as the practices of a range of non-state and quasi-state actors including the International Committee of the Red Cross.[15] On currency flows across borders, the formal rules of the International Monetary Fund set some policy limits on states, but far more important for the overall shape of these flows are the informal mechanisms negotiated among powerful states in semi-regularized meetings of central banks and other officials, as well as the cumulative, international effect of states' domestic regulatory environments for finance. The international legal rules on most issues relate to but transcend formal international organizations, and so to grasp the obligations of states requires taking stock of the broader "regime" on that theme – including but not limited to the formal treaties and organizations. It can be useful as a method for understanding the organizations to see them in relation to this environment, for both its complementarities and its contradictions.

Constructivism

The insight behind constructivism can be illustrated with a simple stylized historical example. The United States acted with alarm when North Korea developed nuclear weapons in the 1990s and 2000s but with support when the United Kingdom did the same thing earlier in the twentieth century. How do we account for the difference? Both developments put extremely powerful weapons in the hands of other governments, and yet the US responded differently to the two situations. To answer that "the UK was an ally while North Korea was not" only begs the question: what's the difference between these two? Alexander Wendt, who developed this example, suggests that "ally" and "enemy" are two ways of seeing other countries (or other people) and these ideas influence how we behave toward them and in turn how they behave toward us.[16] These ideas are generated in the course of past interactions and are not reducible to brute

[15] Alexander Betts gives an excellent case study of the details of the migration regime in *Protection by Persuasion: International Cooperation in the Refugee Regime*. Cornell University Press, 2009.

[16] Alexander Wendt, "Constructing International Politics," *International Security*, 1995, 20: 71–81.

material variables, such as weaponry – they combine material and social content which together give governments ideas about how they want to behave.

This little example illustrates the two key features of constructivism: actors behave toward the world around them in ways that are shaped by the ideas that they hold about the world, and that these ideas are generated by past interactions. It provides a different way of understanding international politics than realism or liberalism. Realism, for instance, would expect the US to behave toward North Korean nuclear weapons in the same way as it did to British nuclear weapons since, after all, a British bomb would do the same (or more) damage than a North Korean bomb. There is no material difference between the two. Liberalism would encourage us to see what mutual advantage might be realized by coordinating between the parties, but has little to say about why one relationship looks conflictual while the other looks friendly.

Constructivism is founded on the fact that much of international politics is shaped by the ideas that people and states have about themselves and the world around them (ideas such as "ally" and "enemy"), and that these ideas can change over time.[17] This is "what makes the world hang together," at the intersection between actors, ideas, and the material world.[18] It highlights the power of their ideas and the power that comes from using these ideas in particular ways.

International organizations are the products of these processes, and also contribute to them, and constructivist scholarship looks at both aspects. For instance, Charlotte Epstein's book on the decline of whale hunting examines how the International Whaling Commission (IWC) was established in 1946 at a time when whale hunting was widely seen as a respectable activity with important industrial and economic functions.[19] She charts how that idea changed over time in many countries, though in not all, such that by the 1990s the rival camps of pro- and anti-whaling members had basically divided the organization in two. The disputes that arise at the IWC today can only be understood in light of the broad but not universal spread of anti-whaling discourse.[20]

In addition to an emphasis on the power of ideas and discourse, constructivism focuses on the constitutive effects of interaction between actors and

[17] See also Ian Hurd, "Constructivism," in Christian Reus-Smit and Duncan Snidal (eds.), *Oxford Handbook of International Organizations*. Oxford University Press, 2009, pp. 298–316.

[18] John G. Ruggie, "What Makes the World Hang Together: Neo-Utilitarianism and the Social Constructivist Challenge," *International Organization*, 1998, 52(4): 855–885.

[19] Charlotte Epstein, *The Power of Words in International Relations: Birth of an Anti-Whaling Discourse*. MIT Press, 2008.

[20] Ian Hurd, "Almost Saving Whales: The Ambiguity of Success at the International Whaling Commission," *Ethics and International Affairs*, 2012, 26(1): 103–112.

structures. In other words, it looks at how the process of interacting in the world shapes the interests and ideas of the actors, without taking autonomous state interests for granted. These might include the ways that the interests of states are shaped by social interaction or by ideas and forces in the external environment, or ways that states use international rules and norms to justify their policies, or the various ways that the actions of states contribute to remaking their international environment. All of these are mutually constitutive, so that they continually remake both the rules and the states that use or interact with them.

Consider the "social" foundation of the UN Security Council: as noted above, the formal parameters of the Council's authority are clearly spelled out in the Charter in Articles 25, 39, 41, and 42, among other places. But the practical content of this power is quite uncertain because the phrase "threat to international peace and security" is both crucial and under-specified. The Charter empowers the Council itself to give meaning to that phrase, and thus one can say that the Council's powers are a function of the Council's practice in interpreting its own powers, rather than simply a function of the Council's formal authority. To know what constitutes a "threat to international peace and security" requires that we study the history of Security Council decisions, including both those moments where the Council decided that a situation qualified as such a threat and those where it decided against it. States present their arguments to and in the Council over whether an issue constitutes a threat to international peace and security, and through both its political processes and its voting rule the Council comes to a determination which stands as the dispositive statement of the matter. There is necessarily room here for competing interpretations that never get reconciled, and ultimately for dis-sensus, all of which leads to the fact that any account of the Council's powers is contingent and contested. As we shall see in Chapter 4, identifying the scope of the Council's authority therefore requires understanding the history of how that authority has been deployed, defined, and argued over in practice, and how it is continually changing as states and others continue to argue over it.

The constructivist approach to international organizations is called for whenever the research question requires that we pay attention to the ways that the relationship between states and international organizations is shaped by the processes of interaction between the two. States and international organizations shape each other in the process of world politics, in contrast with realism and liberalism which primarily see international organizations as instruments of states. As states react to the decisions of international organizations, they can reinforce the organizations' authority and power. For instance, when WTO members argue their cases at the Dispute Settlement Panels, they legitimize that process and strengthen the WTO. Similarly, one consequence of the US strategic manipulation of the Security Council ahead of the Iraq invasion may be an even stronger sense in international politics that Council approval is indeed required to make a military operation legal. This reinforcing of the Council was presumably not the intention of the Americans at the time, but by showing how important that support was to their cause, they may inadvertently have enhanced the legal and political status of the organization.

The interplay between practice and legitimation can also be seen at the International Court of Justice. As we will see in Chapter 8, states often prefer to boycott cases at the ICJ when they believe that the Court has wrongly claimed jurisdiction. They refuse to participate, even though their commitment to the ICJ Statute requires it, and even though their refusal likely increases the chances of an adverse ruling. In doing so they appear to understand that participating validates the institution and its processes. (Keeping their options open, they often find ways to make the Court aware of the substance of their case less directly, perhaps by making secret memos public or by sending the Court unsolicited materials. The Court has become adept at considering some of this evidence despite the boycott, and thereby making its hearings more complete.)

The philosophical setting for constructivism comes from the work of social theorists who are interested in how people operate in their rules-saturated environments.[21] People interact with rules in everything they do, from the constructs of language, to the etiquette norms of their interpersonal interactions, to their legal status as "persons" in the eyes of the state. Action can only make sense in relation to these social structures. Rules are not only external and regulative commands. They also constitute the actors as apparently independent agents in the first place, and they constitute the setting for interaction among those units. This is true for international organization as it is for domestic social institutions.

The constructivist insight is that the interaction of states and international organizations changes both sets of players in the game: the rules change as states invoke and interpret them in particular cases, and states are changed as their decisions and indeed their sovereignty are redefined by international rules.[22] Today's international law on the preemptive use of force, for instance, is the aggregation of past cases, interpretations, and fights over preemption; it

---

[21] For instance, Charles Taylor, "To Follow a Rule ...," in Richard Shusterman (ed.), *Bourdieu: A Critical Reader*. Blackwell, 1999, pp. 29–44.

[22] Martha Finnemore and Kathryn Sikkink, "International Norms and Political Change," *International Organization*, 1998, 52(4): 887–917.

remains binding on states, even though there is no consensus on what the rules forbid or allow and no agreement on how to apply them to particular crises.

Constructivism does not deny that states seek to pursue their interests and that they desire power. Its distinctive contribution is in showing how they come to see certain things as being in their interest, or as being useful tools of power, and how these ideas change in the course in events. It is therefore as much about power and interests as any of the other theories of IO.

Marxism

The Marxist approach to international organizations begins from the premise that international politics and international economics are one singular system, and that this system is inherently unequal. This follows logically from the Marxist analysis of political economy more generally, which argues that there is no analytic separation between politics and economics.[23] Rather than being two separate realms, the economic and the political for Marxists constitute a mostly coherent single social (global) order. This order involves the unequal distribution of power among actors in society, in which rich states and firms share a privileged position against everyone else.

The implication of this approach for IO scholarship is well illustrated by B.S. Chimni's account of the role of international institutions.[24] Chimni examines the practical influence of many international organizations and finds that they generally reinforce the unequal power between rich states and poor states. Rather than lead to greater equality the main global organizations such as the UN, the WTO, and the IMF, contribute to maintaining the existing divisions between rich and poor. The mechanisms by which this happens, Chimni says, include the unequal voting rules and membership of the UN Security Council, the WTO's efforts to reduce tariffs on Third World exports such as textiles but their inaction on reducing rich-country subsidies on agriculture, and the IMF's capacity to force countries to adopt market-based policies that harm the poor in exchange for loans that are used to repay international banks.

Any of the four approaches discussed here could make similar points about the unequal distribution of power in international organizations. What

---

[23] See Ellen Meiksins Wood, "The Separation of the Economic and the Political in Capitalism," *New Left Review*, 1/127, May–June 1981; Justin Rosenberg, *The Empire of Civil Society: A Critique of the Realist Theory of International Relations.* Verso, 1994.

[24] B. S. Chimni, "International Institutions Today: An Imperial Global State in the Making," *European Journal of International Law*, 2004, 15(1): 1–37.

is distinctive about Marxism in IO scholarship is the way that the political and economic domains are linked. For Chimni, there is little reason to differentiate between the political interests expressed by the rich states in meetings of the Security Council and the economic analyses produced by the IMF – both serve the same set of interests, namely to maintain a stable political system that enables the accumulation of wealth in ever fewer private hands.

For Chimni and other Marxists, the expression of political and economic interests in the shape of dominant international organizations constitutes a kind of "nascent global state."[25] The administrative network formed by strong states, transnational firms, and a globalized elite class is woven together into a system of governance that disempowers the vast majority of the world's citizens. This is what Michael Hardt and Antonio Negri called "Empire" and Immanuel Wallerstein called "the World System."[26]

The Value of IR Theory

These approaches can take the same set of circumstances and come to very different conclusions about their politics and their meaning. For instance, when the US invaded Iraq in 2003, it used military force to settle a dispute without the authorization of the UN Security Council. This is a violation of the commitments made by the US under the UN Charter, which include the promise to "settle their international disputes by peaceful means" (Art. 2(3)) and to "refrain in their international relations from the threat or use of force" (Art. 2(4)). What does this mean for the relationship between states and their international obligations? One could interpret the US behavior in many ways: perhaps it is evidence that powerful states can choose to ignore the rules to which they have consented and may do so to accomplish a strongly held goal; perhaps it illustrates that the rules are independent of state behavior in the sense that they persist even when they are violated; or perhaps it is one more instance of the long-running inter-action between states and rules as the former interpret, argue over, and manipu-late the latter, and the latter condition, shape, and constitute the former. The relationship that one sees between states and international organizations, and how one conceives of power in world politics, is different in these views.

It should be clear by now that these approaches are not really comparable one to each other. It is not possible to test one against the others with the intention

---

[25] Ibid., 6.

[26] Michael Hardt and Antonio Negri, *Empire*. Harvard University Press, 2000. Immanuel Wallerstein, *The Modern World System: Mercantilism and the Consolidation of the European World-Economy, 1600–1750*. Academic Press, 1980.

of ruling out any of them. These are not theories that produce discrete hypotheses in the sense demanded by Karl Popper and the positivist tradition in the philosophy of science.[27] One cannot falsify any of these approaches, and they do not lend themselves to predictions about specific future events. They are not independent of how one sees the world, and therefore it is not easy to use them to make causal claims about dependent and independent variables.

Each theory provides a distinctive intellectual framework that makes sense of a complex set of events, forces, and ideas in characteristic ways. They should be thought of as alternative "sense-making" devices, as described by Karl Weick.[28] Reasoned argument is unlikely to cause one theory to prevail over another. But a well-educated person should be able to see the logic in each of them and understand their intellectual foundations.

It should also be clear from these descriptions that I seek to dispel some common myths about International Relations theory as it applies to international organizations.

There are some common caricatures of IR theory that circulate in discussions of international organizations, and these should be resisted. Among the myths, for instance, it is often said that realism is about the pursuit of power by states, that liberals are optimistic about cooperation between states, that constructivists see norms as consequential in explaining international cooperation, and that Marxism lost its influence after the end of the Cold War.

As explained above, each of these are either highly misleading or basically wrong. All four approaches above are about political power and the pursuit of state interests – realism does not monopolize the study of power, just as liberalism does not monopolize the study of self-interested bargains. Marxists and constructivists are just as interested in power politics and national interests as liberals and realists. What the four disagree on is how power should be conceived. They present alternative views of power itself, which lead to different ideas of what constitutes an interesting or important research question and therefore different programs of research. It is wrong to equate realism with "power politics" if this means that the other approaches are not about power.[29]

Equally, it is wrong to assume that realists are "pessimists" about international cooperation while liberals and/or constructivists are "optimists."[30]

[27] On this, see Martin Packer, *The Science of Qualitative Research*. Cambridge University Press, 2011.
[28] Karl E. Weick, *Sense making in Organizations*. Sage, 1995.
[29] As is done, for example, in David Kinsella, Bruce Russett, and Harvey Starr, *World Politics: The Menu for Choice*. Wadsworth, 10th edn. 2013, p. 23.
[30] As does Kelly-Kate S. Pease, *International Organizations: Perspectives on Governance in the Twenty-First Century*. Prentice Hall, 2000, p. 63.

These approaches do not in themselves tell us whether international organizations will be plentiful or few, or successful or not. Instead, they tell us under
what circumstances we might expect international organizations to develop,
and what kinds of features we can expect of them. And they indicate ways of
thinking about the powers and limits of international organizations.

Finally, it is too simplistic to associate constructivism with international
"norms" as distinct from cost-benefit calculations.[31] Constructivists are as
concerned with instrumental, self-regarding behavior as are any other scholars.
What is different about constructivism is the view that one should pay attention to how the actor thinks about his or her self-interest, and how those
perceptions of interests are shaped by the external environment and by the
process of interacting with that environment.

Three Views on Ontology: Actor, Forum, Resource

The international organizations in this book exhibit a range of characteristics and
can be understood in a variety of ways. For different situations, or for different
purposes, each might look like an actor, or a forum, or a resource, or some
combination of these at once. That is, each is a corporate entity capable of taking
action in its own right; each is also a location where other actors (mostly states but
potentially also other kinds of actors) come to discuss, debate, and decide; and each
is a kind of resource, or a set of resources, that states and others can use to advance
their own political agendas. Much of the political and academic disagreement about
global governance and international organization is a product of different views on
which of these characteristics provides the best way of thinking about world politics.
This section examines each of these three in turn before suggesting that they can all
be useful, though at different moments and for different kinds of questions.

IOs as Actors

International organizations are actors in world politics. They are constituted by
international law as independent entities, separate from the states that make them
up as their founders and their members. The practical expression of this independence varies greatly across organizations, but in a formal sense they are corporate

---

[31] As do Stephen G. Brooks and William C. Wohlforth in *World out of Balance: International
Relations and the Challenge of American Primacy*. Princeton University Press, 2008.

"persons" much like firms are "persons" in domestic commercial law. This means they have legal standing, with certain rights and obligations, and can sue and be sued. This was established concretely in the ICJ opinion on Reparations for Injuries,[32] but that case merely affirmed what had existed in custom and in practice for a long time prior: inter- state organizations are legally independent from their founders. Some of this independence is written into the treaties that establish them, and some of it arises by implication. Contemporary treaties on international organization usually include a clause similar to Article 4(1) of the International Criminal Court's Statute, which says "The Court shall have international legal personality." This establishes that the Court is an independent body, separate from both the states that make it up and the individuals who staff it. But even without such a declaration, part of the point of creating an international organization is to have a body that is distinct from any of the states within it, and so agency on the part of the IO is an essential component of its function, purpose, and indeed existence.

Being recognized as an actor requires some kind of social recognition plus some kind of capacity for action. For international organizations, this means they are understood by the international community as actors, and that in that community their decisions must have some impact. International lawyers tend to see this "personality" of IOs as a product of the legal construction of the organization by its treaty, while political scientists and sociologists are likely to see it as a product of a social process of institutionalization. The dilemma of international organization as a practice in world politics is of course that IOs as actors are composed of states, that is of units which are themselves independent actors, and so formal international organizations are always collective rather than unitary actors. When they operate as "agents" they are unitary actors in the same way that national governments, also composed of many individuals and factions, are recognized as unitary actors: that is, widely but uneasily. Alexander Wendt has suggested that one test of "personhood" should be whether the actor can do things that its constituent parts on their own are unable to do.[33] Using that criterion, the substantive chapters of this book help to document the evidence that these international organizations do indeed have the capacity for independent action, though it varies across organizations and it sometimes does not match precisely the powers described in the founding charters.

The impact of IOs-as-actors is evident in the real world whenever an international organization influences the shape or practice of world politics for other

[32] Reparations for Injuries Suffered in the Service of the United Nations, ICJ Advisory Opinion, 1949.

[33] Alexander Wendt, "The State as Person in International Theory," *Review of International Studies*, 2004, **30**(2): 289–316.

actors. For instance, in 2009 the International Criminal Court indicted the president of Sudan for crimes in Darfur and issued a warrant for his arrest. This has a major impact on international politics, despite the fact that the president has stayed in power since then and has not been arrested. Following the indictment, the president's travel had to be carefully calibrated to avoid jurisdictions that might arrest him; the legitimacy of the court itself went both up and down, depending on the audience; governments were provoked to take a stand for or against the indictment and changed their policies in various ways as a result. The president's personal situation changed dramatically and immediately as a result of the warrant, as he found his liberty suddenly at risk in ways it was not before. All of these changes are evidence of the capacity of the ICC to behave as an actor in its own right in world politics. That its impact is not entirely in the direction desired by the ICC is not a suggestion of the lack of power for the organization; it does, however, indicate that its power is complicated (in ways which are the subject of Chapter 9). Similarly, the UN General Assembly resolution that equated Zionism and racism (GA 3379) had an impact in world politics: it generated controversy, defense, and renunciation. These reactions were a result of the fact that states seem to believe that statements of the Assembly are influential moves by a relevant international actor, whether they agree with them or not.

IOs as Fora

International organizations are also places in space and time, in the sense of being physical buildings, conferences, and schedules of meetings. Part of their value is that they act as meeting places where states discuss interests and problems of mutual concern. The players in these discussions are usually the member states themselves, and the IO may have no role other than as a focal point or a physical location with a support staff. Non-state actors sometimes have a role in these negotiations but often find it difficult to get access.[34] This is an important contribution to international law and politics but it is very different than the role of "actor" described above.

In their role as fora, international organizations represent an extension of the nineteenth-century European practice of holding ad hoc themed "conferences" among governments, such as those that produced the first Geneva Conventions.

---

[34] For two examples, see Carne Ross, *Independent Diplomat: Dispatches from an Unaccountable Elite*, 2007, and Rebecca Witter et al., "Moments of Influence in Global Environmental Politics," *Environmental Politics*, 2015, 24(6).

This practice became more standardized in the twentieth century, often in the United Nations, with major UN-sponsored conferences on environment and development (Rio 1993), human rights (Vienna 1994), and the status of women (Mexico City 1975, Beijing 1995) among others. The value of the UN in these cases is that it can provide experienced logistical support for large meetings, even though it itself may not be present as a formal participant. These meetings represent the "forum" function of IOs in its clearest manifestation.

In addition, most international organizations include a plenary body in which all members are represented, and whose purpose is general deliberation about the work or themes of the organization.[35] The ICC has its Assembly of States Parties, the WTO has its General Council, the ILO has the International Labor Conference. The procedures for discussion in these bodies are relatively inclusive and open so that all members have an opportunity to participate. As a consequence, they tend to have either few executive powers or high standards of consensus for decisions, or both. The UN General Assembly fits the former category: it can make recommendations but has few powers to take legally binding decisions. The WTO fits the latter: its members can sit as the "Dispute Settlement Body" with the authority to overturn decisions of the dispute settlement panels but requires a unanimity decision to do so.

The deliberative functions of these assemblies can have a powerful legitimating effect on the organization and its decisions. They are also useful for facilitating side negotiations among members. For instance, the original motivation behind the UN General Assembly was to have a place where states that were not Great Powers could have some voice but its annual meetings in New York have come to include both the formal speeches by governments and the large and unknowable number of informal meetings on the sides that are made possible by virtue of so many diplomats and leaders being in one city at the same time. The transaction costs for diplomacy are thereby reduced, and a benefit is achieved even if the formal speeches generate nothing but hot air.

IOs as Resources

Finally, international organizations are political resources that states use as they pursue their goals, both domestic and international. States use the statements, decisions, and other outputs of international organizations as materials to

---

[35] The exception in this book is the International Court of Justice, with no plenary body and with a mandate (judicial decisions) that would seem to work against an open deliberative body.

support their own positions, and many international disputes include competing interpretations of these materials. States fight over what international organizations should say and what they should do, and then fight over what these acts and statements mean for world politics. For instance, does Security Council Resolution 242 really require that Israel withdraw immediately from the Palestinian territory it seized in the 1967 war as the plain text would indicate, or only that it should negotiate a withdrawal in due time? Competing interpretations allow the parties to maintain that the Council supports their policies, and that the other side is violating its obligations. They use the resolution as a political tool to further their goals. Much of what comes out of international organizations is useful to states in this way, and one might even say that anything that is not useful in some way is not likely to have any impact at all.

States spend significant energy pursuing, deploying, and resisting these resources in and around international organizations, a practice which both illustrates and reinforces the power of the organizations in their social and political contexts. The usefulness of these resources is evidence that the audience is paying attention to the outputs of international organizations and helps to establish the point that they are not just "cheap talk." In addition, where the organization can control who uses its symbols and outputs, it can extract concessions from states in exchange for the right to use them. The Security Council controls "UN peacekeeping" as if it were a trademarked brand, and when it has allowed countries' military operations to be called "peacekeeping" missions it has demanded that they adhere to standards set by the Council.[36] International organizations make themselves stronger when they can act as gatekeepers to their valuable symbols.

More generally, however, international organizations have little control over how their names, decisions, and outputs are used by states, and these resources travel effortlessly between legal and non-legal applications. For instance, governments sometimes blame the International Monetary Fund for forcing them to make unpopular policy changes, even though the Fund does not believe that it has the authority to "force" borrowers to do anything. In making this claim, the governments are using the symbol of the IMF for domestic political purposes in ways that may well irritate the IMF. The value of the symbol for these purposes is only loosely related to the actual powers or demands of the IMF, in the sense that the government may well find political advantage in using the Fund as a scapegoat even if the government would have made the same changes absent the Fund.

---

[36] This was the case with Russian operations in the 1990s. See Ian Hurd, *After Anarchy: Legitimacy and Power in the UN Security Council*. Princeton University Press, 2007, ch. 5.

Similarly, states often seek to have the International Court of Justice hear their disputes even if they doubt that the other party will respect the outcome. The non-compliance of the other state may well be a useful political tool. In these cases, the existence of the international organization gives states tools and options which they would not have otherwise, and their effects must therefore be counted as we assess the impact that international organizations have in world politics.

Seeing international organizations as tools rather than as solutions in themselves helps to emphasize the limits to their power and effectiveness. International organizations can be influential when circumstances are favorable but they can also be thoroughly marginalized when powerful actors seek to keep them out, or when no one sees an advantage in bringing them into action. For instance, the UN Secretary-General had prepared in the early 1980s a diplomatic solution to the contested governance of Cambodia, but he and the entire UN were largely kept out of the process by a few states in the Association of Southeast Asian Nations (ASEAN) group who refused to negotiate with the Vietnamese government that controlled Cambodia.[37] Only after the geopolitics of ASEAN changed in the late 1980s did his plan come to be implemented as the Paris Peace Agreement of 1991. The apparent "failure" of the UN to deal effectively with the Cambodia problem was actually a result of the fact that some powerful states insisted that the UN not be used as a tool for solving the problem. The "tool" view is an antidote to the common but misleading assumption that there is always in principle an international-organization answer to every diplomatic problem or humanitarian crisis. From Darfur to the Haiti earthquake to the Syrian war, the potential contribution of international organizations to solving international problems is in part defined and delimited by the utility that states see in invoking them to those ends.

The three aspects of actor, forum, and tool coexist in tension in international organizations. Each on its own provides an incomplete view. They must be considered together, even though they cannot be entirely combined. To see IOs from only one of these three perspectives leads to an unnecessarily partial view of their nature and power, and makes it too easy to criticize or dismiss them. To see them exclusively for their "forum" properties leads to the mistake made by John Bolton, who maintained that the UN "does not exist."[38] What does exist, he implied, is a

---

[37] See Javier Pérez de Cuéllar, *Pilgrimage for Peace: A Secretary-General's Memoir.* St. Martin's Press, 1997, and Hedi Annabi, Yale-UN Oral History Project, 1995. UN Library, New York.

[38] In a speech at the World Federalist Society, 1994, cited in Jane Perlez, "Arms Control Nominee Defends Shifting View," *New York Times*, March 30, 2001, www.nytimes.com/2001/03/30/world/30ARMS.html. Accessed February 6, 2010.

collection of independent states who sometimes choose to meet in the rooms of the UN building, and perhaps to add a UN label to their collective endeavors (i.e. a forum exclusively). This is a radically reductionist view of international politics and law; it claims that everything that is done through or by the United Nations can be reduced analytically to the behavior of individual states without losing any meaning.[39] It denies the possibility of corporate personhood for international organizations and thus the possibility that they might have positions or take actions independent of their members. This is a hard position to sustain since it requires that we deny that there is any practical difference between states acting alone and states acting through the United Nations. The real world of international relations is full of examples that states react quite differently to what other states do as opposed to what IOs do. Consider, for instance, the American effort to gain Security Council approval for its invasion of Iraq in 2003, while John Bolton was in the US Department of State: the premise of that effort was that the Council could provide collective legitimation for the invasion and this would change how other states reacted to the invasion. The US strategy of seeking Security Council support presumed that the audience of states would see an invasion as more legitimate than they would without Council approval, or than they would if the US gained the state-by-state support of governments individually through bilateral efforts. If there is a difference in how the action is perceived depending on whether it is supported by a collection of individual states and supported by those states through the Council, then the reductionist view must be wrong. That difference represents the independent contribution of the Security Council to world politics, beyond its role as a forum or meeting place.

It is equally hard to sustain an entirely actor-centric view of most international organizations. The independence of even the strongest of international organizations is always conditional on an alignment of social forces that is outside of its control. For instance, the Security Council has the authority to intervene in world politics in any way it sees fit in response to anything it identifies as a threat to international peace and security (Arts. 39, 41, 42), and it operates entirely on its own without oversight by any other institution. And yet, its ability to take action on international security depends on the voluntary contributions of military resources by individual member states. As a result, its actor-like qualities in the international system are legally enshrined by

---

[39] On reductionism in International Relations, see Alexander Wendt, "The State as Person in International Theory," *Review of International Studies*, 2004, 30(2): 289–316.

the Charter but in practice are drastically undercut by member states. Both the independence of IOs and their limits are central to some versions of the "delegation" approach to international organizations, a subset of liberal IR theory that focuses on the delegation by which states endow them with authority.[40] Once empowered by this delegated authority, the organization may have considerable autonomy to deploy its powers as it wishes, and it may be a challenge for member states to control it. To overstate the independence of international organizations is as much a mistake as to understate it, and anywhere along this spectrum all claims about the autonomy of international organizations must be grounded in an empirical study of the particular organization in question. There are no general answers to questions about the distribution of power and authority between states and international organizations.

These three images of international organizations coexist in varying proportions and manifestations in each international organization. The UN General Assembly is, for example, much more of a forum than either the ICJ or the ICC, and many of the more technical organizations such as the Universal Postal Union are much less useful as resources than are those with a higher political profile such as the UN Security Council. Despite these variations, all three aspects are embedded in all IOs, as they are in all complex organizations in society.

All three views must therefore be considered, and the challenge for the scholar of international organizations is to figure out how to combine them and where to put the emphasis to best suit the research problem at hand. When Michael Barnett sought to understand how the UN came to abandon Rwanda at the time of the genocide in 1994, he looked at the positions that the strongest states on the Security Council brought to the debate (a "forum" view of the UN), as well as at the position of the Secretary-General and his staff (thus recognizing that the UN was also an actor in the process), and at how the collective decisions of the Council would be perceived and manipulated by other states and by the *genocidaires* themselves (i.e. how the UN would be used as a tool by other players).[41] This combination resulted in a nuanced history of the decisions of the UN on the matter, and one which belies simplifying attempts to assign to any one player the well-deserved blame for the UN behavior.

[40] See Darren G. Hawkins et al. (eds.), *Delegation and Agency in International Organizations.* Cambridge University Press, 2006. Also, Andrew T. Guzman and Jennifer Landsidle, "The Myth of International Delegation," *California Law Review*, December 2008, **96**(6): 1693–1724.

[41] Michael Barnett, *Eyewitness to a Genocide.* Cornell University Press, 2003.

Conclusion

The fundamental tension in international law, which is central to the field of international organization as well, is between state sovereignty and the commitment involved in international treaties. States are the masters and the servants of international organizations, and this tension must be reconciled somehow. The academic study of international organizations has developed various strands for thinking about this complexity in different ways. The theoretical approaches in this chapter, realism, liberalism, constructivism, and Marxism, adopt different starting points for thinking about international organizations.

This chapter suggested a second three-way typology for analyzing international organizations: that of actor, forum, and resource. These are different lenses for studying, or metaphors for imagining, international organizations, based on different interpretations of their role and function in world politics. At times, international organizations behave like independent actors in international relations, issuing decisions, taking actions, and being talked about as if they were players in their own right. At other times, they provide a forum in which states (or others) carry out their negotiations and their diplomacy. A forum is a place rather than an actor, and there are times when even the most powerful international organizations slip off their corporate personhood and become just a setting for interstate bargaining. Finally, international organizations are also sometimes resources or tools with which states try to accomplish their goals. This is on display on those occasions where states use the organization as a source of status or legitimacy. States strive to associate themselves with organizations that they think will give them status in the international community, and they work to have their causes legitimated by association with those organizations.

The themes of this chapter emphasize the importance of both the legal and the political aspects of international organizations. Indeed, neither can be understood without the other. In doing so, it sets the stage for the case studies of particular international organizations which follow, and primes the argument that the real-world powers and practices of international organizations are equally and at once in the domains of international law and of international politics.

Further Reading

A most helpful guide to studying the legal aspects of international organization is Jan Klabbers, *An Introduction to International Institutional Law* (Cambridge University Press, 2002). For an introduction to international legal theory, see Harold Hongju Koh, "Why Do Nations Obey International Law?" *Yale Law Journal*, 1997, 106: 2599–2659. Two excellent books on the intersection of world politics and international law are Christian Reus-Smit (ed.), *The Politics of International Law* (Cambridge University Press, 2004), and David Armstrong, Theo Farrell, and Hélène Lambert (eds.), *International Law and International Relations* (Cambridge University Press, 2007).

For examples of the contractual approach to international organizations, see the essays in Darren G. Hawkins et al. (eds.), *Delegation and Agency in International Organizations* (Cambridge University Press, 2006). Andrew T. Guzman argues for the importance of reputation in his book *How International Law Works: A Rational Choice Theory* (Oxford University Press, 2008). The regime-theory variant of liberalism is evident in Oran R. Young, *International Governance: Protecting the Environment in a Stateless Society* (Cornell University Press, 1994). Michael Barnett and Martha Finnemore put the constructivist approach to work in their book *Rules for the World: International Organizations in Global Politics* (Cornell University Press, 2004).

3 The United Nations I
Law and Administration

key facts

Headquarters: New York

Members: 193 countries

Mandate: to end international war, and to promote social and economic development.

Key structure: six principal "organs" are the General Assembly (all UN members, to make recommendations to states), the Security Council (fifteen members, to take enforcement action on international security), the International Court of Justice (to decide legal disputes between states), the Secretariat (the Secretary-General and staff), the Economic and Social Council (fifty-four members, to make recommendations on economic and social questions), and the Trusteeship Council (defunct).

Key obligations: member states must give up the use of force except for self-defense, must carry out Security Council decisions, and can conclude no treaty that contradicts the Charter.

Enforcement: the Security Council can take any action it deems necessary, including the use of force, to respond to threats to international peace and security.

Key legal clauses of the UN Charter:

Article 2(1) The Organization is based on the ... sovereign equality of all its Members.

Article 2(4) All Members shall refrain in their international relations from the threat or use of force...

key facts

Article 2(7) Nothing . . . in the present Charter shall authorize the United Nations to intervene in matters which are essentially within the domestic jurisdiction of any state . . .

Article 4(2) Membership in the United Nations is open to all . . . peace-loving states.

Article 10 The General Assembly may discuss any questions . . . within the scope of the present Charter . . . [and] make recommendations to the Members of the United Nations or to the Security Council.

Article 24(1) [T]he United Nations . . . confer on the Security Council primary responsibility for the maintenance of international peace and security.

Article 25 The Members of the United Nations agree to accept and carry out the decisions of the Security Council.

Article 42 [The Security Council] may take such action by air, sea, or land forces as may be necessary to maintain or restore international peace and security.

Article 51 Nothing in the present Charter shall impair the inherent right of individual or collective self-defense if an armed attack occurs against a Member of the United Nations.

Article 103 In the event of a conflict between the obligations of the Members of the United Nations under the present Charter and their obligations under any other international agreements, their obligations under the present Charter shall prevail.

The UN Charter, signed in 1945, created two distinct things: a set of basic rules of conduct for governments and a formal organization with its own powers. Both the organization and the rules are legally binding and are therefore a kind of constraint on the sovereignty of member states, and they also make possible new kinds of international politics that can be very useful to states. They are therefore empowering as well as constraining. The formal organization of the United Nations is composed of separate organs including the Security Council, the General Assembly, and the Secretariat. Each has a specific area of competence and they vary in how much authority they exercise over member states. The basic rules include commitments to refrain from the use of force to solve international disputes, to respect the decisions of the International Court of Justice, and to pay the required dues to the United Nations itself. The two aspects of the UN Charter amount to something like a constitution for the international system.[1]

The United Nations Charter defines the UN as a formal institution of limited powers as well as a generalized system of constitutional principles to govern all of inter-state politics. The institutional parts of the UN, such as the General Assembly and the Security Council, are required to operate within these principles, but the principles themselves are refined and brought to life through the daily practices and actions of the states and others who make use of them. The principles and the practices need to be understood together, as neither is really dominant. When, for instance, the Charter says that the Security Council has "primary responsibility for the maintenance of international peace and security" (Art. 24(1)), the only way to know what is meant by the key terms "primary" and "international peace and security" is to look at how the Council and others have used these terms through the years in debates, justifications, and argument. This chapter therefore looks at the UN with one eye on the legal language of the Charter and the other eye on the artful applications of that language in the practical diplomacy and manipulations of states.

As a formal organization, the United Nations is a system of many constituent sub-organizations of varying degrees of independence and authority. The Charter describes the six principal organs of the United Nations that make up the central core of the system. They are the General Assembly, the Security Council, the Trusteeship Council, the International Court of Justice, the Economic and Social Council, and the Secretariat. Each has a distinct sphere of operation and a set of powers that is delimited by the Charter, and each has the power to act as an independent player in world politics in some limited domain of competence. Beyond these six, lies a vast universe of "specialized" agencies and "related" organizations and funds. These include many of the largest stand-alone organizations discussed in this book (such as the WTO, the IMF, and the ILO) that agree to report their activities to the United Nations but are not formally subordinate to it in any way. It also includes subsidiary bodies of the UN itself, such as the UN Population Fund and the UN Development Program.

---

[1] Whether it really qualifies as a constitution is debated in Bardo Fassbender, "The United Nations Charter as Constitution of the International Community," *Columbia Journal of Transnational Law*, 1998, **36**: 529–723, and Michael W. Doyle, "The UN Charter – A Global Constitution?" in Jeffrey L. Dunoff and Joel P. Trachtman (eds.), *Ruling the World? Constitutionalism, International Law, and Global Governance*. Cambridge University Press, 2009, pp. 113–132.

This chapter is concerned with the six primary organs of the UN and the obligations, compliance, and enforcement that they generate relative to UN member states. The Security Council (SC) is responsible for responding to threats to international peace and security and has the authority to force states to change their policies through military enforcement if necessary. The General Assembly (GA) has a broader scope than the SC in that it can discuss any matter within the jurisdiction of the UN, including and beyond "international peace and security," but its enforcement authority extends only to making recommendations to states and to other parts of the UN. It cannot take "decisions" in a formal sense of acts that create binding obligations for member governments. The Secretariat is the bureaucratic staff of the UN, headed by the Secretary-General. The staff is drawn from member states but they are formal employees of the international organization and so owe their loyalty to the UN rather than to their home governments. The Trusteeship Council (TC) is responsible for supervising any people and territories that have been placed under "trusteeship" with the UN, and is now moribund as there are no more such territories. The TC is interesting today mainly as evidence of how hard it is to amend the text of the Charter to remove outdated provisions, though some have suggested that the Trusteeship Council could be cleansed of its colonialist overtones and become a device for dealing with the administration of "failed states."[2] The International Court of Justice (ICJ) is a judicial body where states bring complaints when other states have failed to live up to their obligations under international law. Its jurisdiction and powers are subtle and interesting, and are the subject of Chapter 8. Finally, the Economic and Social Council (ECOSOC) contains a subset of GA members and has the power to undertake studies and make recommendations on a range of non-security topics.

It is an open question whether the activities of the United Nations actually enhance human or global welfare. This is certainly the aspiration of the organization, committed as it is to reducing war and conflict and to improving the living conditions of people around the world. But it is naive to assume that it necessarily succeeds in doing this. This is true both in the sense that sometimes UN operations go wrong, and people suffer as a result, and also in that the political issues treated by the UN necessarily involve choosing winners and losers.

---

[2] For a discussion of moving "trusteeship" functions around in the UN system, see James D. Fearon and David D. Laitin, "Neotrusteeship and the Problem of Weak States," *International Security*, 2004, 28(4): 5–43.

It is never self-evident what the UN should do; it is always a matter of some contestation. Some people will be put out and others will be privileged. To the winning side, the UN might look like a paragon of international consensualism and common-sense, but to the losers it will look very different. The UN does not erase political disagreements over what should be done and who should decide. It is instead an actor, forum, and resource in the context of those disagreements.

These differences are explored in a case study of Richard Goldstone's inquiry into the 2009 Gaza War. Goldstone, a South African lawyer, was asked by the General Assembly to investigate whether war crimes were committed in that conflict. The powers, limits, and politics of the investigation show in practice how the UN is both empowered and constrained by its position in international politics.

This chapter concludes with a case study of a 2010 cholera outbreak in Haiti to explore what happens when a UN operation goes wrong. In that case, peacekeepers accidentally sparked an epidemic which led to the death of thousands of people. The organization's response is a lesson in how powerful actors like the UN can use their positions to avoid accountability for their own actions. It is a reminder too that UN operations must be judged on their practical effects and not on their best-case assumptions or ideal designs.

Obligations

Under the Charter

Members of the United Nations take on general obligations under the UN Charter as well as specific obligations to particular organs of the UN. This section considers the main obligations of states to the Charter itself and the next section looks at the obligations of states relative to the authority and powers of specific UN organs. It highlights also the legal limits on the UN's authority.

The Charter spells out the general obligations of UN members and the general powers and limits of the UN as an organization. These define the parameters within which the UN exists and within which inter-state relations are supposed to take place. The organs of the UN take their place within this framework and are governed by it. This makes the Charter *the* fundamental international treaty. Its status is explicitly affirmed in Articles 102 and 103, which require that every other inter-state treaty be subordinate to the UN Charter. Article 103 says that "in the event of a conflict between the ... present Charter and [states'] obligations under any other international agreement, their obligations under the present Charter shall prevail" and Article 102(2) says that states cannot invoke their obligations under any other treaty if that treaty has not been registered with the UN Secretariat in advance.

In other words, no treaty that contradicts the UN Charter or that is not put on deposit with the Secretary-General is considered legally binding. The singular importance of the UN Charter is evident in the way the document was physically handled in 1945: at the end of the San Francisco conference, the copy of the Charter that had been signed by the founding states was flown to Washington, DC by an American official, Alger Hiss. The box containing the Charter was equipped with its own parachute, but none was provided for Hiss himself.[3]

Article 2 of the Charter contains several clauses crucial to modern inter-national politics. Article 2(4), in particular, stands ahead of almost anything else in the Charter. It says that "all members shall refrain in their international relations from the threat or use of force against . . . any state." In the eyes of the framers of the Charter at San Francisco in 1945, this was perhaps the single most important component of the new international system they were designing. It means that all UN members (which today includes all 193 of the world's states) are forbidden from using or threatening war against other states. The implica-tions of this are profound, and are explored below and in the following chapter.

For the UN organization itself, Articles 2(1) and 2(7) are extremely important. They have a kind of constitutional status because of the breadth and severity of the limits they place on the organization vis-à-vis state sovereignty. These clauses say that "the Organization is based on the principle of the sovereign equality of all its Members" (Art. 2(1)) and that the UN cannot "intervene in matters which are essentially within the domestic jurisdiction of any state" (Art. 2(7)). These rules address themselves to the United Nations as an institution rather than to its member states, and they therefore define fundamental rules for the operation of all UN business. To understand the impact of these two clauses, it is worth looking at the "chapeau" to Article 2, ahead of the numbered paragraphs, where it says that "the Organization and its Members . . . shall act in accordance with the following Principles: . . ." In other words, everything that the UN does must conform to the principles of legal equality among states and domestic non-interference by the UN. By the standards of public international law these are very strongly stated and clearly marked obligations; to say "the

---

[3] Alger Hiss interview, Yale-UN Oral History Project, October 11, 1990, p. 48. UN Library, New York.

Organization shall act . . ." is an absolute prohibition on acting otherwise. Every peace mission, every development program, and every speech by the Secretary-General must abide by these limits. The rule on sovereign equality ensures, for instance, that each country's representative gets to speak at the annual meeting of the General Assembly for the same amount of time, at least in theory.[4] It is also behind the practice of treating all gifts to the UN art collection with equal dignity and respect, regardless of their artistic merits – since to do otherwise might be interpreted as treating nations as other than fully equal.[5] However, "equality" in this context does not mean that anyone believes that all countries are equal in wealth or power or influence; it only means that they are absolutely equal in their legal rights and obligations as sovereign states and in their relations with the UN. This kind of juridical or legal equality is central to modern international law and to the law and practice of the United Nations.[6]

The rule on non-intervention is equally fundamental. Article 2(7) preserves the domestic sovereignty of governments over anything that is "essentially within" the domestic jurisdiction of the state. The United Nations cannot take any action that interferes with that domestic jurisdiction; as a consequence, the UN's authority extends only to international matters and these are understood as being mutually exclusive with everything that is domestic. For anything that is "domestic," therefore, the UN can only operate with the consent of the local government. It can only intervene in the domestic affairs of states without their consent when these affairs have crossed the threshold and become "international" matters, at which point (by definition) they cease to be within the domain of domestic for the purposes of Article 2(7).

This is perhaps most visible in the area of UN military operations, where forceful "intervention" is an entirely different legal act than a consensual "peacekeeping" operation. Peacekeeping missions are generally negotiated between the UN and the state in question, and thus blue-helmet peacekeeping

---

[4] In practice, leaders often go on for far longer than their allotted time and the UN has few means to limit them. Libya's Colonel Qaddafi produced a memorably long speech in 2009. "Libyan Leader Delivers a Scolding in UN Debut," Neil MacFarquhar, *New York Times*, September 23, 2009.

[5] "Space is Tight at the UN, but Art Gifts Keep Coming," Daniel B. Schneider, *New York Times*, March 31, 2004. Also, "UN Art Collection, Like the UN, Keeps Growing," William G. Blair, *New York Times*, March 13, 1983.

[6] Gerry Simpson provides a very interesting corrective to this doctrine. His book *Great Powers and Outlaw States: Unequal Sovereigns in the International Legal Order* (Cambridge University Press, 2004) shows the many ways that international law over history has treated "great powers" as having more rights and "outlaw states" as having fewer.

troops are sent to a country only with the permission of the government. Aid programs, elections monitoring, and refugee assistance, among other kinds of activities, must equally be premised on the consent of the government to avoid violating Article 2(7). A powerful corollary of this rule is that if a government withdraws its consent to a program in progress, the UN must cease its work and remove its people. It cannot keep personnel or programs in a country that has not consented to them. The clarity of the legal principle had decisive consequences when in 1967 Egypt withdrew its consent to the UNEF peacekeeping mission stationed in Sinai.[7] U Thant, the Secretary-General at the time, ordered the peacekeepers to leave immediately, despite fully expecting that this was a prelude to war with Israel. Israel refused to allow the peacekeepers to move to its side of the border, and as they evacuated from the Sinai, war between Egypt and Israel erupted around them. Fifteen UN soldiers were killed in the process. Thant understood that without an explicit legal mandate from the host country, UN troops would be violating Article 2(7) if they stayed in place. Non-consensual "peace enforcement" missions are different. They are legally defined in Chapter VII of the UN Charter and their legal and political features are the subject of the following chapter in this book.

For Article 2(7) to be meaningful, it can only be in relation to the key phrase "essentially within the jurisdiction of any state." It presumes a bright line between domestic affairs and international matters, and while it is entirely conventional to distinguish between the two, the importance of the distinction in the law and practice of the UN makes for some interesting problems. The basic idea of domestic sovereignty is clear enough but its details, limits, and implications are all highly contested. One might wonder, for instance, what the modifier "essentially" is doing in the sentence. Does this imply that some issues are only partly domestic, and if so can the UN legally take action with respect to them?

From a practical perspective, the line between international issues and matters within the domestic jurisdiction of the state is never self-evident. The line is both unclear and moveable.

Much of the controversy in foreign policy arises over competing arguments about where the legitimate legal boundaries of domestic sovereignty are drawn. The UN system presumes that such boundaries exist but does not give much help on how to determine them. As Sands and Klein point out, there has been great

---

[7] UNEF is "United Nations Emergency Force," and its history is well described in the UN's own archives: www.un.org/en/peacekeeping/missions/past/unef1backgr2.html. Accessed February 9, 2010.

controversy over the years over whether (for instance) apartheid in South Africa, genocide in Rwanda, and colonialism are essentially domestic matters or are of legitimate international concern.[8] In 1999 the Security Council said that the easy availability of small arms and light weapons might constitute a threat to international peace and security and therefore the trade in small arms might not be entirely within the domain of domestic jurisdiction.[9] The tendency has been for the Council to find more and more matters to be within its jurisdiction as threats to international peace and security, with the effect that the areas covered by Article 2(7) protection are shrinking. While there is no formal provision in the Charter for treating past decisions as precedents, the gradual accumulation of Security Council resolutions expanding the "international" sphere results in reducing the "domestic" sphere.[10]

To the UN Organs

It is within the context of these rules that the organs of the United Nations go about their business. Member states are committed to the obligations described in the Charter and therefore also to any new obligations created by UN organs as they carry out their mandates. The principal obligations of UN members involve the General Assembly (GA) and the Security Council (SC), and this section focuses on these. The ICJ is treated separately in Chapter 8. The other main organs (the Secretariat, the Trusteeship Council, and ECOSOC) create minor obligations for UN members, and are best understood in contrast to the GA and the SC.

The General Assembly's powers are clearly set out in Articles 10 through 13 of the Charter. As a general matter, the Assembly "may discuss any questions or any matters within the scope of the present Charter" (Art. 10). There is no limit to the substantive topics that it may address, as long as it abides by rules discussed above for the UN as a whole, notably Article 2(1) and 2(7). The Assembly is the plenary body of the UN, meaning that it includes as members all of the nation-states in the UN. Each state gets one vote in the Assembly and resolutions

---

[8] Philippe Sands and Pierre Klein, *Bowett's Law of International Institutions*, 5th edn. Sweet and Maxwell, 2001, pp. 39–55.

[9] S/PRST/1999/28. Each UN document has a unique reference code, where the first letter represents the body that produced the document ("S" for Security Council, "A" for General Assembly, etc.), and subsequent characters further specify. In this case, this is the 28th Presidential Statement from the Security Council in 1999.

[10] See Bruce Cronin and Ian Hurd (eds.), *The UN Security Council and the Politics of International Authority*. Routledge, 2008.

generally pass if they are supported by two-thirds of the members present and voting. While Article 10 authorizes the Assembly to discuss "any questions or any matters" of concern to the UN, the Assembly's power on any of these topics is limited to making "recommendations" to states or to the Secretary-General, issuing reports, and launching studies.

General Assembly resolutions are therefore (at most) statements of recommendation. They are never legally binding directives. States' obligations to these recommendations are very limited; the Charter implies that states have a duty to take these recommendations seriously, but it does not create any formal legal obligation to implement or even consider them, let alone to take any action. The General Assembly's power is therefore broad but shallow. It can consider and make recommendations on many topics but its outputs have no coercive or binding authority.

The one exception to this pattern is that the Assembly has decisive power over the UN expenditure budget and the allocation of costs among member states. This authority is established by Article 17 and it is noteworthy because it means that the sensitive matters of revenue and spending are decided by the Assembly by a two-thirds majority vote without any special influence reserved for the highest-contributing states. The UN's critics, particularly among conservatives in the US, have taken this as ammunition for the complaint that UN spending is disconnected from or unaccountable to the rich states who contribute the largest shares of the UN's income.[11] That the UN is organized this way reflects the fact that in 1945 there was a dominant view that the spending decisions of the organization were of interest to the general membership and not just the Great Powers. In this case, the democratic impulse trumped the usual tendency for the strong states to keep close control over important decisions.

However, the power of the big contributors is accommodated in more subtle ways, using the procedural rules of the Assembly: the draft budget of the organization only reaches the Assembly as whole after it has passed through a committee on which the major contributors are represented and which takes decisions by consensus. This committee (the Advisory Committee on Administrative and Budgetary Questions (ACABQ)) has sixteen members, elected from the General Assembly, and it receives the draft budget from the Secretary-General before sending it on to the Assembly. By customary agreement, the US always has a member on the

---

[11] For instance Brett D. Schaefer, "A Progress Report on the UN," Backgrounder 1937, Heritage Foundation: www.heritage.org/Research/InternationalOrganizations/bg1937.cfm. Accessed December 3, 2009.

committee.[12] In practice, therefore, the US can veto the budget in this committee stage before it ever reaches the Assembly and thus no budget reaches the Assembly without US approval. In a second accommodation to the influence of political power, the budget for peacekeeping missions is organized separately from the "regular" budget described in Article 17, in an effort to insulate the regular budget from the disagreements that arose when the GA, rather than the SC, launched peace operations in the 1950s and 1960s. (This is discussed in Chapter 5.)

To the extent that GA resolutions have a significant effect in world politics it is due to their political influence rather than to the legal obligations that they carry. General Assembly resolutions can be politically useful tools in the rhetorical struggles between states and for that reason a good deal of attention is devoted to fighting over the language in them. These resolutions can sometimes be successfully presented as reflecting the view of the "international community" of states. Since the GA is the closest thing to a global legislature that currently exists, its products might be seen as statements on behalf of the collective community. They fall far short of "legislation," but GA statements and resolutions are useful in legitimating positions, policies, and ideas.

Several of the most famous GA resolutions illustrate the fact that their political impact sometimes far outweighs their very limited legal status. For instance, the Universal Declaration of Human Rights began its life as a statement issued by the General Assembly in 1948 (it was not a formal "resolution" of the Assembly). This declaration is an excellent example of how the Assembly can be used to create or reinforce international norms or rules of customary international law. Similarly, the GA resolution known colloquially as "Uniting for Peace" (GA 377) is influential, though far more legally uncertain. It includes the claim that the Assembly can use its recommendatory power to create new peace operations in cases when the Security Council fails to execute its "primary" responsibility for peace and security under Article 24. In 1975, the Assembly passed a resolution declaring that "Zionism is a form of racism" because it privileges one religious or ethnic group over all others.[13] This was later revoked (in 1991, with Resolution 46/86), but the controversy it attracted shows the political power of GA instruments. These instances show that, given the right arrangement of circumstances

---

[12] Chesterman, Franck, and Malone detail the political failures that led, in 1996, to the US being denied a seat on ACABQ for the first and only time: Simon Chesterman, Thomas M. Franck, and David M. Malone, *Law and Practice of the United Nations: Documents and Commentary.* Oxford University Press, 2008, pp. 228–229.

[13] A/3379.

and content, GA resolutions can have an impact that is much greater than one might expect from reading the legal terms of the Charter.

States owe few obligations to either ECOSOC or the Trusteeship Council. The Economic and Social Council is a subsidiary body of the General Assembly, though it is formally set out in the Charter as a permanent fixture of the UN. It has the power to "initiate studies and reports with respect to international economic, social, cultural, educational, health, and related matters and may make recommendations with respect to any such matters to the General Assembly, to the members of the United Nations, and to the specialized agencies concerned" (Art. 61(1)). The scope of these powers is broad, and includes the authority to discuss human rights, health, and development, among other topics, but they are also very limited in the sense that they do not include the ability to take decisions or forcefully intervene in any issue. ECOSOC has no power to tell governments what to do. As a result, ECOSOC functions mainly as a coordinating body for the varied agencies and programs that are at work on these topics. It can be politically influential when it uses its administrative capacity to launch high-profile conferences or to publicize a topic that its members believe is important. These have recently included initiatives on sustainable development and the special problems of development in post-conflict societies. ECOSOC's fifty-four members are elected from the General Assembly membership for three-year terms with a system of regional representation similar to that of the Security Council (which is discussed below).

The Trusteeship Council operated until 1994 to oversee what the Charter called "non-self-governing territories." These included both territories that were governed directly by the UN as protectorates (such as Eritrea until 1952) and territories that were held by UN members (such as Somalia by Italy until 1960, and Palau by the US until 1994). It created obligations only on those UN members that controlled these territories, and so when the last such territory (Palau) became an independent state in 1994, these obligations ceased to exist in practice. The Charter still lists the obligations of the trust-governing states in Chapters XI and XII, which center on the hopeful-sounding yet vague responsibility to treat "the interests of the inhabitants of these territories [as] paramount, and accept as a sacred trust the obligation to promote to the utmost . . . the well-being of the inhabitants" (Art. 73).[14] The only substantive obligation of Trust-

---

[14] The relationship between the early United Nations and European colonialism is the subject of Mark Mazower, *No Enchanted Palace: The End of Empire and the Ideological Origins of the United Nations*. Princeton University Press, 2009.

holding states at the Trusteeship Council was "to assist in the progressive development of their free political institutions" and to work toward self-government (Art. 73(b)), and this produced the controversy over the South West Africa trust territory. The trust-governing state (South Africa) refused to allow the Trusteeship Council to oversee its governance of South-West Africa because it did not accept the idea that it should be obligated to contribute toward the self-governance of the polity. This generated a series of crises between South Africa and the rest of the world, including important GA resolutions (especially Res. 2145) and ICJ opinions (the South-West Africa cases and advisory opinions), as well as a protracted civil war and exhausting postwar transition. The area is now Namibia.

The powers of the Security Council are dramatically different than those of any other UN organ. They begin with Articles 25 and 49, which say "The Members of the United Nations agree to accept and carry out the decisions of the Security Council in accordance with the present Charter" and "The Members of the United Nations shall join in affording mutual assistance in carrying out the measures decided upon by the Security Council." These two rules mean that states are legally committed to obeying decisions of the Council whether they agree with them or not, and whether they are themselves members of the Council or not. The scope of Council decision-making authority is defined by Articles 39, 41, and 42: Article 39 empowers it to determine what behavior by states constitutes a "threat to or breach of international peace and security," while Articles 41 and 42 allow it to respond with any measures it deems necessary, including military interventions and programs of economic sanctions. Together with Articles 25 and 49, these rules constitute the Council as a body with historically unmatched powers of collective political and military enforcement. It has, by a wide margin, the most authoritative and complete grant of enforcement power ever made in the history of the system of state sovereignty. No other international organization has anything like this power to centralize and dominate policy-making on any topic, let alone a topic as important as the decision to use military force. As we shall see in Chapter 4, how this power is used in practice is interesting and complicated, and at times it may exceed what is described in the Charter while at others it thoroughly fails to live up to what the Charter envisions.

Upon joining the United Nations, states automatically commit themselves to carry out the Council's decisions, and to allow that the Council takes on "primary responsibility for the maintenance of international peace and security" (Art. 24). At the same time, they also gain some rights toward the

Council, including the right to bring their concerns about international security to the Council (Art. 35(1)) and to participate in Council deliberations that might affect their interests (Art. 31). They also have the right to run for election to the non-permanent seats in the Council (Art. 23(1)). The existence of these rights, however, points to the fact that the Council has a very small membership relative to the size of the UN, and that most of the work of the Council is done with the large majority of states on the outside looking in. The Council has fifteen members, five of which are the permanent members who are listed by name in Article 23(1). These five are the Republic of China, France, the Soviet Union, the UK, and the US, and they have special voting powers. Two of these states no longer exist, but by informal agreement the Council operates as if Russia and the People's Republic of China were listed in Article 23. The remaining ten members of the Council are elected from the General Assembly for two-year terms. When the Council takes decisions it follows the voting formula described in Article 27(3): "Decisions of the Security Council on all other matters [i.e. on non-procedural questions] shall be made by an affirmative vote of nine members including the concurring votes of the permanent members."[15] This is the origin of the Great Power veto in the Council. Decisions in the Council require the agreement of all five permanent members as well as at least four non-permanent members to reach the required nine votes.

The veto, with its obvious hierarchy and inequality, has always been controversial and is a frequent target for complaint by states and activists. It clearly violates the spirit of Article 2(1), but because it is written into the Charter, and is therefore legally equal to Article 2(1), it cannot violate the letter of that rule. In the negotiation of the Charter in 1944 and 1945 the veto was an absolute requirement to secure the consent of the US, the UK, and the Soviet Union. The Big Three fought every attempt by the small and medium states at San Francisco to dilute or qualify the veto, and openly threatened to abandon the effort to create the UN if any changes to it were approved by the majority of San Francisco delegations.[16]

The legal effect of the veto is that the permanent members have an absolute ability to defeat any substantive decision of the Council with which they

---

[15] Before the enlargement of the Council in 1965 from eleven to fifteen members, this Article said "an affirmative vote of seven members including the concurring votes of the permanent members."

[16] Ian Hurd, *After Anarchy: Legitimacy and Power in the UN Security Council.* Princeton University Press, 2007, ch. 4.

disagree for any reason. And since the Council is the only part of the UN that can create new legal obligations on states, this means the permanent members have absolute control over the extent of their commitments to the UN. This broad and ultimate authority over peace and security actions was the sine qua non for the Great Powers at San Francisco.

The existence of the veto is decisive proof against the frequently repeated claim that the Charter presumed that a concord among the Great Powers would continue after World War II – quite the opposite: the Americans, British, and Soviets clearly understood that they would likely have major disagreements about how international stability should be organized, and they demanded a veto over Council decisions precisely to protect their interests in those disagreements. The veto was included so that each of the Great Powers could individually kill collective measures that threatened their interests. Far from being naive or unrealistic about power politics, as Michael Glennon and others have suggested, the framers of the Charter saw the Council as a forum for continuing their struggles over power.[17] The veto ensures that the UN cannot take any collective measures on international security without the consent of the five permanent members. It is absolute and without exception.[18]

The Security Council is a select body of limited membership and strong powers. This naturally turns it into a place where great controversy arises over the distribution of those limited seats. The non-permanent seats are allocated to countries from the General Assembly under a formula described in Articles 23(1) and (2) and in the procedural rules of the Assembly.[19] States are elected to the Council by their regional caucuses so that five states come from the African and Asian group, one from Eastern Europe, two from Latin America and the Caribbean, and two from "Western Europe and Other." These regional groups are the invention of the General Assembly, and they put into effect the Charter provision in Article 23(1) that "due regard ... [be paid] to equitable geographical distribution" of non-permanent seats.

The "Western Europe and Other" group (WEOG) is a remarkable construction. It reflects the effort to contain Western Europe, Canada, Australia, and New

[17] Michael Glennon, "Why the Security Council Failed," *Foreign Affairs*, May/June 2003, 82(3): 16–35. See also the responses by Anne-Marie Slaughter, Edward Luck, and Ian Hurd, *Foreign Affairs*, July/August 2003, 82(4): 201–205.

[18] Notice, for instance, that the qualification in Article 27(3) about a party to a dispute refraining from voting only applies to some kinds of pacific dispute settlement by the Council. It does not apply to the legally binding enforcement actions that are at the core of the Council's powers.

[19] The Procedures of the General Assembly are available at: www.un.org/ga/ropga.shtml.

Zealand in one group, and as such it is more of a conceptual than a regional group. It assumes an affinity of interests among these states whose foundation is historical or cultural or perhaps racial. Until 2000, when it was allowed to join WEOG, Israel did not belong to any regional group because none would accept it, and so it was structurally unable to run for or vote in Security Council elections. The US is not formally a member of any group but it participates in the WEOG as an observer. Each regional group is free to decide its own method for choosing its candidates and these vary greatly.[20] The Western Europe and Other group allows any member to contest an open seat, thus generating interesting open contests with plenty of intrigue, lobbying, and side payments. The African and Asian group splits itself roughly in half and allocates three of its seats for Africa and two for Asia. Within this subset, the African contingent (like the Latin American group) decides in advance on its candidate and so avoids competitive elections in the GA. The Asian group does not decide in advance.

A very different kind of controversy surrounds the permanent seats and their voting rights. A permanent seat is a valuable thing, both because of the veto and because it guarantees a voice and influence in every Council deliberation. There was not much controversy in 1945 over which countries should be the permanent members, though the Soviets made efforts to impede China's participation, and at one point the US favored including Brazil as a sixth member.[21] Because they are explicitly named in the Charter, the permanent members cannot be removed, changed, or added to without going through the formal process of Charter amendment, which is described in Article 108 (and which requires approval of the five permanent members). A lively diplomatic melee has been going on since the early 1990s as the General Assembly has tried to find a formula for revising the membership combination in the Council. This has taken place in part within a GA subcommittee called the "Open-Ended Working Group on Security Council Reform,"[22] and in part directly among capitals.

---

[20] These are described in research by Security Council Report. See "UN Security Council Elections 2008," Research Report #2, 2008 at: www.securitycouncilreport.org/site/c.glKWLeMTIsG/ b.4464545/k.3006/Special_Research_Report_No_2brUN_ Security_Council_Elections_ 2008br29_August_2008.htm.

[21] Townsend Hoopes and Douglas Brinkley, *FDR and the Creation of the UN*. Yale University Press, 1997, Ch. 9; Stephen C. Schlesinger, *Act of Creation: The Founding of the United Nations*. Westview Press, 2003, p. 49.

[22] Its full name deserves quoting. It is the "Open-Ended Working Group on the Question of Equitable Representation on and Increase in the Membership of the Security Council and other Matters Related to the Security Council."

It is not surprising that no solution is in sight to the problem of Council expansion. It is stuck on at least two dilemmas: first, the apparently irreconcilable tensions among the desires to keep the Council relatively small and relatively diverse by region and wealth; and second, the regional jealousies that surface as potential new members are named. Because changes require near-consensus among UN members, every new formula that has been proposed to or by the Open-Ended Working Group has produced enough unhappy states to prevent it from going forward. And yet many governments say that they find the status quo to be unacceptable as well. In the absence of either consensus or a hegemon to force the issue, the entire project seems mired.

When the Security Council issues a decision, it is binding on all states. The Council therefore has the power to create new legal obligations for states without requiring their consent. Decisions are contained in resolutions, and stand out because of their declaratory and active language. For instance, the SC resolution on removing Iraq from Kuwait in 1990 says that the Council "demands that Iraq comply fully with Resolution 660" (on withdrawing from Kuwait) and "authorizes Member States ... to use all necessary means to uphold and implement Resolution 660" (SC Res. 678). These specific obligations are not contained in the Charter. They are "merely" the operational products of the Council and yet they are as binding on UN members as the Charter itself.

The contrast between the Assembly and the Security Council neatly illustrates a trade-off in the UN between democracy and authority. The Assembly is the much more democratic body, with its one-state one-vote procedure and majority rule, but as a consequence it was allowed only much weaker authority at San Francisco. The Security Council is highly undemocratic but has dispositive authority to impose obligations on all member states. This inverse relationship between democracy and power is no accident: at San Francisco, none of the Big Three who dominated the negotiations over the Charter were willing to give real authority over important matters to any body that worked according to majority rule. The limited membership of the Council, and more importantly its veto and permanent seats, were essential for the Big Three to accept its broad authority on collective peace and security.

This discussion of the obligations that states accept under the Charter reveals that there is a relatively short list of formal legal obligations. These include paying one's dues to the organization, carrying out the decisions of the Security Council, and refraining from the threat or use of force in foreign policy. Beyond these, we can identify a wide range of aspirations in the UN that are not backed by formal legal obligations (such as to promote economic development, respect human rights, and respectfully consider the recommendations of the General Assembly and ECOSOC). As we consider the ways that states choose to comply or not comply with their obligations under the Charter, and the mechanisms in the UN that are designed to induce compliance, the conversation about compliance comes to focus on the smaller set of very specifically legal obligations rather than the broader goals and aspirations of the Charter.

Compliance

What devices does the UN use to encourage states to fulfill these legal obligations of the Charter? The Security Council has special powers of enforcement, which are discussed in Chapter 4, and aside from these there are few coercive instruments available within the UN to induce compliance. In the absence of coercion, the Charter is largely designed around taking advantage of the interests of states in either preserving their good international reputations or in maintaining an organization that is broadly useful to them. These two incentives, each tuned to states' own interests, are evident throughout the law and practice of the United Nations.

The way that compliance has unfolded with respect to the financial obligations of members to the organization helps to show the complicated and symbiotic legal and political relationship that exists between states and the Charter. The clause that obligates states to pay their dues to the UN is contained in Article 17(2), which says "the expenses of the Organization shall be borne by the Members as apportioned by the General Assembly." This article is the foundation of the budget process of the UN, in which the General Assembly sets both a revenue and an expenditure budget. The expenditure budget is a two-year budget that travels through the ACABQ process discussed above. The revenue side is controlled by a schedule of "assessments" in which states are asked by the General Assembly to contribute specific amounts of money based on their ability to pay. By a special agreement (i.e. negotiated among powerful players outside the framework of the UN Charter), the US is asked to pay 22 percent of the UN's regular budget. This makes it the largest single contributor to the UN but is less than the US would contribute if the normal assessments formula were followed. The smallest assessment category is just 0.001 percent of the budget.

There have been significant controversies over state compliance and non-compliance with the financial terms of the Charter, and many states have put themselves into deep debt with the UN. This has included superpowers and very poor states as well as many in between.

When a member fails to pay its dues, the Charter specifies a formal penalty in Article 19, which says in part "A Member of the United Nations which is in arrears in the payment of its financial contributions to the Organization shall have no vote in the General Assembly if the amount of its arrears equals or exceeds the amount of the contributions due from it for the preceding two years." There have been many instances in which states have been barred from voting in the Assembly as a result, normally through the device of simply not calling on the country during a roll-call vote. At any given time, there might be several dozen members of the Assembly in this situation. For some special cases, however, the suspension of voting rights has become an inflammatory legal and political matter: France, China, and the Soviet Union have all at times been more than two years behind in their payments; the US has teetered at the edge many times, but has always paid just enough in time to remain under the debt limit.[23]

The politics of Great-Power arrearages are entirely different than those of the smaller states. The US has used its withholding as an instrument to force the UN to change policies that the US opposes, and to reduce the American share of the overall budget. An agreement in 1999, for instance, led the US to promise to repay large parts of its debt in exchange for the American share of the overall budget falling to its current level of 22 percent. Some of this has been accomplished, though the US still owes over $1 billion today (if one includes debt to the peacekeeping fund). The Soviet Union and France accumulated large arrears in the 1960s as a form of protest against the General Assembly's assertion of authority to launch peace operations in the Middle East and Congo. These governments maintained that the Assembly had overstepped its legal authority in authorizing these missions and so their costs could not be considered the legitimate expenses of the organization under Article 17. The US and many Western states disagreed, and the ICJ affirmed their view in its advisory opinion in Certain Expenses of the United

---

[23] Calculating the amount owed is controversial since it involves estimating the worth of US "in-kind" contributions to peace operations and other reimbursements. See Frederic L. Kirgis, "US Dues Arrearages in the United Nations and Possible Loss of Vote in the GA," ASIL Insight, July 1998, www.asil.org/insigh21.cfm. Accessed December 4, 2009.

Nations.[24] Despite the ICJ opinion resolving the legal question, the issue produced something of a stalemate in that the Soviets and others insisted that they were complying with Articles 17(1) and 17(2) and defending the UN against unconstitutional misuses of GA power, while others insisted they were in flagrant non-compliance with the Charter.

Many in the Assembly both wanted to defend the principle of paying dues as required and feared the political consequences should two of the five permanent members be denied their right to vote in the Assembly. As the two-year window in Article 19 closed, the parties decided to prolong rather than resolve the stalemate by agreeing that the Assembly would operate by consensus rather than formal votes, and so the non-paying states would not in practice lose their votes and yet Article 19 would not be obviously violated. The Soviets eventually paid their debts in the 1980s.[25] The controversy has accentuated two unresolved questions: Is the ban on voting in Article 19 automatic, or does it only come into effect when the General Assembly explicitly decides to invoke it against a state? And, what is to be done if an organ of the UN is acting outside its legal powers? The withholding of dues has raised both questions and on both the arguments continue.

The politics over UN finance show the complexities that are attached to questions of compliance and non-compliance in the UN. Problems of non-compliance are always situated in a broader political context where it matters very much who the non-compliant state is and what are the political objectives it is pursuing through its non-compliance. China, for instance, was not prevented from voting in the Council in the 1970s when its arrears were very large, but the Dominican Republic and the Central African Empire were.[26] The financing cases provide concrete instances where the Charter has clear rules for defining non-compliance and a clear sanction for those who violate it, and even in these cases non-compliant behavior does not automatically lead to the sanctions envisioned in the Charter.

This leads to a broader point: most of the controversy in and around the United Nations has very little to do with formal compliance and non-compliance with the Charter. What should count as compliance is heavily debated; states provide highly self-serving interpretations of their own

[24] Certain Expenses, ICJ Reports (1962).
[25] "Article 19," *The Charter of the United Nations: A Commentary*, edited by Bruno Simma. Oxford University Press, 1994, p. 330.
[26] Ibid., p. 334.

behavior; and they often claim to be complying with one set of obligations as an explanation for why they are apparently violating another. The US invasion of Grenada in 1983 was called by the General Assembly "a flagrant violation of international law" (UN GA 38/7) but was defended by the US as a rightful exercise of the principle of protecting one's citizens. The Cuban missile crisis of 1963 centered on what the Cubans saw as lawful arming for self-defense and the Americans said was illegal provocation. These competing interpretations are the standard practices of international politics, and in the context of the United Nations they are compounded by the fact that most goals of the UN Charter are written in aspirational language rather than as firm commitments. For instance, the Charter combines sweeping and vague language on human rights in the preamble with specific but weak legal obligations to cooperate in Article 56. The Preamble says "We the peoples of the United Nations determined . . . to reaffirm faith in fundamental human rights, in the dignity and worth of the human person . . . have resolved to combine our efforts to accomplish these aims." But the implementation of this aspiration is limited, in Article 56, to "All members pledge themselves to take joint and separate action" toward these goals. The result is that it is essentially impossible to make an uncontested finding of violation with these weakly written obligations, and that the cases of clear violation of the Charter are relatively few compared with the much larger set of cases where states are hard at work arguing for why their behavior should be counted as compliant.

Enforcement

In this environment, what are we to make of enforcement? What powers are there in the Charter for organs of the UN to enforce against states who insist on breaking these obligations? Setting aside the powers of military enforcement held by the Security Council (for which, see Chapter 4), the UN has few tools for enforcing its decisions. However, there are some interesting channels in the Charter for enforcement which fall short of military action and which mostly travel through pathways separate from the Security Council. These are conceptually at least as interesting as the Council's military powers since they illustrate ways in which international organizations strive for influence and impact in the absence of military coercion.

The General Assembly has tried in various ways to interpret its power under the Charter so that it might have some capability to take action beyond the "recommendations" described in Article 10. The issues for which it has been most mobilized include anti-apartheid in South Africa and the Israel-Palestine problem. As mentioned above, it has also claimed the authority to send UN peace operations to conflict zones: to Korea in 1950, to the Middle East in 1956 (UNEF), and to Congo in 1960 (ONUC). These are important enforcement actions for which it claimed legal authority after it decided that the Security Council was failing in its "primary responsibility for the maintenance of international peace and security" in Article 24. It was these operations that sparked the Soviet and French withholding of their UN dues. The GA's approach was to read the Council's "primary" authority as implying logically that some other organ, presumably the Assembly on behalf of the UN as a whole, must therefore have a "secondary" or "subsidiary" or "residual" authority. It therefore essentially wrote itself this power in the resolution known as "Uniting for Peace" in 1950 (Res. 377). It was used to develop the UN's operations in the Korean War, and later for UNEF and ONUC. This is a dramatic extension of the Assembly's powers and a close reading of the Charter provides little support for it. Its use has been highly contentious in international politics and highly questionable in international law.

Much more conventional are the many instruments the Assembly has deployed with respect to South Africa and Israel-Palestine, as these have generated state policies which the Assembly has interpreted as being non-compliant with Charter obligations. On these topics, the Assembly has been relatively united over the years, and has therefore had the chance to become frustrated by its lack of coercive tools under the Charter. It has been motivated to think creatively about how to leverage what influence and authority it does possess for maximum effect. On South Africa, for instance, the Assembly passed many resolutions condemning apartheid and calling for the South African government to reform itself. These were of course "recommendations" in the legal language of the Charter and did not create any legal obligations for the government. The Security Council in 1963 decided that apartheid "is seriously disturbing international peace and security" and called for apartheid to be abandoned (SC Res. 181), but the Assembly continued to strive for more powerful enforcement action than the Council was willing to provide. The Assembly variously called for economic sanctions, arms embargoes, cultural isolation, and an end to cooperation over sports, all with the force of recommendations. In 1974 it used its internal procedures to suspend South Africa from participating in the Assembly, a condition that continued into the 1990s. This power is nowhere set out in the Charter, but rests instead on the authority of the Assembly's credentials committee to decide on the qualifications for occupying a seat. It also took what action it could to interfere with South African control over the territory of Namibia, then known as South-West Africa, which South Africa claimed to manage under an old League of Nations mandate but which the General Assembly believed it was occupying illegally.[27] The Assembly argued that it and the Trusteeship Council had legal authority over the territory because the League's trust territories transferred to the UN in 1945, and it therefore issued what it believed were legally binding instructions to South Africa to remove itself from the territory. It also formally changed the name of the territory to Namibia in 1968, against the wishes of South Africa, and recognized an anti-South African militia as the legitimate government in 1973. The Assembly's actions spurred the Security Council and the ICJ into action, and these bodies issued their own decisions, in 1970 and 1971 respectively, and legally binding, that South Africa was not legally entitled to rule Namibia. The matter remained contested by South Africa until the combination of armed struggle, changing international politics, and changing South African domestic politics led to Namibian independence in 1990.

These devices show ways that bodies in the UN strive to enforce their recommendations and decisions in world politics, quite separate from any power of direct military or legal enforcement. The tools of enforcement held by the General Assembly are all indirect, resting on its capacity to mobilize other political resources in the international system including ICJ decisions, public contempt and shaming, Security Council actions, and coalitions for economic sanctions. The Assembly does indeed have some paths by which it can try to enforce its collective will, but they lie almost entirely in the political register rather than the more explicit military category. As we look at the Security Council in the next chapter, we can see how the Council's enforcement capacity is equally political but is backed up with the possibility of military force, and as a result the Council's politics are very different than those of the rest of the United Nations.

---

[27] See Cedric Thornberry, "Namibia," in David M. Malone (ed.), *The UN Security Council: From the Cold War to the 21st Century.* Lynne Rienner, 2004, pp. 407–422.

CASE I: The Goldstone Report

The legal and political aspects of the United Nations are well illustrated by the 2009 report on possible war crimes in Israel's invasion of Gaza. This was the product of the Human Rights Council, a subsidiary body of the General Assembly and itself a recent invention that is worth some attention. It is also one small piece of a long UN history on Palestine and Israel that began in 1947 with a resolution calling for the British "mandate" territory of Palestine to be divided between an "Arab" state and a "Jewish" state and the city of Jerusalem (UN GA Res. 181).

The Human Rights Council came into existence in 2006, and replaced the former Commission on Human Rights. It was created by the Assembly and has powers that are delegated to it from the Assembly. Its membership is a subset of the Assembly's members. It therefore operates within the terms of the Assembly's own powers and does not expand the UN's authority in any way.

The mandate of the Human Rights Council is to address human rights violations in UN member states. It is composed of forty-seven members, elected by secret ballot for three-year terms by the General Assembly. Following Article 2(1) of the Charter, all states are eligible for membership in the new body. This offended the US administration at the time for it neither guaranteed the US a permanent seat nor guaranteed that states with lousy human rights practices would be excluded; the Council's composition therefore reflects the inclusive view of the UN as a place where all states gather rather than the view that this should be a kind of body of experts on human rights who monitor poorly behaved others. The body has set out for itself a mission to periodically review the human rights situation in every UN member state, as well as to make inquiries or recommendations on specific issues or situations, such as on ways to further protect the rights of children. As a subsidiary construct of the Assembly, its authority is limited to making recommendations about human rights, and these recommendations are not legally binding on states or on the UN. They are nonetheless influential in the practical politics of international relations, as evidenced by the aftermath of the Goldstone Report.

Richard Goldstone, a prominent international lawyer from South Africa, was asked by the Human Rights Council "to investigate all violations of international human rights law and international humanitarian law that might have been committed at any time in the context of the military operations that were conducted in Gaza" from December 2008 to January 2009.[28] This meant two things: a "fact-finding" mission to the region in order to assess the behaviors of Israel, Hamas, the Palestinian Authority, and assorted militias, and a set of legal interpretations on what constitutes lawful conduct in war. He found significant evidence of violations of the laws of war by all parties in the conflict, and much of the report is devoted to documenting specific cases of war crimes. The report is strongly shaped by the difficulties inherent in gathering evidence in such cases, and as a result the report focuses on a few illustrative instances where evidence was relatively available. The difficulties were many, including the basic problem of determining responsibility for destruction after the fact, as well as the facts that many civilians were reluctant to discuss what they had seen and that Israel refused all cooperation with Goldstone's team. Backed by only the General Assembly's powers of "recommendation," a mission of the Human Rights Council has no authority to compel states or others to cooperate with its investigations.

The report's conclusions are therefore also limited to the status of "recommendations." In this case, it recommended that the parties in the conflict begin to respect the humanitarian laws that apply to their conduct, that Israel cease interfering in the politics of the Occupied Territories and pay reparations to the UN and others for damaged property, and that all sides release political prisoners and begin to respect human rights and the freedoms of civil society. It also made recommendations to other international organizations, notably to the UN Security Council, that it use its enforcement authority to force Israel to follow international humanitarian law in war and more generally in its occupation of the region, and to the International Criminal Court that it investigate the possibility of prosecutions of those responsible for war crimes on all sides. It also called on the states of the Geneva Conventions to take action to enforce their rules.

The report's legal context emphasizes the obligations of states and non-state actors in military conflicts. It is concerned mainly with the obligations that armies and militias owe to civilians, rather than with the more general obligations that states owe to other states under public international law. Goldstone says that his effort is devoted to "the protection of all victims in accordance with international law." These obligations arise from the existing framework of international humanitarian law, including the rules on belligerent occupation, on the use of chemical weapons, on the protection of civilians in war, and on

---

[28] UN Human Rights Council, Fact Finding Mission on the Gaza Conflict UN A/HRC/12/48, p. 39.

self-determination. The report therefore has much in common with the legal framework of the International Criminal Court discussed in Chapter 9.

In finding that there were significant war crimes committed in the conduct of the war, and indeed that the war itself was initiated by Israel in violation of the laws on war, the Goldstone Report added the language of international law to the politics of the conflict. Despite being limited by the General Assembly's constrained authority (i.e. only "recommendations"), it nonetheless had a significant effect in the broader regional and international politics that encompass the situation. The Report motivated many states and international organizations to take it seriously, and in doing so these states and IOs added their weight either against or behind its recommendations. Israel rejected the report as unfair and insisted that "military necessity" was sufficient legal rationale for both the war and its conduct in the war.[29] Human Rights Watch and other advocacy groups endorsed the report and used it to push further for judicial accountability for those who commit war crimes, no matter their home government's position.[30] The US has used the report as evidence that all sides in the conflict need to strengthen their internal mechanisms for investigating the possibility that their own personnel may have violated international humanitarian law.[31]

The politics surrounding the report demonstrate the practical effect that the United Nations can have in world politics even without any stronger legal instrument than the relatively weak "recommendation" power of the General Assembly. With its capacity to investigate and recommend, the Assembly can package information into new international instruments of great political consequence. Reports such as this one become tools in the hands of states and others who wish to use them as resources in their political fights. The capacity to create such resources is an important power for the United Nations. This power can be significant, and it is in a fundamental way separate from the legal authority of the Human Rights Council and of the General Assembly.

[29] "UN Human Rights Chief Endorses Goldstone Gaza Report," Haaretz, November 2, 2009, www.haaretz.com/hasen/spages/1121045.html. Accessed December 3, 2009.
[30] www.hrw.org/en/news/2009/11/03/un-endorse-goldstone-report. Accessed December 3, 2009.
[31] See for instance David Kaye, "The Goldstone Report," American Society of International Law Insight, October 1, 2009, 13(16).

CASE II: Cholera in Haiti – Who Pays?

When things go wrong with a UN operation, who pays the costs? The UN has had a presence in Haiti on and off since the early 1990s, including peacekeepers, police officers, election monitors, aid workers, and more. It added more logistical resources after the 2010 earthquake including soldiers from Nepal who, it turned out, unwittingly brought with them the cholera bacteria. Endemic in Nepal, cholera was non-existent in Haiti. The peacekeepers built a camp along the Artibonite River with substandard latrines and thus allowed the bacteria into the public water supply. Cholera is an infection of the small intestine that causes watery diarrhea and, if untreated, leads to death by dehydration. The epidemic launched by the UN in Haiti killed almost 10,000 people and made a million people sick. It added immense suffering and loss in what was already a major natural disaster in one of the poorest countries in the world.

It took only a few weeks for local people to realize that the UN base was the source of cholera. The Nepalese soldiers began to arrive on October 9, 2010; the first hospitalization for cholera was on October 17; on October 22 it was officially declared an epidemic; and by mid-November there were widespread protests against the United Nations for its carelessness. The peacekeepers responded with violence, and killed at least one person in these protests.

But it took almost six years for the United Nations to admit that the disease came from its peacekeepers. Only in the summer of 2016 did it begin talking about its responsibility and consider the possibility of compensating victims and their families.

In the intervening years, the UN used its political and legal powers described in this chapter to insulate itself in what Scott Veitch has called a "zone of irresponsibility" where the harms it caused were, legally speaking, not its responsibility. In the face of both private claims and public lawsuits the UN successfully deployed legal arguments to avoid accountability. In 2011, a group of activists organized 5,000 families in Haiti affected by cholera and presented a set of claims to the United Nations. They requested compensation, new investment in water treatment, and an apology.[32] The UN refused to respond to their claims, saying only that they amounted to an illegitimate demand to

---

[32] The petition for relief can be read here: www.ijdh.org/2011/11/topics/law-justice/chief-claims-unit-minustah-log-base-room-no-25a-boule-toussaint-louverture-clercine-18-tabarre-haiti-ijdh-bai.

second-guess "political and policy matters" within the organization.[33] The petitions for relief ended there. A second attempt was made using more formal legal channels, with a series of lawsuits against the UN and its officials in US federal courts. By 2016, these cases were all rejected by the courts on the grounds that the United Nations enjoys immunity from all domestic legal actions. This comes from the UN Charter and from a subsequent treaty in 1946 that defines the "privileges and immunities" of the organization relative to national governments.

The UN's immunity from domestic courts is typical for international organizations. It is usually seen as essential to facilitating the kind of work the organization is meant to do: it is protected from interference by local officials who might entangle it in local regulations. But it has a broader political effect too in that it takes away from local people an important tool for holding powerful institutions accountable. It shifts power away from the people and decisively to the organization. In Haiti, as in other places governed by similar Status of Force Agreements, the UN operates in its own legal environment – it is subject to local law in a nominal sense but cannot be taken to court if it violates the law. The latrines of the peacekeepers did not meet local (or international) building codes and the result was the cholera epidemic – if a regular person had done this they might be charged with criminal negligence or sued in civil court for the damage that followed, but the UN cannot face those possibilities. It exists in a privileged legal bubble, accountable only to its member states and not to any courts.

Legal immunity empowers the UN over the people in the places where it operates. It shifts the terrain of globalization even further against regular people and in favor of the global institution. It shifts the costs of negligence and bad behavior from the organization to the people it is supposed to serve. This is amply clear in the many cases of sexual assault by peacekeepers: when on a mission, peacekeepers are exempt from local law and are subject to the law of their home country. The local police cannot arrest or prosecute them; they can only request that the UN send them back home.

In the end, the Haiti episode shows how the UN's legal status protects it from accountability in local courts. The harms that it might cause cannot be pursued through the usual channels of criminal cases or lawsuits. In many cases, they cannot be pursued at all. When things go wrong with UN operations it is often the local people who pay the costs, not the organization itself.

---

[33] Patricia O'Brien, UN Legal Counsel, letter to Brian Concannon, February 21, 2013.

Conclusion

The United Nations presents states with a set of authoritative rules for international politics and with a set of institutions of varying power and scope. The rules define the basic parameters of legal international conduct, including a ban on the use of force to settle disputes among states, the essential equality of countries as sovereign states, and an obligation to assist the United Nations in various ways when it takes collective action against threats to international peace and security. The organizations that make up the six principal organs of the UN can also create obligations for UN members, as when the General Assembly decides on the budget and assessments for UN financing and when the Trusteeship Council would in the past supervise the administration of trust territories. These organs have powers that are explicitly delimited by the UN Charter and they can be seen as possessing authority that states have delegated to them from their own stock of sovereign prerogatives. The Security Council is an exceptional creature, however, in that to it states have delegated powers of enforcement and collective action that are broad, open-ended, and binding. The Council is the only part of the UN with the authority to create new obligations for member states on the key issues of war, peace, and sanctions, and so it possesses the potential to upend the traditional hierarchy in which states are always legally superior to their international organizations. This power is unprecedented both conceptually and in practice, and is treated more fully in the following chapter.

The complexities of the organization make it an excellent location in which to observe all three of the roles of IOs described in Chapter 2. There are elements of actor, forum, and resource evident throughout the political life of the United Nations. The annual meetings of the General Assembly provide a classic example of an international forum, where states take advantage of the existing institutional body to give their statements greater political impact. It also operates as an actor when it issues statements and resolutions that may represent something like the sentiment of the international community. The collective nature of its outputs may give them a special weight in world politics and may therefore make the Assembly appear to be a unified actor. These resolutions are highly coveted by states as symbolic resources with which they can influence the global perception of the issues that interest them, and in this way the Assembly may also perform as a resource in the hands of other actors.

The UN's high level of political salience in international relations is remarkable given that most of its organs do not have the legal authority to make decisions that are binding on states. Most, including the General Assembly, ECOSOC, and the Secretariat, have very limited legal powers relative to the UN member states, and in most cases they can do no more than make recommendations to governments. The few exceptions to this rule are all the more interesting and contested because they stand out so clearly from the larger set of recommendatory powers. These binding powers include the GA's power over the UN budget and the Security Council's authority to enact military interventions. The UN has political power in many dimensions in world politics which come about incidentally from the much more limited legal powers described in the Charter.

Further Reading

The UN Charter is essential reading and it is best read in print rather than online. The famous little blue book is available at: https://unp.un.org/details.aspx?pid=4769. The best reference work that explains each article line by line is *The Charter of the United Nations: A Commentary*, edited by Bruno Simma (Oxford University Press, 1994). For the history of negotiations at San Francisco and before, see Stephen C. Schlesinger, *Act of Creation: The Founding of the United Nations* (Westview Press, 2003), Robert C. Hilderbrand, *Dumbarton Oaks: The Origins of the United Nations and the Search for Postwar Security* (University of North Carolina Press, 1990), and Townsend Hoopes and Douglas Brinkley, *FDR and the Creation of the UN* (Yale University Press, 1997).

On the practical side of the UN's history, many excellent books exist. These are indispensable: *The Oxford Handbook on the United Nations*, edited by Thomas G. Weiss and Sam Daws (Oxford University Press, 2009), *The Procedure of the UN Security Council*, edited by Loraine Sievers and Sam Daws (Oxford University Press, 4th edn., 2014), and *Law and Practice of the United Nations: Documents and Commentary*, edited by Simon Chesterman, Thomas M. Franck, and David M. Malone (Oxford University Press, 2008). The Secretary-General's role is well described in Simon Chesterman (ed.), *Secretary or General? The UN Secretary-General in World Politics* (Cambridge University Press, 2007).

For daily developments at the UN, subscribe to the "UN Wire" email briefing memo from the United Nations Foundation, an independent advocacy and monitoring group that covers the broad spectrum of UN issues at www.unfoundation.org/what-we-do/campaigns-and-initiatives/un-wire.

On the early UN's role in Palestine and the partition, see Elad Ben-Dror, *Ralph Bunche and the Arab-Israeli Conflict* (Routledge, 2015) and the UN's own history in "The Question of Palestine & the United Nations," DPI/2276 2003.

The Haiti claims and lawsuits were instigated by the Institute for Justice and Development in Haiti. An excellent account of the UN in Haiti after the earthquake is in Jonathan M. Katz, *The Big Truck that Went By: How the World Came to Save Haiti and Left Behind a Disaster* (St. Martin's, 2014). On the law and politics of UN immunity in Haiti and elsewhere, see Mara Pillinger, Ian Hurd, and Michael N. Barnett, "How to Get Away with Cholera: The UN, Haiti, and International Law," *Perspectives on Politics*, March 2016, 14(1). On how the UN might cause human rights problems, and then how it responds, see Guglielmo Verdirame, *The UN and Human Rights: Who Guards the Guardians?* (Cambridge University Press, 2011).

APPENDIX 3
Charter of the United Nations (excerpts)

Article 1

The Purposes of the United Nations are

1. To maintain international peace and security, and to that end: to take effective collective measures for the prevention and removal of threats to the peace, and for the suppression of acts of aggression or other breaches of the peace, and to bring about by peaceful means, and in conformity with the principles of justice and international law, adjustment or settlement of international disputes or situations which might lead to a breach of the peace;
2. To develop friendly relations among nations based on respect for the principle of equal rights and self-determination of peoples, and to take other appropriate measures to strengthen universal peace;
3. To achieve international co-operation in solving international problems of an economic, social, cultural, or humanitarian character, and in promoting and encouraging respect for human rights and for fundamental freedoms for all without distinction as to race, sex, language, or religion; and
4. To be a centre for harmonizing the actions of nations in the attainment of these common ends.

Article 2

The Organization and its Members, in pursuit of the Purposes stated in Article 1, shall act in accordance with the following Principles.

1. The Organization is based on the principle of the sovereign equality of all its Members.
2. ...

3. All Members shall settle their international disputes by peaceful means in such a manner that international peace and security, and justice, are not endangered.

4. All Members shall refrain in their international relations from the threat or use of force against the territorial integrity or political independence of any state, or in any other manner inconsistent with the Purposes of the United Nations.

5. All Members shall give the United Nations every assistance in any action it takes in accordance with the present Charter, and shall refrain from giving assistance to any state against which the United Nations is taking preventive or enforcement action.

6. The Organization shall ensure that states which are not Members of the United Nations act in accordance with these Principles so far as may be necessary for the maintenance of international peace and security.

7. Nothing contained in the present Charter shall authorize the United Nations to intervene in matters which are essentially within the domestic jurisdiction of any state or shall require the Members to submit such matters to settlement under the present Charter; but this principle shall not prejudice the application of enforcement measures under Chapter VII.

Chapter II: Membership

Article 3

The original Members of the United Nations shall be the states which, having participated in the United Nations Conference on International Organization at San Francisco, or having previously signed the Declaration by United Nations of 1 January 1942, sign the present Charter and ratify it in accordance with Article 110.

Article 4

1. Membership in the United Nations is open to all other peace-loving states which accept the obligations contained in the present Charter and, in the judgment of the Organization, are able and willing to carry out these obligations.

2. The admission of any such state to membership in the United Nations will be effected by a decision of the General Assembly upon the recommendation of the Security Council.

Article 5

A Member of the United Nations against which preventive or enforcement action has been taken by the Security Council may be suspended from the exercise of the rights and privileges of membership by the General Assembly upon the recommendation of the Security Council. The exercise of these rights and privileges may be restored by the Security Council.

Article 6

A Member of the United Nations which has persistently violated the Principles contained in the present Charter may be expelled from the Organization by the General Assembly upon the recommendation of the Security Council.

. . .

Chapter III: Organs

. . .

Article 8

The United Nations shall place no restrictions on the eligibility of men and women to participate in any capacity and under conditions of equality in its principal and subsidiary organs.

Chapter IV: The General Assembly

COMPOSITION

Article 9

1. The General Assembly shall consist of all the Members of the United Nations.

. . .

FUNCTIONS AND POWERS

Article 10

The General Assembly may discuss any questions or any matters within the scope of the present Charter or relating to the powers and functions of any organs provided for in the present Charter, and, except as provided in Article 12, may make recommendations to the Members of the United Nations or to the Security Council or to both on any such questions or matters.

. . .

VOTING

Article 18

1. Each member of the General Assembly shall have one vote.
2. Decisions of the General Assembly on important questions shall be made by a two-thirds majority of the members present and voting . . .

3. Decisions on other questions, including the determination of additional categories of questions to be decided by a two-thirds majority, shall be made by a majority of the members present and voting.

Article 19

A Member of the United Nations which is in arrears in the payment of its financial contributions to the Organization shall have no vote in the General Assembly if the amount of its arrears equals or exceeds the amount of the contributions due from it for the preceding two full years. The General Assembly may, nevertheless, permit such a Member to vote if it is satisfied that the failure to pay is due to conditions beyond the control of the Member.

. . .

Chapter V: The Security Council

COMPOSITION

Article 23

1. The Security Council shall consist of fifteen Members of the United Nations. The Republic of China, France, the Union of Soviet Socialist Republics, the United Kingdom of Great Britain and Northern Ireland, and the United States of America shall be permanent members of the Security Council. The General Assembly shall elect ten other Members of the United Nations to be non-permanent members of the Security Council, due regard being specially paid, in the first instance to the contribution of Members of the United Nations to the maintenance of international peace and security and to the other purposes of the Organization, and also to equitable geographical distribution.
2. The non-permanent members of the Security Council shall be elected for a term of two years. In the first election of the non-permanent members after the increase of the membership of the Security Council from eleven to fifteen, two of the four additional members shall be chosen for a term of one year. A retiring member shall not be eligible for immediate re-election . . .

FUNCTIONS AND POWERS

Article 24

1. In order to ensure prompt and effective action by the United Nations, its Members confer on the Security Council primary responsibility for the maintenance of international peace and security, and agree that in carrying out its duties under this responsibility the Security Council acts on their behalf . . .

Article 25

The Members of the United Nations agree to accept and carry out the decisions of the Security Council in accordance with the present Charter.

. . .

VOTING

Article 27

1. Each member of the Security Council shall have one vote.
2. Decisions of the Security Council on procedural matters shall be made by an affirmative vote of nine members.
3. Decisions of the Security Council on all other matters shall be made by an affirmative vote of nine members including the concurring votes of the permanent members; provided that, in decisions under Chapter VI, and under paragraph 3 of Article 52, a party to a dispute shall abstain from voting.

. . .

Chapter VII: Action with Respect to Threats to the Peace, Breaches of the Peace, and Acts of Aggression

Article 39

The Security Council shall determine the existence of any threat to the peace, breach of the peace, or act of aggression and shall make recommendations, or decide what measures shall be taken in accordance with Articles 41 and 42, to maintain or restore international peace and security.

. . .

Article 41

The Security Council may decide what measures not involving the use of armed force are to be employed to give effect to its decisions, and it may call upon the Members of the United Nations to apply such measures. These may include complete or partial interruption of economic relations and of rail, sea, air, postal, telegraphic, radio, and other means of communication, and the severance of diplomatic relations.

Article 42

Should the Security Council consider that measures provided for in Article 41 would be inadequate or have proved to be inadequate, it may take such action by air, sea, or land forces as may be necessary to maintain or restore international peace and security. Such action may include demonstrations, blockade, and other operations by air, sea, or land forces of Members of the United Nations.

Article 43

1. All Members of the United Nations, in order to contribute to the maintenance of international peace and security, undertake to make available to the Security Council, on its call and in accordance with a special agreement or agreements, armed forces, assistance, and facilities, including rights of passage, necessary for the purpose of maintaining international peace and security.

. . .

Article 49

The Members of the United Nations shall join in affording mutual assistance in carrying out the measures decided upon by the Security Council.

. . .

Article 51

Nothing in the present Charter shall impair the inherent right of individual or collective self-defence if an armed attack occurs against a Member of the United Nations, until the Security Council has taken measures necessary to maintain international peace and security. Measures taken by Members in the exercise of this right of self-defence shall be immediately reported to the Security Council and shall not in any way affect the authority and responsibility of the Security Council under the present Charter to take at any time such action as it deems necessary in order to maintain or restore international peace and security.

. . .

Chapter XII: International Trusteeship System

Article 75

The United Nations shall establish under its authority an international trusteeship system for the administration and supervision of such territories as may be placed thereunder by subsequent individual agreements. These territories are hereinafter referred to as trust territories.

Article 76

The basic objectives of the trusteeship system, in accordance with the Purposes of the United Nations laid down in Article 1 of the present Charter, shall be:

1. to further international peace and security;
2. to promote the political, economic, social, and educational advancement of the inhabitants of the trust territories, and their progressive development towards self-government or independence as may be appropriate to the particular circumstances

of each territory and its peoples and the freely expressed wishes of the peoples concerned, and as may be provided by the terms of each trusteeship agreement;

3. to encourage respect for human rights and for fundamental freedoms for all without distinction as to race, sex, language, or religion, and to encourage recognition of the interdependence of the peoples of the world; and

4. to ensure equal treatment in social, economic, and commercial matters for all Members of the United Nations and their nationals, and also equal treatment for the latter in the administration of justice, without prejudice to the attainment of the foregoing objectives and subject to the provisions of Article 80.

. . .

Chapter XIV: The International Court of Justice

Article 92

The International Court of Justice shall be the principal judicial organ of the United Nations. It shall function in accordance with the annexed Statute, which is based upon the Statute of the Permanent Court of International Justice and forms an integral part of the present Charter.

Article 93

1. All Members of the United Nations are ipso facto parties to the Statute of the International Court of Justice.

. . .

Article 94

1. Each Member of the United Nations undertakes to comply with the decision of the International Court of Justice in any case to which it is a party.

2. If any party to a case fails to perform the obligations incumbent upon it under a judgment rendered by the Court, the other party may have recourse to the Security Council, which may, if it deems necessary, make recommendations or decide upon measures to be taken to give effect to the judgment.

. . .

Chapter XVI: Miscellaneous Provisions

Article 102

1. Every treaty and every international agreement entered into by any Member of the United Nations after the present Charter comes into force shall as soon as possible be registered with the Secretariat and published by it.

2. No party to any such treaty or international agreement which has not been registered in accordance with the provisions of paragraph 1 of this Article may invoke that treaty or agreement before any organ of the United Nations.

Article 103

In the event of a conflict between the obligations of the Members of the United Nations under the present Charter and their obligations under any other international agreement, their obligations under the present Charter shall prevail.

Article 104

The Organization shall enjoy in the territory of each of its Members such legal capacity as may be necessary for the exercise of its functions and the fulfilment of its purposes.
. . .

Chapter XVIII: Amendments

Article 108

Amendments to the present Charter shall come into force for all Members of the United Nations when they have been adopted by a vote of two thirds of the members of the General Assembly and ratified in accordance with their respective constitutional processes by two-thirds of the Members of the United Nations, including all the permanent members of the Security Council.
. . .

4 The United Nations II
International Peace and Security

key facts

Headquarters: New York

Members: 193 countries

Mandate: to end international war, and to promote peace and security.

Key structure: the Security Council has fifteen members, five of which are listed in Article 23 as permanent members, and the remaining ten are elected for two-year terms; decisions are passed when nine members (including the five permanent members) support a resolution.

Key obligations: member states must give up the use of force except for self-defense, must carry out Security Council decisions, and must provide military resources to the Council for its enforcement actions.

Enforcement: the Security Council can take any action it deems necessary, including the use of force, to respond to threats to international peace and security.

Key legal clauses of the UN Charter:

Article 24(1) [T]he United Nations ... confer on the Security Council primary responsibility for the maintenance of international peace and security.

Article 25 The Members of the United Nations agree to accept and carry out the decisions of the Security Council.

Article 39 The Security Council shall determine the existence of any threat to the peace, breach of the peace, or act of aggression

key facts

and shall ... decide what measures shall be taken in accordance with Articles 41 and 42, to maintain or restore international peace and security.

Article 41 The Security Council may decide what measures not involving the use of armed force are to be employed to give effect to its decisions.

Article 42 Should ... measures provided for in Article 41 ... be inadequate, [The Security Council] may take such action by air, sea, or land forces as may be necessary to maintain or restore international peace and security.

Article 43(1) All Members of the United Nations, in order to contribute to the maintenance of international peace and security, undertake to make available to the Security Council ... armed forces ... necessary for the purpose of maintaining international peace and security.

Article 46 Plans for the application of armed force shall be made by the Security Council with the assistance of the Military Staff Committee.

Article 49 The Members of the United Nations shall join in affording mutual assistance in carrying out the measures decided upon by the Security Council.

Article 51 Nothing in the present Charter shall impair the inherent right of individual or collective self-defense if an armed attack occurs against a Member of the United Nations.

On matters relating to "international peace and security" the United Nations has decisive authority to impose itself on any country or dispute in the world. This power goes far beyond the power ever given to any other international organization and it introduces a radically new kind of legal hierarchy into inter-state relations. There are strict limits, both legal and political, on how this authority can be used, and these limits are in large part responsible for the patchwork of activism and seizure that characterizes the UN's record on international security crises since 1945. The UN Security Council controls this authority, and decisions to intervene must pass through the peculiar membership and voting rules of the Council. The combination of these rules and the political interests of influential states produce the controversies, actions, and limits that define the UN's behavior on international security.

The UN's power over international security begins with Articles 24(1) and 39. These define an organization that has the "primary responsibility for the maintenance of international peace and security" (Art. 24(1)) in world politics and that has the authority to decide what kind of collective response is warranted in times of crisis (Art. 39). There are many other points in the Charter at which this power is modified, elaborated, and limited, and equally important are the ways these powers have been interpreted and applied in practice since 1945. Together, the rules of the Charter and the instances in which those rules have been invoked and fought over by states create the legal regime for international war that exists today. They define both the laws that govern the use of force by states and the military powers and capacity of the UN itself. As a result, no use of force by states can ignore the rules and practices that originate in the UN Charter – and though they may frequently be misinterpreted, abused, and manipulated by states, the rules on force in the Charter create the inescapable context for state behavior.[1]

This chapter examines the law and practice of the UN with respect to international peace and security. This is the most important contribution of any international organization to international security, and it puts the UN at the center of the high-politics concerns of nation-states. The obligations that states take on with respect to international security are highly constraining on state sovereignty, and as a result the politics of compliance and enforcement are extremely interesting. These obligations are also changing over time as the Security Council interprets the Charter for particular crises. That this may take place without the explicit consent of the rank-and-file membership of the UN is conceptually puzzling to state-centric theories of International Relations.

The UN has enforcement powers unlike any other international organization in the history of the inter-state system. This chapter begins by examining states' obligations regarding international security under the UN Charter, and then looks at peacekeeping and peace-enforcement to illustrate the means at the Council's disposal to encourage state compliance with those obligations and to enforce them when states fail to fulfill them. Peacekeeping operations rest on the consent of the parties in the conflict and peace-enforcement refers to missions that use the full coercive power of the United Nations against a member state. The law and politics of the two are very different.

---

[1] A broad view of this legal context is provided in the excellent book by Christine Grey, *International Law and the Use of Force*, 3rd edn. Oxford University Press, 2008.

Finally, the chapter considers the case of Darfur to explore how the legal authority of the Security Council, set out formally in the Charter, translates into practical politics. The Darfur case is exceptional in its scale and its historical importance, but it also provides an archetypal instance of the kinds of security problems that fall under the authority of the Security Council. It shows in practice how all the main rules of the Charter relating to peace and security play together to shape the real-world politics of the most pressing problems of international security, and how these rules are no guarantee of peace or decency.

Obligations

The Security Council is the organ of the United Nations responsible for international peace and security. It is the only body in the UN with the authority to take action in defense of the collective security needs of the international community. This includes the authority to take military action to enforce its decisions. It was designed in 1945 as something like the executive committee of the most powerful states to enforce against threats to the post-war international order that they were constructing. The Charter clauses that define the authority of the Council create novel and compelling legal obligations for states that join the United Nations.

The members of the United Nations concede a tremendous amount of their legal autonomy to the Security Council. In Article 25 of the Charter, they "agree to accept and carry out the decisions of the Security Council in accordance with the present Charter." In Article 49, they agree to "join in affording mutual assistance in carrying out the measures decided upon by the Security Council." In Article 103, they concede that "in the event of a conflict between the obligations ... under the present Charter and their obligations under any other international agreement, their obligations under the present Charter shall prevail." These provisions apply even to states that oppose or disagree with the decisions of the Council. Together, these commitments mean that every member of the United Nations is legally bound by what the Council decides and that there are no avenues by which they can escape that legal subordination short of withdrawing from the organization.[2]

---

[2] Even withdrawing from the UN may not end a state's obligation to comply with a decision imposed on it by the Security Council.

The scope of that subordination is further refined when the Charter explains over what areas the Security Council has the authority to issue decisions, and on this there are two key provisions. The first comes in the combined effects of Articles 24(1) and 39, which give the Council authority over matters of "international peace and security," and the second comes in the general prohibition on UN involvement in "matters essentially within the domestic jurisdiction of any state" (Article 2(7)). These two are logical exclusives of each other, in the sense that any matter that constitutes a threat to international peace and security under Article 39 is by definition not a matter within the domestic jurisdiction of a state under Article 2(7). Conversely, in the absence of a threat to international peace and security, the Security Council has no authority at all. As we shall see, all decisions of the Council that impose legal obligations on states must be premised on a finding by the Council of a breach of, or threat to, international peace and security.

State obligations to the Council therefore hinge on how the phrase "international peace and security" is interpreted. The Charter has nothing to say on the subject, except to make clear in Article 39 that it is up to the Security Council itself to determine case by case what situations constitute threats to or breaches of the peace. We therefore must look at the practice of the Council in making these determinations in order to learn how much sovereignty states are giving up. Each time the Council adopts a resolution invoking the phrase "international peace and security," its meaning in international law is clarified a little and shifts a little. Overall, there has been a gradual expansion over the years in how the Council has interpreted its key phrase, and so the grant of authority to the Council has been expanding as well. For instance, Bruce Cronin has listed nation-building, war crimes, peacekeeping, apartheid, humanitarian crises, civil wars, and restoring democracy as recent areas of high activity by the Council, all of which stretch the understanding of "international peace and security" from where it rested when the Charter was written.[3]

Two recent moves have shifted the type, not just the scope, of the Council's authority over states. Both are related to the response to international terrorism networks since the mid-1990s. In 1999, the Council issued the first in a series of resolutions (Res. 1267) to impound the assets of individuals supporting the Taliban in Afghanistan. This has been expanded several times since then and

---

[3] Bruce Cronin, "International Consensus and the Changing Legal Authority of the UN Security Council," in Bruce Cronin and Ian Hurd (eds.), *The UN Security Council and the Politics of International Authority*. Routledge, 2008, pp. 57–79.

has led to a new norm that UN economic sanctions should primarily take the form of "smart" sanctions (or "targeted" sanctions) that attack individuals responsible for threats to international peace and security, rather than a state and all its citizens as a whole.[4] The second development involves Council resolutions that create a broad requirement that all states must conform to some policy framework set out by the Council. Demands such as these, extending indefinitely into the future, in essence define certain choices in the domestic laws of states (i.e. loopholes that allow for underground financial transactions, or weak controls on nuclear material) as potential threats to international peace and security, and then require that states bring their policies up to a Council-determined standard. These have been used to pursue the financial transactions that support terrorist networks, among other goals. These two moves mean that the Council now has established the practice of identifying individuals rather than states as "threats to international peace and security," and has also decided that its resolutions can function essentially as legislation for states. Both claims to power are innovations in the history of the Council, and they further expand the effective meaning of the Charter's language defining the Council.

Both have also been controversial. The move to regulating individuals has created a string of practical and legal problems for the Council because all the Council's work in the preceding decades had been premised on dealing with inter-state problems, and its quick adaptation to dealing directly with individuals has meant it has had to learn (often by trial and error) of the importance that individuals and their domestic courts attach to due process. The Council's early experience with maintaining lists of suspected "terrorists" has been riddled with complaints about errors and unfairness, and many harmed individuals are suing the Council or states for wrongs done to them.[5] The Council's efforts to demand changes to domestic regulations have also been conceptually interesting and practically controversial. The novelty arises in these resolutions because the Council is using its international authority to require that states adopt particular standards or legislation; these demands are addressed to all states, unbounded by a particular crisis or a limit in time, and are backed by the Council's authority under Chapter VII of the Charter.[6] A more normal way of

---

[4] This is reviewed in a very interesting report of the Watson Institute at Brown University, "Strengthening Targeted Sanctions through Fair and Clear Procedures," March 2006.

[5] See the discussion in José Alvarez, *International Organizations as Law-Makers*. Oxford University Press, 2005, pp. 174–175.

[6] Ian Johnstone, "The Security Council as Legislature," in Bruce Cronin and Ian Hurd (eds.), *The UN Security Council and the Politics of International Authority*. Routledge, 2008, pp. 80–81.

operating for the Council would be to make demands of specific states that they should change their peace-threatening behaviors. For instance, in the famous Resolution 678 in 1990, the Council insisted that Iraq should "fully comply with resolution 660" (which demanded that Iraq withdraw its forces to the positions of August 1, 1990) and if it failed then other states would use force to compel it to do so. Ian Johnstone has suggested that the new approach, as illustrated by Resolution 1373 on terrorist financing, indicates a move into something that looks more like issuing legislation than the crisis-response model envisioned in 1945. This may be a shift in the practical power of the Council, making it more general and perhaps governmental than had been the case prior to 1999, and its legality depends on one's interpretation of Articles 39, 41, and 42 of the Charter, which are discussed further below.

Compliance

The entry into force of the Charter ushered in a new international legal system, one by which member states are legally subordinate to the Security Council to a striking degree. This, of course, does not translate automatically to state compliance with these obligations, and this section investigates the ways that states and the UN approach the question of compliance. The Council aims to produce compliance by states by a combination of political suasion and the threat of military enforcement. The latter is rarely used but its possibility rests in the background and helps activate the Council's political influence. This section focuses on how the UN has used the practice of peacekeeping to negotiate with states over compliance, while the next, on enforcement, looks at the practice of military coercion by the Council through its peace-enforcement power.

The Security Council is at once a legal actor and a political forum, and so the dynamics of compliance by states have both legal and political features. The legal content of the Council's powers derives from the Charter clauses discussed above that establish the absolute legal subordination of member states to the Council's decisions on international peace and security. These legal powers are immense, and therefore are often hard to put into practice. They engender great controversy and often great resistance by the states against which they are used or who may fear the precedent that their use may set. As a result, there are relatively few instances in which the Council is able to mobilize its full coercive legal authority against a state, its "peace-enforcement" powers (Iraq in 1990–91 is one example), and it is far more common to see the Council's authority used as a resource or tool to shift the political grounds of a dispute among states, in a "peace-keeping" mode. In these cases, the threat of enforcement remains but it is sent to the background of the dispute, and compliance by states is achieved (or sought) more through negotiation and compromise. In other words, the Council often seeks compliance with its decisions through political means rather than by brute force, and the history of peacekeeping is testament to the centrality of nuance, diplomacy, and even ambiguity in UN power. It is a mistake to necessarily interpret this nuance as a sign of weakness in the Council or as an unfortunate by-product of Great-Power dissensus; rather, it may instead be evidence that the Council is looking for whatever means it can find to influence states amid, and around, the realities of international politics.

To study how and whether states comply with the Security Council requires that we recognize that there is rarely a situation in which the Council can achieve its goals by itself. Its accomplishments are ultimately a result of its ability to influence the choices of states in directions that it desires. The Council has some instruments that might influence these choices but, as with all international organizations, the most the UN can do is to shape the legal and political context in which states make their choices. It hopes that in such a way compliance with its decisions is made more likely than non-compliance. Sometimes, this influence is decisive and explicit, as with enforcement action in Libya in 2011, and sometimes it is decisive and subtle, as when the UN created the idea of peacekeeping and thus changed the language of intervention for all players. Often, it is just one influence among many: for instance, on Darfur, the Council catalyzed action by the International Criminal Court by issuing a resolution that authorized the ICC to investigate international crimes in Sudan, as discussed in Chapter 9.

The Council has learned to maximize its influence by leveraging its legal powers into the more subtle currency of political persuasion. It has reserved the exercise of its absolute legal authority over states for a small subset of disputes that appear before it. The difference between these two modes of operation is evident in practice in the difference between peacekeeping and peace-enforcement missions, as mentioned above. Peace-enforcement missions are coercive invasions of countries by a UN-authorized force, intent on eliminating or mitigating a threat to international peace and security. Peacekeeping missions, by contrast, are negotiated between the UN and states or other parties, and have the consent of the government in the state where they are operating; they often occur in the shadow of a threat from the Council, but in legal form they are always present with the formal consent of the country. A peacekeeping mission is characterized by three key components. It is a multinational force authorized by the UN that is (i) impartial between the sides in the conflict; (ii) authorized to use force only to defend their own lives; and (iii) consented to by the relevant governments. These three features, of impartiality, force only in self-defense, and consent of the states, are the hallmarks of a peacekeeping force.[7] They reappear time and again across cases, including the UN missions in Cyprus (UNFYCIP, monitoring a cease-fire between Greek and Turkish Cypriots since 1964), in southern Lebanon (UNIFIL, since 1974, though substantially changed over time, especially after the Israel–Lebanon War in 2006), in Nicaragua (ONUCA, 1989–92), in El Salvador (ONUSAL, 1991–95), and elsewhere.

The military operation against Qaddafi in Libya in 2011 represents the peace-enforcement model, while the Rwanda mission from 1993–94 is an example of a peacekeeping mission (at least at the start). Both operations were intended as responses to threats to international peace and security, and they included demands by the Council that the states involved comply with certain conditions set out in the Council's Resolutions, but the logic by which they induced compliance was dramatically different between the two. The two resolutions governing these operations are excerpted below in Appendices 4.A and 4.B, and the differences in language are striking.

The concept of peace-enforcement is clearly set out in the Charter (in Chapter VII) but in practice the Council in fact has far more experience with the peacekeeping type, and this is not explicitly described in the Charter. The idea of the "peacekeeping mission" was launched in the context of the Suez War in 1956, and was initiated by the Secretary-General and the General Assembly rather than the Security Council. After an invasion of Egyptian territory in the Sinai by France, the UK, and Israel, the General Assembly established a multi-national "emergency force" of soldiers to patrol the area and monitor a cease-fire agreed to by the warring governments. This was given the name United Nations Emergency Force (UNEF) and it lasted until 1967 (it became known as UNEF I after a new force was sent to Sinai in 1973 to prop up an Israel–Egypt cease-fire). The UNEF mission has come to define the category of "peacekeeping" with the following features.

---

[7] The key UN documents that define this and other peace-mission categories are An Agenda for Peace (1992) and Supplement to an Agenda for Peace (1995). These were originally reports by the Secretary-General to the Security Council, www.un.org/Docs/SG/agpeace.html. Accessed October 5, 2009.

The Security Council created a classic peacekeeping mission in the 1993 Rwandan civil war. After the government of Rwanda and the forces trying to overthrow it (the Rwandan Patriotic Front, RPF) signed a cease-fire agreement, the Council agreed to send a multinational peacekeeping force to the country to monitor the compliance of both sides with its terms. These included monitoring the demobilization of troops on both sides and a weapons-free area around Kigali, the capital, training workers to clear land mines, coordinating aid supplies, and monitoring the return of refugees.[8] The mission, known as UNAMIR, was initially composed of around 2,500 military personnel, largely Belgians, under a Canadian commander with a political leader from Cameroon. Its powers were negotiated between the United Nations, the Rwandan government, and the RPF, and were set out formally in SC Resolution 872. The resolution made it explicit that the mission was "at the request of the parties" (i.e. the government of Rwanda and the RPF) and rested on the twin premises of "peaceful conditions" and "the full cooperation of all the parties." These terms were important to the character of the mission, both in theory and in practice, because they ensured the mission would operate as a partnership between three players: the government, the RPF, and the UN. This partnership is paradigmatic of a classic peacekeeping mission. In practice, it meant the mission was in a poor position to adapt to the new circumstances that arose once the genocide began in April 1994, leaving it a bystander amid mass atrocities.

The consent of the Rwandan government was essential because UNAMIR could not otherwise legally be present in the country. As a sovereign state, Rwanda enjoyed the protection against UN interference afforded by Article 2(7) of the UN Charter. Its domestic affairs are legally insulated from all branches of the UN. It follows therefore that the Council can only impose military solutions on countries by following the procedures of Articles 39, 41, and 42, which permit it to identify threats to international peace and security and to respond in any way it deems necessary. These clauses lead to peace-enforcement missions described below, rather than to peacekeeping. Peacekeeping is the UN's mode of operation when, for whatever reason, it does not pursue these more forceful and interventionist powers. For Rwanda, the Council declined to use its power to impose itself on the parties until well after the government had largely succeeded with the genocide by mid-1994.

[8] The mission is described at: www.un.org/Depts/dpko/dpko/co_mission/unamir.htm. Accessed October 9, 2009.

The set of three principles that defines peacekeeping is the necessary and logical consequence of the UN's absence of legal authority in instances when the Council has not taken its more forceful route. Without a finding under Chapter VII, the UN is left with whatever influence it can organize with the consent of the states involved. This often, perhaps always, requires substantive compromises in order to gain the support of the target state, and can produce mandates for peacekeeping missions that are seriously impaired as compared with what the UN's Department of Peacekeeping Operations might want. It also often means no mission at all, when states refuse to agree. In the case of Rwanda, it meant a mandate for UNAMIR that did not include the right to use force to protect innocent civilians or to challenge the genocidaires.

Without legal authorization to do these things UNAMIR became, once the genocide started, a witness to the killing and did almost nothing to stop it. Such are the legal limits on UN action, and to respond differently to the killing UNAMIR would have been likely to violate some aspect of the international legal agreements that had brought it into being in the first place. In one very stark case in April 1994, UNAMIR soldiers from Belgium were stationed at a school, providing de facto protection to 2,500 people inside the school from a crowd outside who wanted to murder them. The soldiers could in principle have used their guns to defend those they were protecting, but this would have meant exceeding UNAMIR's authority as set by the Security Council. It would also have meant breaking the Council's promise to the Rwandan government not to take sides in the conflict. It would likely further mean that the peacekeepers would become targets of the killers as well, both at the school and around the country. In deference to the law and politics of the United Nations the peacekeepers left the school when they were challenged by the killers, and the people in it were massacred within hours of their departure.[9] The faithful adherence to the law of the UN Charter in this case contributed to a tragedy.

A peacekeeping mission is expressly designed around terms that the target state can agree to, and as such it aims to get states to voluntarily follow the Council's wishes. It represents an exercise in subtle power by the United Nations, where the terms of compliance are negotiated between states and the organization and are consented to by both. This is more in the style of the ILO or the ICJ than of centralized enforcement or punishment. Threats and coercion, where

---

[9] The story of the school, the École Technique Officielle, is recounted in the film *Beyond the Gates* (IFC Films, 2004).

they exist in such cases, take place behind the scenes and in advance of the public agreement represented by the mission's mandate.

There remains of course the category of peace-enforcement, explained in the next section. This is the logical complement to peacekeeping, and the characteristics of each help to explain the peculiarities, and strengths and weaknesses, of the other.

Enforcement

In many ways, what was needed in the Rwandan conflict was a peace-enforcement mission rather than a peacekeeping mission. In peace-enforcement, the three features that define peacekeeping are each reversed: the UN's military force is neither neutral nor consensual, and it is authorized to wage war to accomplish the political goals set out by the Security Council. The military operation to force Iraq from Kuwait in 1991 illustrates this in practice. The Security Council in that case declared that by refusing to leave Kuwait the government of Iraq had "usurped the authority of the legitimate Government of Kuwait" and had thereby breached international peace and security. It further declared that the UN was "determined to bring the invasion and occupation of Kuwait by Iraq to an end and restore the sovereignty, independence and territorial integrity of Kuwait" (Res. 660). To achieve this it authorized "Member States cooperating with the Government of Kuwait ... to use all necessary means to uphold and implement Resolution 660 [restoring Kuwait's independence]" (Res. 678). These resolutions and the war that followed show the contours of a peace-enforcement mission: the UN identified an enemy whose conduct was threatening international peace and security, and authorized a full military campaign to reverse it. Such missions, which remain rare, do not have the consent of the target government, they take sides in the conflict, and they deploy force in a war-like fashion to accomplish their goals. This is the reverse of peacekeeping's consent-based model.

Enforcement by the Security Council is governed by Chapter VII of the UN Charter. Here, the Council is given the power to identify threats to international peace and security (Article 39) and decide what measures are necessary to respond to those threats. These measures may include economic sanctions, blockades, and other non-military means (Article 41) as well as collective military force (Article 42). This power is in principle unbounded, making the Council on paper the most powerful international organization in the history of the states system.

The Council can decide on collective military action on behalf of the entire United Nations and all its member states. These decisions must come in the form of a resolution of the Council, passed according to its voting formula set out in Article 27 and described in Chapter 3: "an affirmative vote of nine members including the concurring votes of the permanent members." The voting rules mean that these enforcement actions can take place only when all five permanent members are willing to support it, or at least abstain from vetoing it, and also at least four of the non-permanent members must vote in favor. This sets a high standard of inter-state agreement before enforcement by the Council can take place and is the main reason that the Council has used its full power only a handful of times.

A second constraint on Council activism is that the Council itself (and the UN more generally) possesses no military resources and it must rely on voluntary contributions from UN member states. These contributions (of troops, money, and equipment) are negotiated case by case by the Secretary-General or the members of the Council, and require separate legal agreements in each case between the troop-contributing country and the United Nations.[10] States are paid a per diem reimbursement by the UN for their contributions, though these are far below the carrying costs of all but the most ill-equipped and ill-trained troops. The diversity that is characteristic of most multinational forces, and is a source of both strength and weakness, is the result of this organizing system. When too few contributions are forthcoming for a proposed mission, the mission cannot take place. In Rwanda, a shortage of willing contributors helped to delay the launch of UNAMIR II, a peace-enforcement mission, until after the genocide was over, by which point its raison d'être had largely dissipated.

When these obstacles are overcome, the Council can be a very efficient and powerful military force. This was well illustrated in the 2011 military intervention against Libya. The intervention was motivated by the imminent threat of a massacre of citizens in Benghazi by the Libyan government, in the context of a widespread uprising against Muammar Qaddafi's dictatorship. The Security Council had previously made various demands of Qaddafi to refrain from using his military to defeat the political opposition, and when these were ineffective

---

[10] Kofi Annan's autobiography describes some of these negotiations. Kofi Annan and Nader Mousavizadeh, *Interventions: A Life in War and Peace.* Penguin, 2012.

the Council agreed to Resolution 1973 on March 17, 2011. This resolution is reproduced in Appendix 4.A below. Its key legal components include:

- identifying Qaddafi's violence against his citizens as a threat to international peace and security (using Article 39 of Chapter VII of the Charter)
- banning "all flights in the airspace of" Libya in order to protect civilians
- authorizing UN member states "to take all necessary measures" to enforce this no-fly zone
- authorizing UN member states "to take all necessary measures... to protect civilians... under threat of attack"

These measures together constituted the legal foundation for NATO and others to use their military forces to defeat the Libyan army, in the name of protecting the Libyan population against the depredations of its government. This took the form of air and naval power, since Resolution 1973 explicitly ruled out "a foreign occupation force" in Libyan territory. The war that ensued was a hybrid of civil war, inter-state war, and UN peace-enforcement operation. It ended in late October 2011 when Qaddafi himself was killed by anti-government forces.

The Charter includes provisions (in Articles 43 and 45) that require members to make available to the UN some proportion of their national military forces. These were intended to allow the Council to have more direct control over troops so that it could be more independent and expeditious in launching new enforcement missions, but these clauses have never been enacted. No state has concluded the kind of agreement envisioned in Article 43, which imagined that states would negotiate bilateral agreements with the Council on the types and terms of available resources. There is little enthusiasm among UN members for a more militarily independent Security Council; neither the Great Powers, who would likely supply the capacity for these missions, nor the small and medium states, who see themselves as the likely targets of such missions, have pushed to further empower the Council. There does exist a coalition of activists and middle-power states who defend the idea, on the grounds that a UN "rapid-reaction force" could be more efficient and effective than the current practice of generating new contributions each time the Council decides on an operation.[11]

The categories of peacekeeping and peace-enforcement define ideal-types, and as much as the UN might try to keep them separate in practice many

---

[11] For instance, Brian Urquhart, "A Force behind the UN," *New York Times*, August 7, 2003.

missions end up blurring the lines between them.[12] As Michael Matheson has said, "UN operations do not fall into well-defined, mutually exclusive categories, any more than do the conflicts they address."[13] However, keeping them distinct is important both legally and practically. In law, they have entirely different sources of legal authorization under the Charter, and these legal foundations produce characteristic features and problems in the missions themselves. In practice, the needs and the dangers associated with each type of mission are significantly different, so that mixing up the two can be counter-productive and even dangerous. The Somalia operations of 1992–94 provide a classic example of the dangers: these missions included both UN and US operations designed at the start to follow the classic peacekeeping model and to assist with the delivery of humanitarian aid. Once they discovered the extent to which local militias were impeding that aid, the US and the UN began using their military capacity to defeat the militias. They shifted, in other words, from peacekeeping to peace-enforcement, from having the consent of the government and using force only in self-defense to actively using force to defeat local enemies.[14] The transition left the foreign troops vulnerable to counterattacks, and several dozen were killed, and it alienated many local people by making them the targets of foreign militaries. These together made the original humanitarian mission impossible and led to the collapse of the whole enterprise, though the operation succeeded in increasing the supply of humanitarian assistance for a time.

The peace-enforcement mission is a seldom-used tool of the United Nations, but it represents the starkest application of the UN's powers of enforcement in response to threats to international peace and security. It is far more common for the Council to invoke its enforcement power as a leverage tool to induce states to change their policies. Thus, the Council relatively frequently identifies some particular crisis or state behavior as "a threat to international peace and security," and it uses that language from Article 39 to signal that it is making a legally binding call to UN members to respond as it demands. By using this language, it is indicating unambiguously that it is conscious of its enforcement capacity under Chapter VII of the Charter and is implicitly threatening to take

---

[12] A third type of operation, known as peace-building, occurs when the UN takes a direct role in the administration of a state, generally after the collapse of the existing government or its complete capture by one side in a civil conflict.

[13] Michael Matheson, *Council Unbound: The Growth of UN Decision Making on Conflict and Postconflict Issues after the Cold War*. United States Institute of Peace Press, 2006, p. 100.

[14] Resolution 794 (1992) made the legal change to the mandate of the UN mission.

more forceful measures if states fail to act as it requires of them. The enforcement powers of the Council therefore form part of the inescapable background to its political influence.

The interaction between law, politics, and enforcement is characteristic of the Security Council's place in international relations, and this was very much part of its original design when the United Nations was formed in 1945. It was the intention of the UN's framers that the Security Council would be a place where the political negotiations among the Great Powers over the management of the international system would be framed within an explicit grant of legal authority by all the other states. It created a legal hierarchy on top of the traditional dynamics of power politics between Great Powers and the rank-and-file states of the international community.[15] This is a dramatic development for international politics: it means that governments have given up their legal primacy regarding questions of international peace and security. Sovereign states in the UN system accept that the Council (and the Charter) has the ultimate legal authority over international peace and security. This directly contradicts the mythology of sovereign statehood, and the assumption that world politics takes place in an international "anarchy."

CASE I: Darfur 1990s–2000s

The international response to the Darfur crisis is thoroughly shaped by the rules, powers, and paradoxes of international organizations, and none more importantly than those of the UN Security Council. Within the UN, the rules on domestic sovereignty (Article 2(4)), threats to international peace and security (Article 39), voting in the Council (Article 27), and troop-contributing countries are central, and beyond the UN the case involves also the International Criminal Court, the African Union, the ambiguous and changing norms of humanitarian intervention, and the nascent doctrine of the Responsibility to Protect.

The "problem" of Darfur centers on the fact that the Sudanese government has organized and encouraged attacks on the people in the Darfur region, in the west of Sudan, often using para-state militias. The purpose of this violence appears to be to destroy three ethnic groups, the Fur, the Masalit, and the

---

[15] Gerry Simpson provides an excellent history of legal hierarchies in world politics in *Great Powers and Outlaw States: Unequal Sovereigns in the International Legal Order.* Cambridge University Press, 2004.

Zaghawa, and to eliminate, through mass killing, a potential source of political opposition for the government. As a consequence, something like 400,000 people have been killed and millions more made landless and homeless or turned into refugees.[16] The scale of the violence, and the fact that it is directed by the government against innocent civilians, places it in the top rank of modern crimes against humanity, alongside the Holocaust, the Khmer Rouge in Cambodia, and the Rwandan genocide. To many it looks precisely like the type of case for which United Nations intervention was invented, and indeed the United Nations has been reacting to it in one way or another since at least 2004. In the shape of these reactions, and in their successes and their failures, we can see on display the powers and the limits of the UN Security Council.

The first step to any Council action, as we saw in Chapter 3, is to satisfy the requirement that there be a breach of, or threat to, international peace and security. This language appears in Article 39 of the Charter, at the opening of Chapter VII, and it defines an unbreachable outer limit on the authority of the Security Council; all of the enforcement powers available to the Council, described later in Chapter VII of the Charter, are possible only if the Council finds that there is a threat to or breach of international peace and security.

In the Darfur case, this has been extremely controversial. The predations of the Sudanese government have been almost exclusively addressed to people who are Sudanese citizens and living in the territory of Sudan. The politics of the conflict are part of the internal politics of the country. In what sense, therefore, can the problem be said to be one of "international peace and security" as opposed to a problem of domestic turmoil and civil war? The Security Council cannot act on any matter "essentially within the domestic jurisdiction" of a member state (from Article 2(7)), and a government's behavior toward its own citizens has traditionally been understood in international law as largely within the confines of its domestic sovereignty. Even gross mistreatment of innocent people seems to be within the bounds of the domestic exclusion from international authority, as long as the people are not the citizens of another state. In an exclusively state-centric view, the Darfur case could fall within the domestic space, both territorial and conceptual, of the Sudanese government. The Council, with its state-centric construction and the state-centric Charter, has in

---

[16] John Hagan and Wenona Rymond-Richmond, *Darfur and the Crime of Genocide.* Cambridge University Press, 2009, ch. 4.

consequence struggled to reconcile this with the self-evident urgency with which massive human suffering pushes itself back on to the policy agenda.

The same problem arose in 1994, as the Security Council considered whether and how to act in response to the Rwandan genocide. Much like Darfur a decade later, in Rwanda the government of the country organized and encouraged mass killing of innocent people as a tool to tighten its hold on power. The government drew its political power from sections of the Hutu population of the country, and it decided that the Tutsi population constituted a threat to the continuation of that power. It sought to massacre the Tutsi people, along with many Hutus, to avoid implementing a power-sharing compromise negotiated by the United Nations. In its own way it succeeded: the genocidaires killed in the range of 800,000 people in three months. In the first days of the genocide, the Security Council met to consider the problem and through informal conversations among the most powerful countries on the Council it was decided this was a domestic matter within the meaning of Article 2(7): the killing was within the borders of Rwanda, and targeted Rwandans rather than foreigners, and so the diplomats in the Council decided that the killing did not constitute a threat to international peace and security under Article 39. It was seen instead as part of a civil war, which by definition was "a matter essentially within the domestic jurisdiction." The UN could therefore have no authority (or obligation) to respond.

This interpretation of the situation, and of Charter law, led to the conclusion that the United Nations should, and could, do nothing in response to the killing, and produced the policy of inaction which allowed the killing to continue unbounded. It is clear today that this policy conclusion was in fact the preferred policy of the US and many other powerful governments, and so the legal interpretation of the Charter and of the situation in Rwanda looks to have been driven by the desire to find a way not to take action to help end the genocide quickly. The US was cowed by its experience in Somalia in 1993, discussed above, and saw the possibility of intervening in Rwanda as an opportunity to repeat the failure. Many in the UN felt the same fear and similarly preferred inaction over action.[17] The consequence of these choices was that the Council allowed the genocide to continue for several weeks, and allowed thousands to be killed, on the grounds that this was made necessary by the language of Article 2(7). As the killing progressed, the Council's inaction became unbearably shameful. While it

---

[17] See Michael Barnett, *Eyewitness to a Genocide.* Cornell University Press, 2003. Also Kofi Annan and Nader Mousavizadeh, *Interventions: A Life in War and Peace.* Penguin, 2012.

remained committed to the idea that the killing was part of a civil war, the Council decided that the increasing refugee flows out of Rwanda, as people sought to escape the massacres, were themselves a threat to international peace and security. In these refugee movements the Council found the trans-border element that it needed to activate its powers under Article 39. It eventually authorized a peace-enforcement mission in Rwanda to protect civilians, though by the time any troops arrived to carry out the mission the genocidal government had already been overthrown by the RPF army and the killing had stopped.

The Rwanda case shows that the legal interpretation of "domestic matters" is extremely powerful, both legally and politically. It is the device by which governments insulate themselves from outside (i.e. UN) interference. It limits what the United Nations can say about, among other things, how the Myanmar government reacted to the devastating flooding after cyclone Nargis in 2008, how the Iranian elections of 2009 were conducted, how Bashar al-Assad maintains himself in power in Syria, and how the death penalty is applied in the United States. In all these cases, the relevant governments claim that their actions are protected by the domestic exclusion of Article 2(7), and therefore neither the Security Council nor any other part of the UN system has any legal authority.

However, the final word on the legal interpretation of such claims appears to lie with the Security Council rather than with the governments or any other institution. This follows from the fact that the Council has the authority to decide what is or is not a threat to international peace and security under Article 39. The meaning of the domestic exclusion is the inverse of what is meant by "a threat to international peace and security," and so it is in the power of the Council to decide how a given crisis should be understood. The Council is effectively unlimited, from a legal perspective, in its ability to declare new things to be threats to international peace and security.

The inverse relationship between matters of domestic jurisdiction and of international security is being continually remade with each decision of the Council. We only know the extent of state sovereignty by observing the practice of the Security Council in identifying threats in specific situations. State sovereignty is therefore an uncertain category, despite being so highly prized by governments. As discussed earlier, the Council has found that terrorist financing is a threat to international peace and security, along with the proliferation of weapons of mass destruction, the use of children in war, and sometimes rape and sexual assault as tools of war. With each move, the areas protected by Article 2(7) shrink a little further and the scope of Council authority grows a little broader. Sovereign authority is being transferred from states to the Security Council.

Genocide, however, is different – and it is the possibility of genocide in Darfur that changes the legal environment for the Security Council. Genocide is one among a small number of behaviors that automatically and in themselves are considered breaches of international peace and security – the others include crimes against humanity and war crimes. These crimes have special status in international law; they are acts that by their very nature are violations of the laws of nations and there is no need for the Council to specifically identify them as such. They may also permit cross-border military or criminal responses that do not require separate legal authorization from either the local government or an international body.

It is this special status that explains why the United States in 1994 refused to call the massacres in Rwanda "genocide," because to acknowledge it as genocide would immediately void the legal interpretation that the problem was a domestic matter and not a threat to international peace and security. Security Council inaction would therefore be much harder to justify. William Schabas, in his excellent survey of international law on genocide, notes that genocide has been recognized "as anti-social since time immemorial" but that there was little effort to prosecute its perpetrators since it "was virtually always committed at the behest and with the complicity of those in power."[18] After 1945, it was quickly institutionalized around the Nuremberg Trials as a rule of jus cogens (that is, a law that binds all states by virtue of their being states, regardless of their consent or opposition).

The United States declared in 2004 that the Sudan killings were part of a genocide, though the Security Council to date has not. In the American perspective, the Council therefore already has the authority to take enforcement action in Darfur. For the UN, though, the matter remains open to intervention based on a Council finding of threat to international peace and security. In large part the Council has operated on the basis of negotiation with the Sudanese government rather than by force. The UN has approved a "hybrid" peace operation in Darfur, under Council resolution 1769 in 2007. It is hybrid in two distinct ways: first, it was grafted on to a peace operation of the African Union (AU), known as AMIS (African Union Mission in Sudan), and it is meant to support the political reconciliation negotiated by the AU in the Darfur Peace Agreement; and second, it has aspects of both a peacekeeping and a peace-enforcement mission. Both issues arise from the Council's unwillingness to make Darfur a clear-cut case of

---

[18] William Schabas, *Genocide in International Law*, 2nd edn. Cambridge University Press, 2009.

humanitarian international intervention, and the consequent need to maintain a working relationship with the Sudanese government.

China and Russia are both opposed to finding that the Sudanese government is breaching international peace and security, and have used the veto threat to stop resolutions that make formal demands of the Sudanese. Instead, the Council's response to Darfur incorporates the government as a partner rather than as an enemy, meaning that it negotiated the mandate of the Darfur mission with Sudan and made changes in response to Sudanese demands, such as accepting limits on the countries that would be considered qualified to be troop-contribution countries. This is typical of a peacekeeping mission, where the mission must have the consent of the host country. The hybrid nature of the UN–AU partnership was also a result of this process, as Sudan insisted on an "African" rather than international mission.

However, the resolution itself complicates things, and leads to the second dimension of hybridity in the mission. The preamble to Resolution 1769 reaffirms the Council's earlier decision that "the situation in Darfur, Sudan continues to constitute a threat to international peace and security," which has traditionally been coded language in Council resolutions for the authority of enforcement given to the Council by Article 39 and the rest of Chapter VII. Invoking that phrase should set the UN mission safely beyond the domain of Article 2(7) and its domestic protections, though in the operative paragraphs the resolution does not use this authority to set any legal limits on the Sudanese government. Subsequently, one paragraph of the resolution (para. 15) opens with the explicit declaration that for that paragraph alone, the Council is "acting under Chapter VII of the Charter of the United Nations." This paragraph contains the rules that govern when troops of the mission can use force, and these say that they may "take the necessary action … in order to

i) protect its personnel, facilities, installations and equipment, and to ensure the security and freedom of movement of its own personnel and humanitarian workers,
ii) support early and effective implementation of the Darfur Peace Agreement, prevent the disruption of its implementation and armed attacks, and protect civilians, without prejudice to the responsibility of the Government of Sudan."[19]

---

[19] S/RES/1769 (2007).

These clauses therefore give the UN mission the legal right to use force in self-defense (i.e. "to protect its personnel, facilities . . .") but also more broadly in defense of the goals of the mission itself (i.e. to protect "humanitarian workers" and to "protect civilians"). This broader grant of authority is what was missing from the UNAMIR mandate in Rwanda and caused that mission to actively seek the minimum of impact in preventing killings, and it gives the Sudan operation the potential for direct confrontation with those forces who are punishing the Darfur population. It could well become a peace-enforcement mission. However, this is unlikely to happen in practice, as indicated by the last words of 15(ii): "without prejudice to the responsibility of the Government of Sudan." This clause, though it is ambiguous, would seem to return the mission back under the authority of the government of Sudan, and reinforces the sense that it is a peacekeeping mission consistent with the sovereignty of Sudan, at least with respect to the broader goals of the mission (notice that this clause modifies the authority to use force to protect civilians and not the previous section that defines the right to use force to defend UN troops or humanitarian workers).

In the end, the mission is a hybrid between peacekeeping and peace-enforcement: it deploys the forceful legal language of Chapter VII of the Charter with an implied threat of military enforcement, but its ability to exercise authority on the ground is circumscribed by the Sudanese govern-ment. The mission ultimately defers to the local government and makes no demands of it.

The Darfur mission shows how the law of the Charter mixes with the politics of international affairs to constitute a UN peace operation. The powers, limits, and dilemmas of these missions make sense when seen through the lens of Council politics. The Council can authorize extremely powerful interventions when it has the collective will to do so, and when it lacks a consensus in favor of intervention it may do nothing or may make only a symbolic but ineffective gesture. Its successes and failures have much to do with the private interests being sought by the Permanent Members. Even "success" and "failure" need to be carefully defined – the Rwanda operation could be considered a "success" from the point of view of those permanent members whose objective was to avoid involving the Council and themselves in another civil war, and the Sudan mission is a "success" if one's goals are to protect the Sudanese government from the "illegal" intrusion of the Council. They are both failures in terms of improving the fortunes of those targeted by their governments.

CASE II: Syria in the 2010s

The patterns evident in Darfur and Rwanda appear again in the UN's response to the Syrian war since 2011. A people's revolution against the dictatorship of President Bashar al-Assad was met with widespread violence by the government against the civilian population. This cost the government much of its domestic support and its international legitimacy. As large areas of the country fell to various opposition groups, the tenure of Assad looked shaky which prompted his government to escalate even further its indiscriminate killing of civilians in opposition areas. The US began openly bombing Da'esh (ISIS) forces which took over some areas as the government retreated. Russia began openly attacking rebel forces and neighborhoods in 2015 to support Assad. What began as a street-level uprising against a long-standing dictator has become a thoroughly internationalized regional war with superpowers backing opposite sides and regional powers including Israel, Turkey, Hezbollah from Lebanon, Saudi Arabia, Iran, and others deeply involved. Under the weight of this militarization, civilian society has been crushed: perhaps 500,000 people have been killed, 2 million more wounded, and 10 million people (half the country's pre-war population) displaced from their homes.

At every stage of the conflict – from street protests to civil war to a regional "world war" – the UN Security Council has been watching carefully and continually failing to take constructive action. It has issued statements in favor of peace and condemning human rights violations, violence against civilians, and the use of chemical weapons. It has declared cease-fires, supported UN envoys, demanded humanitarian access, and supplied some aid. It endorsed an inspection team to monitor the government's promise to dispose of its chemical weapons.

But the Security Council has not made use of its enforcement powers to impose a solution that resolves the underlying "threat to international peace and security." The reasons for this are clear, and will be familiar from the stories about Rwanda in 1994 and Darfur in the 1990s: the Permanent Members in the Council disagree on how the Syrian conflict should be resolved. The US, UK, and France among others have for many years wished to see the Assad government overthrown, though the US at least since 2015 has appeared more interested in "stability" in the country that excludes Da'esh. Russia supports Assad and increases its military commitment any time he appears to be weakening. Without Great Power consensus, the Security Council cannot do anything; it is irrelevant by design. On Syria, it has produced a series of relatively weak statements of aspiration for peaceful settlement, because this is all that the P-5 can agree on. When the Secretary-General told the Council in 2016 that it has "no higher responsibility" than ending the Syrian war, he is speaking in a sense against the institutional framework that undergirds the organization.[20] The Council has the legal authority to act forcefully in Syria but its permanent members have conflicting ideas about what it should do and whom it should protect. When the Great Powers in the Council agree with each other, the organization can act like a global imperial power, imposing itself as it sees fit anywhere. But when they do not agree, it disappears.

Conclusion

Every peace mission of the United Nations must be built on two foundations, and each contributes to the shape of the final structure: a legal mandate under the Charter, and a grant of resources (military or otherwise) from the member states. The legal mandate defines what are the powers and limits of the mission (usually though not always in the form of a formal resolution of the Security Council) and how the mission relates to Article 2(7) on domestic sovereignty. Peace-enforcement missions use the coercive authority of Chapter VII of the Charter and are therefore not covered by the domestic exclusion in Article 2(7). Peacekeeping missions, with their foundation on the consent of the states involved, use that consent to avoid violating Article 2(7): what is consented to by the government cannot, by definition, be considered interference in "matters which are essentially within [its] domestic jurisdiction."

In addition to a legal mandate, all missions also must have the resources to enact that mandate, and these resources always come from loans by member states. The United Nations has no military capacity of its own, despite the plain language of Articles 43 and 45, and it has little leverage to force states to contribute what it needs. Therefore, the resources that make up peacekeeping and peace-enforcement operations are given at the discretion of the contributing states and often fall short of the ideal. In the case of Darfur, the possibility

[20] See www.un.org/apps/news/story.asp?NewsID=55002#.WB4GCDKZNp8.

of a humanitarian intervention on behalf of the local population has thus far failed on both the legal and the resource fronts: the states on the Council are not in sufficient consensus to authorize a forceful legal mandate for a peace mission, and even if they agreed to authorize an enforcement or humanitarian mission against the wishes of Sudan there are not at present sufficient contributions from UN members to make it work.

The Security Council is the institutional expression of the enforcement powers of the United Nations. The Charter gives to the Council the right (or the responsibility) to identify threats to international peace and security and the authority to respond to them. Its menu of options in crafting its response is partly contained in Chapter VII of the Charter, especially in Articles 41 and 42, and partly exists at the uncertain intersection between the Council's political power and the details of the dispute in question. The formal powers in Chapter VII can be clearly ascertained, and amount to everything from economic sanctions to military invasions. Its practical powers are seen in particular cases, where the Council uses its influence to cajole states into cooperating with it. It is also seen in the cases where the Council does not use its full influence – for instance, the absence of a forceful response to the Darfur situation is a function of the arrangement of interests on the Council that do not permit a veto-proof coalition in favor of intervention.

The Council is an excellent example of an international organization that displays all three of the functions set out in Chapter 2. It is at times primarily a forum that brings together senior diplomats from its fifteen member states and where high-level negotiations can take place. Members are required to be continuously available so that Council meetings can take place on very short notice, and the result is a well-institutionalized forum of inter-state crisis diplomacy. When these states are sufficiently in agreement to take a decision, the Council becomes more like an actor in its own right. It takes collective decisions and appears to have a collective opinion, and it stands independent of any of its members. This collective personality may well be a fiction, but this does not diminish its power – it is an effective fiction. Finally, these collective decisions enter into a broader international society where they can be used by other actors as tools in their own political strategies, perhaps even in ways that are quite dislocated from the original intentions of the Council. States use the decisions and statements of the Council among the raw materials for their foreign policies, and in so doing they help constitute the broader world of international politics. The complexities in the nature of the Security Council help to account for its usefulness to states – it can be used and interpreted in a number of ways, subject of course to certain limits set by the legal terms of the UN Charter.

Further Reading

The best resource for insight into the practical operation of the Council, including how it has interpreted its powers in various crises over the years, is Loraine Sievers and Sam Daws, *The Procedure of the UN Security Council* (Oxford University Press, 4th edn., 2014). David Malone's edited volume is an excellent collection of essays across the broad range of Council history and activity: David M. Malone (ed.), *The UN Security Council: From the Cold War to the 21st Century* (Lynne Rienner, 2004).

For primary documents and facts on specific peace operations, the annual Global Peace Operations *Review* is excellent (NYU – Center on International Cooperation), as is the UN's own series of "blue books," documents on its main missions, organized by country. For further analysis of some of these operations, see Roland Paris, *At War's End: Building Peace after Civil Conflict* (Cambridge University Press, 2004), Katharina P. Coleman, *International Organizations and Peace Enforcement: The Politics of International Legitimacy* (Cambridge University Press, 2007), and Nigel White, *The United Nations System: Toward International Justice* (Lynne Rienner, 2002). On the UN's involvement in Rwanda, see Michael Barnett, *Eyewitness to a Genocide: The United Nations and Rwanda* (Cornell University Press, 2003). On Darfur, see John Hagan and Winona Rymond-Richmond, *Darfur and the Crime of Genocide* (Cambridge University Press, 2009). The documentary film *Refuge: A Film about Darfur* (Juju Films, 2009) is also revealing of the relationships between environmental change, political conflict, and the local people.

On Syria, two short documentary films provide particularly striking personal perspectives on the war: *Return to Homs* highlights a young soccer star who joins the anti-Assad movement after his home is destroyed by government forces, and *#chicagoGirl* shows some of the social networking behind the early protest movement from the perspective of a woman in the Chicago suburbs coordinating with protesters in Syria.

APPENDIX 4.A
UN Security Council Resolution 1973 on Libya (2011)

S/RES/1973 (2011)

17 March 2011

RESOLUTION 1973 (2011)

Adopted by the Security Council at its 6498th meeting on 17 March 2011

The Security Council,

Recalling its resolution 1970 (2011) of 26 February 2011,

Deploring the failure of the Libyan authorities to comply with resolution 1970 (2011), Expressing grave concern at the deteriorating situation, the escalation of violence, and the heavy civilian casualties,

. . .

Reiterating the responsibility of the Libyan authorities to protect the Libyan population and reaffirming that parties to armed conflicts bear the primary responsibility to take all feasible steps to ensure the protection of civilians,

. . .

Determining that the situation in the Libyan Arab Jamahiriya continues to constitute a threat to international peace and security,

Acting under Chapter VII of the Charter of the United Nations,

1. Demands the immediate establishment of a ceasefire and a complete end to violence and all attacks against, and abuses of, civilians

. . .

4. Authorizes Member States that have notified the Secretary-General, acting nationally or through regional organizations or arrangements, and acting in cooperation with the Secretary-General, to take all necessary measures, notwithstanding paragraph 9 of resolution 1970 (2011), to protect civilians and civilian populated areas under threat of attack in the Libyan Arab Jamahiriya, including Benghazi, while excluding a foreign occupation force of any form on any part of Libyan territory

. . .

6. Decides to establish a ban on all flights in the airspace of the Libyan Arab Jamahiriya in order to help protect civilians

. . .

8. Authorizes Member States that have notified the Secretary-General and the Secretary-General of the League of Arab States, acting nationally or through regional organizations or arrangements, to take all necessary measures to enforce compliance with the ban on flights imposed by paragraph 6 above

. . .

29. Decides to remain actively seized of the matter.

APPENDIX 4.B

UN Security Council Resolution 872 on Rwanda (1993)

S/RES/872 (1993)

5 October 1993

RESOLUTION 872 (1993)

Adopted by the Security Council at its 3288th meeting, on 5 October 1993

The Security Council,

Reaffirming its resolutions 812 (1993) of 12 March 1993 and 846 (1993) of 22 June 1993,

. . .

Welcoming the signing of the Arusha Peace Agreement (including its Protocols) on 4 August 1993 and urging the parties to continue to comply fully with it, Noting the conclusion of the Secretary-General that in order to enable the United Nations to carry out its mandate successfully and effectively, the full cooperation of the parties with one another and with the Organization is required,

Stressing the urgency of the deployment of an international neutral force in Rwanda, as underlined both by the Government of the Republic of Rwanda and by the Rwandese Patriotic Front and as reaffirmed by their joint delegation in New York,

. . .

Resolved that the United Nations should, at the request of the parties and under peaceful conditions with the full cooperation of all the parties, make its full contribution to the implementation of the Arusha Peace Agreement,

1. Welcomes the report of the Secretary-General (S/26488);
2. Decides to establish a peace-keeping operation under the name "United Nations Assistance Mission for Rwanda" (UNAMIR) for a period of six months subject to the proviso that it will be extended beyond the initial ninety days only upon a review by the Council based on a report from the Secretary-General as to whether or not substantive progress has been made towards the implementation of the Arusha Peace Agreement;
3. Decides that, drawing from the Secretary-General's recommendations, UNAMIR shall have the following mandate:
   (a) To contribute to the security of the city of Kigali inter alia within a weapons-secure area established by the parties in and around the city;
   (b) To monitor observance of the cease-fire agreement, which calls for the establishment of cantonment and assembly zones and the demarcation of the new demilitarized zone and other demilitarization procedures;
   (c) To monitor the security situation during the final period of the transitional government's mandate, leading up to the elections;
   (d) To assist with mine clearance, primarily through training programmes;
   (e) To investigate at the request of the parties or on its own initiative instances of alleged non-compliance with the provisions of the Arusha Peace Agreement relating to the integration of the armed forces, and pursue any such instances with the parties responsible and report thereon as appropriate to the Secretary-General;

(f) To monitor the process of repatriation of Rwandese refugees and resettlement of displaced persons to verify that it is carried out in a safe and orderly manner;

(g) To assist in the coordination of humanitarian assistance activities in conjunction with relief operations;

(h) To investigate and report on incidents regarding the activities of the gendarmerie and police;

. . .

7. Authorizes the Secretary-General, in this context, to deploy the first contingent, at the level specified by the Secretary-General's report, to Kigali for an initial period of six months, in the shortest possible time, which, when fully in place, will permit the establishment of the transitional institutions and implementation of the other relevant provisions of the Arusha Peace Agreement;

. . .

11. Urges the parties to implement the Arusha Peace Agreement in good faith;

. . .

13. Demands that the parties take all appropriate steps to ensure the security and safety of the operation and personnel engaged in the operation;

14. Urges Member States, United Nations agencies and non-governmental organizations to provide and intensify their economic, financial and humanitarian assistance in favour of the Rwandese population and of the democratization process in Rwanda;

15. Decides to remain actively seized of the matter.

5 The World Trade Organization

Website: www.wto.int.

Members: 164 members and observers, including some that are not states.

Main bodies:

- Ministerial Conference: annual meeting of trade ministers.
- General Council: plenary body of trade officials, meets in various guises to consider trade in goods, trade in services, trade in agriculture, intellectual property, and so on.
- Dispute Settlement Body: General Council session to consider trade disputes.
- many working groups, working parties, and committees.

Area of competence:

- sets limits on what policies members can choose that have an impact on international trade.
- strives to create a stable regulatory environment for international trade.
- aims for "rule-governed" trade, rather than free trade.
- settles disputes between members regarding violations of these rules, and authorizes retaliatory tariffs under the Dispute Settlement Understanding.

Principal obligations of members:

- "most-favored nation": generally treat goods from all trade partners the same (Art. I), qualified by many other rules.
- "schedule of concessions": maintain a public and fixed set of tariffs for imports (Art. II).
- "national treatment": treat imports no worse than domestically produced goods (Art. III).

The World Trade Organization enforces a set of rules limiting the choices of governments with respect to international trade. These rules define what is legal and illegal when it comes to a wide range of state policies that might affect international trade. These include import tariffs, industrial subsidies, and all manner of taxes and regulations. For WTO member countries, any government policy that might have an impact on private firms that trade across its borders could conceivably come under the scrutiny of the organization. However, not all goods and services are covered, and not all trade-influencing policies are prohibited, and so interpreting the WTO's rules has become an important industry both inside the organization and its Dispute Settlement Body and outside the organization in the universe of international trade lawyers, lobbyists, and activists.

The World Trade Organization is among the key institutions that govern the international political economy, and as such it is central to a great number of the controversies associated with globalization. Its main component is the General Agreement on Tariffs and Trade (GATT), a treaty from 1947 which specifies how countries can regulate their imports and exports of most goods. The WTO also oversees an agreement on the trade in services (GATS), rules on intellectual property (TRIPS), trade dispute-resolution processes, and rules on agricultural trade and subsidies, among many other elements. The WTO is a formal organization that was given the task of implementing these agreements on trade starting in 1995. Most of the substantive commitments on trade are contained in the agreements themselves, rather than in the WTO. This chapter uses the GATT and its rules to illustrate the international legal regime for trade. It does not strive to explain all the agreements in detail. This is justified by the facts that the GATT forms the historical and legal core of the international trade regime, and that GATT rules are the baseline from which these other agreements were negotiated.[1]

The WTO itself is a small formal organization and bureaucracy (with a staff of just 640), but it has a reach that is both broad and deep: it has been joined by 164 member governments and the substantive scope of the trade agreements that it manages is comprehensively global. As a consequence, virtually all world trade takes place under WTO rules: 97 percent of world trade is between WTO members, and 99 percent of the import tariffs of developed countries are bound

---

[1] See the Further Reading suggestions for more detailed examinations of the WTO's wide range of sub-agreements.

by the WTO.[2] Some of its members are not formally recognized as states, including Hong Kong, China; Chinese Taipei; and the European Union. The WTO will accept as members political entities that control the trade policy for a territory – this allows it to build a trade network that reflects actually existing political-economy units in international trade, as opposed to only those that are widely accepted as "sovereign states." This membership criterion makes it possible for non-states to join the WTO and is unique among the organizations in this book.

As the dominant legal regime in world trade, the WTO makes three main contributions to the international economic system: (i) it establishes rules that govern how members can set domestic policies that affect international trade; (ii) it requires that members maintain public lists of import tariffs for all products which cannot be altered except through multilateral negotiation; (iii) and it sets up court-like dispute-settlement procedures to hear complaints when one member believes another is breaking these rules. These three developments radically transformed economic policy-making for member governments, so much so that there is a clear disjuncture between policy-making for these governments before this system was created and since then. After 1947, with the General Agreement on Tariffs and Trade in place, governments inside the system must take into account this highly regulated international-legal environment; governments that are WTO members are much less autonomous in their policy-making than non-WTO members. In return, however, they expect to be wealthier by virtue of participating in a world where international trade is made easier and cheaper for firms.

The WTO system includes different rules for different kinds of products – rules for agricultural bulk goods are different than for manufactured products and different again from traded services such as accounting, banking and professional services. In agriculture, for instance, direct subsidies from governments to producers are permitted, and for textiles and apparel import quotas were common into the 2000s. Both quotas and subsidies are generally prohibited for manufactured goods. Government procurement has its own rules, permitting discrimination in favor of domestic suppliers in ways that would be illegal if applied elsewhere in the economy. Many other categories, special rules, and side-deals exist and ensure that one must pay close attention to details in order to know which rules apply to which products and among which trading partners.

---

[2] David Jolly, "WTO Grants Russia Membership," *New York Times*, December 16, 2011. And www.wto.int/english/thewto_e/whatis_e/tif_e/fact2_e.htm. Accessed January 7, 2013.

The key to understanding the pattern of this patchwork is to look for the desires of powerful governments. All negotiators try to shape the rules around their own interests but the strongest governments in WTO negotiations clearly dominate the results. The leading power players include the US, the European Union, and Japan, with China and Brazil exerting new influence and Australia and Canada having notable influence in agriculture and some natural resources. The fact that, for instance, agricultural subsidies are permitted while industrial subsidies are not comes directly from the strongest states' desire to continue to underwrite their farm industries while simultaneously wanting market competition in manufactured goods.

The trade rules should therefore be understood in political terms: they are designed with the interests of the strong in mind. It is easier for the strong than the weak to comply with the rules since the rules generally do not demand things of the strong that are politically very difficult – though we will see below how interesting are those cases where this does happen. Friedrich List diagnosed the power politics of free trade back in the 1840s, as he noticed that Britain became an advocate of open trading systems only once it became the leading industrial nation, at which point it sought to prevent poorer countries from using managed trade to develop their own competitors. In trade negotiations, weak states are generally rule-takers not rule-makers.

This chapter looks at the changes brought about by the GATT and the WTO in domestic policy and international political economy. It begins by looking at the GATT agreement to identify what it is that states are committed to doing when they join the WTO. These obligations are not what many people assume when they think about the WTO. It then considers the formal organization set up by the WTO treaty and examines how the organization induces compliance with its rules. Enforcement of WTO rules is done by member states themselves, not by the central authority of the WTO, in a unique arrangement that takes advantage of conflicting self-interests among WTO members.

To see the WTO's rules in action, this chapter looks at one case in depth: the "Shrimp–Turtle" dispute in which a group of countries complained that the US was breaking its commitments under the GATT. Their complaint was that the US was using environmental protection laws as a disguise for trade protectionism. In following how the case traveled through the dispute-settlement process we can see many intriguing facets of the WTO system. The case is useful not only because it shows how the dispute process works, but also because it brings up two substantively important problems for the future of international trade and international law: first, it shows the tangled relationship between trade policy and environmental consequences; and second, it leads directly to a puzzle over the relationship between how things are made and how they are traded. The "how things are made" question is not often talked about in scholarship on the WTO but it may end up being the most important question in international trade in the coming decades.

Obligations

In joining the WTO, governments commit to specific limits to their domestic economic policies. These are shared obligations on all members and together they create the framework within which most international trade in goods takes place. They are spelled out in the clauses of the original GATT agreement from 1947, and were subsumed under the broad WTO umbrella in 1995. For instance, Article XVI sets rules on when governments can subsidize their domestic industries; Article XI forbids setting quotas on imports or exports; Article VI discourages "dumping" goods in an export market at less than their regular price in the home market. All of these rules are subject to exceptions and provisos and so the ultimate effect of the rules depends on precisely how they are written and interpreted. As a result, much of the action around the WTO consists of lawyerly argument about the meaning of the words – for instance, the anti-dumping rule in Article VI says that exporting goods "at less than the normal value ... is to be condemned if it causes or threatens material injury to an established industry" in the importing country. Precisely what is "normal value," "material injury," or an "established industry," and what it means for a practice to be "condemned," are left mostly undefined.[3] Behind these vague terms are political battles of enormous consequence.

Three of these obligations are particularly important as they make up something like the constitutional order of world trade. These are the idea of "bound" tariffs and the rules of most-favored nation and of national treatment, and they appear in the first three Articles of the GATT agreement.

---

[3] A separate agreement, added in the Uruguay Round ending in 1995, tries to spell them out. It is the "Agreement on the Implementation of Article VI of the GATT."

"Bound" Tariffs

Upon joining the World Trade Organization, each country is required to agree to a ceiling for the import tax it charges on each imported good. This maximum tariff can be different for each item but the country must publish a list (called a "schedule") of all its tariff rates (called "concessions") and must agree not to unilaterally raise those rates above the published levels. These become the "bound" tariffs of the country, and the schedule automatically becomes part of the WTO treaty. The tariff rates are therefore legally binding commitments by the government – sticking to them is an obligation of the government just like any other commitments it might make under international law.

Article II (1a) of the GATT says "each contracting party shall accord to the commerce of the other contracting parties treatment no less favorable than that provided for in the appropriate Part of the appropriate Schedule annexed to this Agreement." As these commitments are made by all members, the result is a comprehensive set of maximum tariffs on almost all international trade, organized into thousands of categories and subcategories. Almost all categories of traded goods are now covered by bound tariffs: 99 percent of developed country imports and 73 percent of developing country imports, according to the WTO.[4] The binding rates need not be zero, and therefore free trade is not necessarily the outcome, but they cannot be changed except through the multilateral processes of negotiations among members that take place at the big review conferences of the WTO itself. Firms that seek to import or export goods therefore know with great certainty the taxes that will be charged on their commerce as it crosses borders, and tariff rates generally remain stable for the years between the negotiating "rounds."

In the US, the list of tariffs is published by the US International Trade Commission and is known as the Harmonized Tariff Schedule (HTS). A selection from the US HTS is reprinted in Box 5.1. Each kind of item is assigned an eight-digit code and a brief description. The HTS lists the ad valorem duty that the US government charges for imports that originate in three categories of countries (the three "Rates of Duty" columns in the table): these are (i) WTO members ("general"), (ii) special trade-agreement countries ("special"), and (iii) everybody else (column "2"). The distinctions among items are very fine-grained such that, in the example in Box 5.1, chandeliers of brass are charged a 3.9 percent import tariff and chandeliers of other metals are charged

---

[4] www.wto.org/english/theWTO_e/whatis_e/tif_e/agrm2_e.htm#con

7.6 percent (for imports from WTO members). On imports from non-WTO members, the rate is 45 percent for both, and the rate is zero (i.e. free trade) for many trading partners that have signed "special" free-trade agreements with the US (such as Bahrain (BH), Dominican Republic (P), and Canada (C)). (These agreements are discussed below.)

There are two further interesting things to note in the Harmonized Tariff Schedule. First, the rates of tariffs themselves are decided by negotiation between the US and its trading partners. These negotiations are complex and multidimensional, and so the differences in rate between similar items (such as a higher rate on non-brass than on brass chandeliers) may come about because of a concession by other countries on a completely unrelated category of traded goods, or because of the influence of a domestic interest group or a politician seeking to protect a particular factory making non-brass lighting in their own country. These negotiations and concessions take place among governments, generally behind closed doors, at the periodic "rounds" of WTO conferences such as the Doha round that began in 2001.

The second thing to notice is the apparent arbitrariness of the categories themselves, and yet their power to influence trade and production decisions around the world. All goods within a category must be charged the same duty, but items in different categories can have different duties. As a result, it matters a great deal to firms and governments how the categories are defined. If chandeliers of all metals were grouped together under one HTS heading then the distinction in tariffs between brass and non-brass imports could not be sustained. Everything within one tariff "line" is understood to be homogeneous – in the language of the WTO, it is "like product" and should be treated consistently.

It becomes an important question who decides when categories should be subdivided, and how? Could (for instance) Christmas tree light sets (9405.30.00) be subdivided so that white bulbs and green bulbs were distinct categories and had different tariff rates? Should glass and plastic bulbs be separated into distinct tariff lines? The categories of the HTS are themselves governed by another international organization, the World Customs Organization (WCO), based in Brussels. It maintains the harmonized system down to the six-digit subheadings; beyond that, countries are free to make their own sub-subheadings to the 10-digit level, for instance between "brass" and "non-brass" lamps in Box 5.1. Changes to the categories are possible only by multilateral agreement among the WCO members. The Shrimp–Turtle dispute discussed below shows some of the controversy that arises over interpreting the HTS categories – that dispute raised the question of whether shrimp caught with fishing nets that accidentally trapped sea turtles should be considered different than shrimp caught with turtle-friendly nets. The HTS in its current form does not allow this. It permits distinctions between categories based only on the qualities of the final good itself, not on the manner in which they were produced. The Shrimp–Turtle case, however, suggests that this may one day change.

Box 5.1 **Harmonized Tariff Schedule of the United States (2009) (Rev. 1)**

Annotated for Statistical Reporting Purposes

Heading/ Subheading	Stat Suffix	Article Description	Unit of Quantity	Rates of Duty		
				1		2
				General	Special	
9405		Lamps and lighting fittings including searchlights and spotlights and parts thereof, not elsewhere specified or included; illuminated signs, illuminated nameplates and the like, having a permanently fixed light source, and parts thereof not elsewhere specified or included:				
9405.10		Chandeliers and other electric ceiling or wall lighting fittings, excluding those of a kind used for lighting public open spaces or thoroughfares: Of base metal:				
9405.10.40		Of brass.	. . . .	3.9%	Free (A,AU,BH, C,CA,CL,E,IL,J, JO,MA,MX, OM,P,PE, SG)	45%
	10	Household.	No.			
	20	Other.	No.			

Box 5.1 (*cont.*)

Annotated for Statistical Reporting Purposes

Heading/ Subheading	Stat Suffix	Article Description	Unit of Quantity	Rates of Duty 1 General	Rates of Duty 1 Special	2
9405.10.60		Other..............	....	7.6%	Free (A,AU,BH, C,CA,CL,E,IL,J, JO,MA,MX, OM,P,PE,SG)	45%
	10	Household........	No.			
	20	Other..............	No.			
9405.10.80		Other..............	....	3.9%	Free (A,AU,BH, C,CA,CL,E,IL,J, JO,MA,MX,OM, P,PE,SG)	35%
	10	Household........	No.			
	20	Other..............	No.			
9405.20		Electric table, desk, bedside or floor-standing lamps:				
9405.20.40		Of base metal:				
		Of brass...........		3.7%	Free (A,AU, BH,CA,CL,E, IL,J,JO,MA, MX,OM,P,PE, SG)	40%
	10	Household........	No.			
	20	Other..............	No.			
9405.20.60		Other..............	....	6%	Free (A,AU, BH,CA,CL,E, IL,J,JO,MA, MX,OM,P,PE, SG)	45%
	10	Household........	No.			
	20	Other..............	No.			

Box 5.1 (*cont.*)

Annotated for Statistical Reporting Purposes

Heading/ Subheading	Stat Suffix	Article Description	Unit of Quantity	Rates of Duty		
				1		2
				General	Special	
9405.20.80		Other.	. . . .	3.9%	Free (A,AU,BH, CA,CL,E,IL,J, JO,MA,MX, OM,P,PE,SG)	35%
	10	Household.	No.			
	20	Other.	No.			
9405.30.00		Lighting sets of a kind used for Christmas trees.	. . . .	8%	Free (A,AU,BH, CA,CL,E,IL,J, JO,MA,MX, OM,P,PE,SG)	50%
	10	Miniature series wired sets.	No.			
	40	Other.	No.			
9405.40		Other electric lamps and lighting fittings: Of base metal:				
9405.40.40	00	Of brass.	No.	4.7%	Free (A,AU,BH, CA,CL,E,IL,J, JO,MA,MX, OM,P,PE,SG)	45%
9405.40.60	00	Other.	No.	6%	Free (A,AU,BH, CA,CL,E,IL,J, JO,MA,MX, OM,P,PE,SG)	45%
9405.40.80	00	Other.	No.	3.9%	Free (A,AU, BH,CA,CL,E,IL, J,JO,MA,MX, OM,P,PE,SG)	35%

"Most-Favored Nation"

The second key rule in the World Trade Organization is the idea of "most-favored nation" (MFN). This is defined in Article I of the GATT treaty which says in part "any advantage, favour, privilege, or immunity granted by any contracting party to any product originating in or destined for any other country shall be accorded immediately and unconditionally to the like product ... of all other contracting parties." This rule requires that members maintain a single set of trade tariffs and rules for their trade with all other WTO members. Members may not treat different WTO members differently, and may not negotiate bilaterally with other states for special treatment (except in free-trade areas, discussed below). This rule accounts for the fact that the HTS contains just one column of "general" rates of duty, and that this column accounts for all WTO members. The tariff is set based on the product not the country of origin. In a non-WTO world, it is conceivable that the US would maintain a different rate of tariff for the imports of brass chandeliers from every country and customs union in the world. The number of entries in the US HTS would then in principle expand exponentially to account for different duties for the same item for each of the 163 or so other WTO members.

The principle of most-favored nation is central to the entire mission of the WTO. Along with the rule of "national treatment" discussed below, it creates a uniform web of trade rules across the WTO trading zone and helps to drive down both the rates of tariff applied by countries and the transaction costs of trading firms. It simplifies the trading system enormously. As countries negotiate concessions with each other under the harmonized system at WTO conferences, all players know that whatever is agreed to between two members in their closed bilateral negotiation will then become the standard tariff offered to all other WTO members. In general, it is thought that this has led to a consistent downward pressure on tariff rates over time. For trading firms, it means fewer rules to deal with, as they know that tariffs and other national policies that affect the costs of trade will be more consistent across the countries in which they seek to do business.

Much of the controversy in contemporary trade policy comes from the fact that Article I of the GATT covers "any advantage, favour, privilege" and not just tariff rates. As a result, any policy with implications for international trade may end up under scrutiny for treating different sources of imports differently. For instance, a country that requires safety inspections for imported machinery must ensure that these inspections are equally mandatory, equally available, and equally strict for all trading partners. This equality must be maintained in practice, not just in writing, and so governments must be constantly alert to how they are implementing their rules. Any hint that a policy produces in effect an informal barrier to trade that is not equal across WTO members might generate a formal WTO complaint by the harmed member(s). The Shrimp–Turtle case was lost by the US because the American policy was deemed to treat some shrimp-exporting countries more favorably than others, which is a violation of MFN and Article I. Arguing over whether policies are faithful to the most-favored nation principle in practice makes up the majority of controversy in WTO disputes.

The "special" column of the HTS represents an enduring irony of the GATT and WTO. Entries in this column reflect the "better-than-MFN" import tariff on the product when it is among countries that have agreed to regional free-trade pacts. For the US, these agreements include the North American Free Trade Agreement (NAFTA), the US–Jordan free-trade area, and the US–Israel free-trade area, among many others. Each is listed by a short code in Box 5.1 in the "special" column along with the special tariff rate, which is usually zero. In the original GATT negotiations in 1947, there was concern that a truly comprehensive MFN system might make it impossible to negotiate local free-trade agreements because these would involve tariffs that were lower than were granted to countries outside the free-trade area. And yet, the spirit of the GATT was to produce lower tariffs in general, not to block those who wanted to go even lower than the general MFN rate. Article XXIV embodies a compromise between the principle that the best rate negotiated between two trading partners should be offered automatically to all other trading partners (i.e. MFN) and the reality that regional trading partners might be willing to eliminate tariffs among themselves but not to the wider world.

The GATT includes two potentially important limits to this right to form free-trade areas. It requires that the agreement be limited within a region (reflecting the original idea that these would be agreements to unite a set of local economies), and that the agreement cover "substantially all" of the trade among those regional partners (Article XXIV (8)). Thus, NAFTA qualifies as a regional trading zone in which nearly all GATT-qualifying trade is done without tariffs. The American agreements with Israel and with Jordan qualify in quantitative terms but are harder to justify as "regional" agreements. That these still stand despite their regional implausibility is a product of the particular relationship between WTO members and the rules: rule-breaking by WTO members is only investigated if another member can show that it has been harmed by the action and chooses to lodge an official complaint. To date, no country has complained about the non-regional nature of some of these American free-trade areas and so the countries have not been forced to justify or change their agreements.

"National Treatment"

The principle of "national treatment" is the natural complement to that of "most-favored nation." Where MFN requires that countries not discriminate among their trading partners, national treatment requires that they not discriminate between imported goods and domestically produced goods. Article III(4) of the GATT defines national treatment (NT): "The products of the territory of any contracting party imported into the territory of any other contracting party shall be accorded treatment no less favourable than that accorded to the like products of national origin." Countries are forbidden to apply rules, taxes, or any other costly burden to imported goods unless they are also applied (and equally applied) to domestically produced units of the same good. Safety standards, sales taxes, and labeling requirements, for instance, must not discriminate between imports and domestic goods. The goal of the NT rules together with those on MFN is to create a seamless environment in which goods are treated equally regardless of their status as traded goods. This, it is thought, will reduce the non-market barriers to international trade and allow market forces a greater role in production and consumption decisions.

The national treatment obligation is expressly designed to prevent countries from favoring their domestic producers over their international competitors. For instance, the US complained in 2004 that China was taxing imported integrated circuits more onerously than the same goods produced by domestic Chinese factories. This, the US claimed, undermined the competitiveness of US exports to China and shifted the pattern of trade artificially in favor of Chinese producers (the case was settled by mutual agreement). Similarly, the EU has maintained for several years that India and its states charged higher domestic taxes on imported wines and spirits than on domestic production. The US and Canada have fought a series of cases in which the US complained that Canadian provinces were discriminating against US beer imports with a host of indirect non-tariff barriers, such as imposing environmental charges on beer cans at a time when US beer was disproportionately in cans rather than bottles. Canada lost. What looked like a straightforward environmental policy designed to encourage recycling had the effect of discriminating between domestic and imported beers and the US claimed it was essentially a disguised trade restriction prohibited under the "national treatment" rules. In adhering to these rules, states clearly lose some of their traditional capacity to manage access to their local markets; they cannot adopt policies, even on non-trade matters, if they lead to trade-discriminating effects.

This may also apply to purchases made by governments themselves. The Government Procurement Agreement (1979), an optional protocol to the WTO, requires that government spending be done on non-discriminatory grounds, subject to some exceptions. The Agreement has been signed by most of the largest governments, including the US, the EU, and Japan, though not by China. In the US, it means that government-sponsored "Buy American" programs are legally suspect.[5] This is often seen by economic nationalists as an unwelcome limit on state sovereignty and as such it is often used to exemplify excessive authority in the WTO. The full paradox of state consent and international authority is on display in these disputes: the rules that empower the WTO to override government decisions were brought into being by the consent of those same governments. Can states claim to have lost their sovereignty when the rules that they themselves agreed to are applied against them?

In the GATT, both national treatment and most-favored nation are defined in terms of "like products," mentioned above. They require that "like products" be treated the same regardless of which WTO member they are imported from and whether they are imports or domestically produced, which of course presumes that we know what products are alike. Rajesh Pillai discusses the evolution of the criteria by which "likeness" is determined in trade law, most importantly by the Working Party on Border Tax Adjustments in 1970.[6] The designation of "like products" is codified in the harmonized system of classification, and so for WTO purposes, "like products" are those that fall under a single category within the

---

[5] See for instance the controversy over one "buy American" provision in the US 2009 stimulus package: http://internationallawobserver.eu/2009/02/17/buy-american-and-the-wto. Accessed February 5, 2010.

[6] Rajesh Pillai, "National Treatment and WTO Dispute Settlement," *World Trade Review*, 2002, 1(3): 321–343. Also, Working Party on Border Tax Adjustments L/3464, BISD 18S/97.

harmonized schedule of tradable goods. This again signals the importance of how these categories are defined and interpreted.

Compliance

Conventional macroeconomic models of international trade suggest that trade produces gains for both trading partners. It is said to increase efficiency by allowing countries to specialize in the products that they make relatively more efficiently and by encouraging production on a larger scale. It is also said to increase the choice available to consumers by making available products that otherwise would not be produced in the home market. Prices should fall and diversity should increase in a market that is opened to imports and exports, as compared to what would obtain in a non-trading (i.e. autarkic) market. As a result, countries should have a self-interested motive to encourage stable and open trading relationships of the kind facilitated by the rules of national treatment, most-favored nation, and fixed tariff schedules. There should therefore be an internal push in countries to comply with the WTO out of purely self-interested motives. However, as many have noted, there are also strong countervailing reasons why countries often find it advantageous to try to circumvent their commitments to freer trade. The WTO's record in encouraging compliance with its rules is therefore mixed. This section looks at why states may shirk on free trade, and argues that the WTO's rules are structured to raise the costs of non-compliance and therefore induce countries to comply. The subsequent section, on enforcement, examines the process that follows when states refuse to comply.

There are two main incentives of governments for violating the trade-policy rules of the WTO: (i) to protect a politically important sector or company, and (ii) to unilaterally increase trade barriers or export subsidies while your partners refrain from retaliating. The first is a function of the uneven distribution of costs and benefits from trade, while the second is closer to outright cheating.

The distributional problem arises because while there may be overall gains from trade for both trading countries, the aggregate outcome obscures the fact that the costs and benefits of trade are unevenly distributed across domestic industries and between the trading partners. States often find that the patterns of trade that result from following WTO rules are not the same as the patterns they favor for other reasons. They may have very parochial political interests in protecting one sector of their economy from foreign competition, despite the costs this imposes on the rest of their society. For instance, the United States discovered in the 1980s that imported cars were winning market share in the US away from the big three American car makers. This change in the composition of the US car market, following in part from freer trade in autos, created a threat to industrial employment in the US that was highly geographically concentrated in Michigan. It therefore created a political threat to office holders from Michigan, and led to a series of legal moves in Washington, DC to protect American car makers from imports. Most significantly, the US forced Japan to accept "voluntary export restraints" on its auto industry, which caused the retail price of cars in the US to rise 41 percent from 1981 to 1984, far faster than other prices were rising.[7] While US consumers, and the US economy as a whole, would have benefited from the cheaper cars and greater diversity of choice that the auto trade would have brought, the way that the costs were distributed in the US pushed the federal government to move against the imports. The net wealth of the US was likely lowered by the move, but the trade-off was deemed worth it by the politicians threatened by the potential unemployment in Michigan and other auto-producing areas. A similar pattern was at work in the decision in 1947 (and reaffirmed many times since) to treat agricultural exports differently than most others. Agricultural goods are exempt from the rules of the GATT described above because few powerful countries are willing to bear the political impact of allowing free trade in agriculture. This is one area in which powerful governments in world trade prefer 'supply-management' to market-based outcomes. As a result, agricultural trade is covered by a separate and much weaker set of rules adopted as an annex to the rest of the WTO charter and the politics of agricultural trade and subsidies remain hotly contested.

Economists often deride these political trade-offs as irrational since they mean countries are in effect choosing a policy that makes them poorer than they would otherwise be. However, from the perspective of the politicians (and perhaps of their citizens) there is nothing irrational about being sensitive to the costs of trade as well as to its benefits. Governments have been overthrown, by elections and by force, as a result of the social upheaval that quickly changing trade flows can create. To protect an industry, whether it be agriculture or steel or shipbuilding or airplanes, from collapse as a result of cheaper, better imports may sometimes be smart public policy. It may also sometimes be crass

---

[7] www.wto.int/english/thewto_e/whatis_e/10ben_e/10b04_e.htm. Accessed January 8, 2013.

opportunism by politicians pandering to a coddled special-interest group. The trick, of course, is to be able to tell the difference between the two.

The WTO agreement includes a series of exemptions that aim to allow governments to respond to the political pressures of their citizens while remaining faithful to WTO rules. Understanding these exemptions and their limits is important for assessing whether states are complying with their obligations. There are exemptions for national security concerns (Art. XXI), for relief against unexpected surges in imports (the "safeguards" clause in Art. XIX), for some cultural products such as films (Art. IV), and for a range of public policy goals including health and safety standards, public morals, and protecting endangered species (Art. XX). The extent of each exemption is defined by the legal language of its article, and a close reading is necessary to grasp what is allowed under each (note, for instance, how the "chapeau" paragraph in Article XX modifies the exemptions in the lettered subparagraphs).

The second set of incentives for non-compliance comes from the fact that states might be able to win short-term gains by cheating on their WTO obligations. Governments face an incentive to displace the costs of freer trade onto other countries while retaining the benefits for themselves. The WTO is organized around a reciprocal arrangement in which the member governments all agree to give up certain trade barriers simultaneously. By making it reciprocal each member is supposed to see increased access to others' markets in exchange for allowing increased access to its home market. The incentive to cheat in this bargain is easy to see.[8]

Around the WTO, this often takes the shape of countries creating non-tariff barriers to trade. These have the effect that the rates that appear in the published tariff schedule do not accurately reflect the true barriers to trade. For instance, the US and Canada complained that an EU ban on beef that had been injected with growth hormones was in fact a disguised way to exclude their beef from the European market and thus to favor domestic European producers. They suggested the ban had less to do with protecting human or animal health and more to do with accomplishing through non-tariff barriers what the EU had promised not to do through tariffs.[9] The WTO eventually agreed, after some complex legal machinations. Similarly, in a 1990s case involving photographic film, the US complained to the WTO that Kodak was effectively barred from exporting film to Japan due to the peculiar structure of the internal market for film in Japan. Regardless of the published tariff rate in

---

[8] John H. Jackson's discussion is unrivaled. See Chapter 1 of his *The World Trading System: Law and Policy of International Economic Relations*, 2nd edn., MIT Press, 1997.

[9] The case is the European Hormone Case.

the Japanese Tariff Schedule, the US argued that the distribution system for film effectively blocked imports and favored Fuji film, a domestic Japanese product. The US ultimately lost the case because the WTO dispute panel did not blame the Japanese government for the ways private Japanese firms were organized and the market structure that resulted.[10]

The outcome in this case provides a reminder of the interestingly complicated position of the WTO at the boundary between government policies and private firms' behavior. The trade that is regulated by the WTO and its agreements is almost all conducted by private firms, but as an intergovernmental agreement the WTO can only create obligations on governments, and not on firms. The WTO's effect on trade must therefore be doubly indirect, mediated through both governments (which the WTO regulates) and firms (which it does not).

The dynamics of members' compliance and non-compliance with the WTO circle around two facets of states' self-interest: on the one hand, the system is designed to make it easier for countries to realize the wealth gains that are believed to come from increased imports and exports, while on the other hand these very same rules create the possibility of cheating and manipulation to shift costs to others and gains to oneself. The system tries to align the self-regarding interests of its members so that there is a reward for choosing to comply with the rules. In other words, the benefits of long-term compliance, enhanced by the reciprocity that this engenders, are designed to outweigh the local payoff that might come from a once-off episode of cheating. Compliance remains a self-motivated and self-interested practice. The grand design of the system also assumes that collective benefits come from all of this coordinated, self-interested behavior. To the extent that the system works, it is because it provides sufficient rewards to states that voluntarily comply with the rules and sufficient costs for non-compliance.

Enforcement

When states find that the benefits of compliance are not enough to outweigh the incentives for cheating, we expect them to begin cheating. At that point, the WTO system shifts to an enforcement mode. As we have seen already in

[10] See the discussion in Bernard M. Hoekman and Michel M. Kostecki, *The Political Economy of the World Trading System*, 2nd edn., Oxford University Press, 1998, pp. 86–87.

Chapters 1 and 2, the power of enforcement is inherently problematic for international organizations, and all international organizations must somehow address the fact that they are striving to enforce rules on sovereign states that retain both the political power and the legal status of autonomous, self-regarding actors. As with compliance, the enforcement system in the WTO works by mobilizing the self-interest of the members in defense of the rules. Rather than centralizing the enforcement function within the WTO itself (as is the model for the UN Security Council, for instance), it relies instead on the members to retaliate directly against those who violate the rules, though they must perform this retaliation according to rules set down by the WTO. The WTO's powers over enforcement are limited to identifying what counts as a violation of the rules and then authorizing members to punish the violator. This produces very different patterns of rule-enforcement than would emerge under any other system.

The formal dispute-settlement mechanism in the WTO is activated when a member complains to the WTO that it believes another member has failed to meet its obligations under the treaty. The initiative for the complaint must come from a member that has suffered some economic harm from the misbehavior of another, and complaints can only be brought to the WTO after the sides have tried to settle the matter by consultations among themselves.[11] That all disputes originate with a harmed party is important in showing that the WTO secretariat itself is not in the business of monitoring compliance or taking independent action in defense of the rules; the spirit of the WTO is very much that the members have made commitments to one another and decisions on compliance and enforcement are in their hands as well. Those who complain are those members with a selfish interest in seeing the rules followed. That said, the WTO provides an institutional path for disputes which is designed to reinforce the incentives for self-interested compliance.

Once a member formally submits a dispute, the WTO creates a "panel" of three trade experts who are asked to hear arguments from the parties and from interested others and to report recommendations on the legal questions in the case. These panelists are supposed to act impartially, not as representatives of their home countries, and to judge the legal merits of the complaint. Their report

[11] The Dispute Settlement Understanding, which governs this process and is mandatory for WTO members, can be read at: www.wto.org/english/docs_e/legal_e/28-dsu_e.htm. Accessed February 5, 2010.

is then distributed to the complaining and responding countries, who may appeal any aspect of the legal interpretations it contains to a separate Appellate Body, and then to the general membership of the WTO. The WTO membership, meeting as a "committee of the whole" called the Dispute Settlement Body (DSB), then either approves or rejects the report. If approved, then the report's recommendations become binding on the parties to the dispute. These may include finding that the responding country has violated its obligations to other members and must change its policies. It would then be under legal obligation to do so. No panel report has ever been rejected by the Dispute Settlement Body.[12]

Many disputes are resolved before they reach this ultimate stage. About two-thirds of disputes are resolved in the consultations phase and never reach the point of needing a panel.[13] Of the cases that continue, many are resolved before they reach the end. For instance, in a case against the US for its special tariffs against imported steel in 2002, both the panel and the Appellate Body found that the US was breaking the rules on "safeguards" in Article XIX. The US repealed the rules on its own initiative (without admitting fault) in December 2003, just six days before the WTO Dispute Settlement Body would have accepted the report.[14] Because the DSB never reached its decision, in formal legal terms the US can be said to have not been found in violation of the rules in the case.

States, of course, sometimes refuse to comply even when they are told by international bodies that they must change their policies. A finding against a state by the Dispute Settlement Body represents a definitive legal and political judgment that the country is not living up to the promises it made upon joining the WTO. However, only the state itself has the capacity to change its policies to conform to its obligations, and the politics of doing so are always complex. Recognizing this, the dispute-settlement process in the WTO includes the possibility of economic sanctions against countries that refuse to comply with DSB decisions. These must be authorized by the DSB itself, and they can come only after the target state has been given opportunities to change its policies or to negotiate compensation to harmed states. In authorizing sanctions, the DSB

---

[12] Reports can only be rejected by a unanimous vote of the WTO members. Anything short of consensus against the report, including the parties to the case, counts as approving it. The barriers to rejection are therefore very high.

[13] www.wto.org/english/thewto_e/whatis_e/tif_e/disp1_e.htm. Accessed March 12, 2009.

[14] See American Society of International Law Insight Brief, November 2003, www.asil.org/insigh120.cfm. Accessed March 12, 2009.

judges the size of the harm done by the violations and permits states to impose trade measures that compensate equally for that harm.

States are supposed to impose these sanctions on the same area of trade where possible, but in practice retaliation is usually carefully crafted so as to maximize their political impact. For instance, in the US steel "safeguards" case mentioned above, the Appellate Body report authorized the EU to impose sanctions on $2.2 billion of US exports to Europe, which would have begun once the report was adopted by the DSB. The EU publicized in advance that it would target citrus exports from Florida and textile exports from North Carolina, among other goods, and that these choices were designed to add pressure in politically sensitive regions ahead of the 2004 presidential election.[15] This was, in a sense, a response in kind to the fact that the American steel tariffs were widely seen as being motivated by the political needs of the Bush administration in steel-producing regions.

This system builds a legal regime around the old practices of inter-state trade disputes. It aims to encase trade disputes in a predictable and rule-governed process, where both complaining and responding states have obligations, rather than leaving it to the play of power politics between countries. In the WTO process, states that believe themselves to have been harmed by the rule-breaking of others are obliged to refrain from unilateral countermeasures, and wait for the DSB to authorize its retaliation. This system generally works well in disputes between the EU and the US because they are more or less equally balanced in political power and economic diversity. It works less well when a small or poor country wishes to complain against a large or rich country: to the small or poor country, imposing retaliatory tariffs on the goods it imports from the large or rich country might well cause more harm to its own domestic economy than it does to the large country it seeks to punish. Retaliation may be self-defeating, and strong countries may see their policies challenged less often than fairness and the rule of law would require. In this sense, the WTO's effort to create a uniform legal framework for trade and trade disputes runs against the political and economic realities of a world with huge power disparities.[16]

---

[15] Benjamin H. Liebman and Kasaundra M. Tomlin, "Safeguards and Retaliatory Threats," *Journal of Law and Economics*, May 2008, **51**: 351–376.

[16] In response to this problem, Gregory Shaffer has very interesting work on enhancing poor countries' access to, and capacity to engage in, the WTO's dispute settlement process. See for instance Shaffer, "The Challenges of WTO Law: Strategies for Developing Country Adaptation," *World Trade Review*, July 2006: 177–198.

CASE: Shrimp–Turtle

The long-running and multi-episode drama over how shrimp are caught and traded provides an excellent illustration of the legal, political, and conceptual life of the WTO. The dispute wound its way through the GATT and WTO dispute systems in the 1990s and along the way touched on many of the most important aspects of WTO law and practice, including most-favored nation, trade's effects on environmental management and endangered species, the relation between WTO rules and state sovereignty, and problems lurking within the concept of "like-products." It is therefore a neat case study of both the rules of the WTO and the controversies that arise from them.

The controversy begins with the mechanics of fishing for shrimp in the ocean, where shrimp are caught by trawling nets that are pulled through the water. These nets trap shrimp as well as other animals, many of which are killed in the process. These animals become something like the industrial-waste by-product of the shrimp industry. The waste in the process is particularly concerning in areas where endangered species share the water with shrimp. This is the case with several species of sea turtles. The US took action to reduce this waste and protect the turtles by legislating that shrimp must be caught in a "turtle-friendly" manner. The US passed a new law in 1989 which banned imports of shrimp from countries that had not proved that their shrimping industry used nets with "turtle excluder devices" or something comparable. The law is an example of how trade law and environmental policy interact. The legislation used trade law as a tool for achieving a conservation goal or – as interpreted by some critics – used an environmental pretext to pursue protectionism in trade policy.

Several trade partners of the US objected to how the rule was implemented, leading to a formal dispute case at the WTO beginning in 1996. The complaint, initiated by India, Malaysia, Pakistan, and Thailand, had many facets. One centered on the fact that the US was not treating all sources of imported shrimp equally because some Caribbean countries "were given technical and financial assistance and longer transition periods" than the Asian countries.[17] They also claimed that the US was attempting to force other countries to adopt domestic policies modeled on American law, which would constitute the extra-territorial

---

[17] "India etc. versus US: 'shrimp–turtle,'" WTO memo, www.wto.org/english/tratop_e/envir_e/ edis08_e.htm. Accessed June 29, 2004.

application of US trade law and unacceptable foreign domination. The case also raised the question of whether Art. XX(g), on the conservation of "exhaustible natural resources," should be read broadly to include animal species or more narrowly to include only minerals and similarly inanimate materials. It also required the WTO to figure out the legal status of trade laws focused on the process by which products were made, rather than on the final attributes of the products themselves.

The ultimate outcome of the dispute-settlement process was that the US was found to be violating its commitments to WTO partners by discriminating among trade partners. This aspect of the case was decided by the original dispute panel and affirmed by the Appellate Body, and it stands as a relatively uncontroversial part of the case. The US implementation of the rule favored some trade partners over others by giving them more support and longer times in which to comply, and this is clearly forbidden by the plain language of the most-favored nation clause in Article I. Other parts of the decision are more interesting and more controversial with long-term consequences for the relationship between governments and the WTO that are still not clear. These include the relationship between environmental rules and trade policy and the hidden problems of determining "like-products."

The environmental consequences of the Shrimp–Turtle case have received a great deal of attention. Many people were concerned that the practical effect of the decision was that a law designed to protect endangered species was ruled to be unacceptable and the country that enacted the law was forced to abandon it. In this broadest view, the outcome suggested that the rules of trade policy would trump the rules of environmental protection, and many environmental groups were profoundly disappointed with the decision. They argued that the case set precisely the wrong precedent for managing the tensions between the economic and the social/environmental aspects of globalization, by apparently refusing to accommodate environmental protection in the interpretation of states' obligations under the WTO.

However, a closer look at the reasoning of the DSB report and at the behavior of the United States suggests that a more nuanced conclusion is warranted. For instance, the Appellate report objected primarily to the terms of implementation that the US applied in the law – that is, the problem with the US rules was that they were implemented in such a way that they created very different burdens on different trading partners. It did not object to the environmental goals of the law. Indeed, a WTO-compliant law on shrimping methods would have been simpler for the US to write than the one it imposed: applying the same rules to everyone would have been easier than crafting the more complicated rules that differentiated among trading partners. Thus, had the US been genuinely interested in its professed environmental goals and in its trading obligations, it would have been relatively easy to reconcile the two. It is therefore true that the WTO ruling demanded that the US make its environmental rules cleave to the existing structures of trade law, and in that sense it represents the triumph of economic globalization over the protection of endangered species. However, the ruling also showed a simple path for reconciling the two: following MFN. In that sense, it revealed that at least in this case there is no necessary trade-off between the trade regime and the goal of environmental protection. The problem arose because the US insisted on its right to favoritism among its trade partners, in obvious violation of its commitments under the WTO.

The case also raises a deep question about how to know what count as "like-products." The phrase "like-products" appears frequently in the WTO and it is crucial for interpreting all of the core rules on trade: most-favored nation, national treatment, and bound tariffs are all premised on our ability to know whether two items from different sources constitute identical goods (and so require similar treatment in trade law) or not (and so can be taxed or regulated differently). The Shrimp–Turtle case includes ambiguity over whether shrimp caught with turtle-excluder nets are "like-products" with those caught in any other way. Do the different processes by which the shrimp were caught make them different goods? This is a specific instance of a more general question regarding what are known as "production and process methods" questions in trade law. The original DSB panel report decided the two kinds of shrimp were indeed like-products – in other words, they were not actually two different kinds of shrimp – and the implication was that therefore the US was generally forbidden from treating the two differently through its trade policies. This is the traditional view in trade law.

The Appellate Body report, however, did not make reference to this argument from the panel report, and Gregory Shaffer (among others) has suggested that this absence is revealing: it suggests that the WTO may be coming to accept that in some instances distinct production methods might lead to distinct products.[18] It would seem that there are many instances in which the pursuit of environmental or other political goals via trade requires understanding production

---

[18] Gregory Shaffer, "WTO Shrimp–Turtle Case," *International Trade Reporter*, 1998, 15(7): 294–301.

methods as leading to distinct products. For instance, cotton shirts produced by slave labor might look and perform the same as shirts produced by paid workers, and so they would pass the traditional test to be considered "like-products," but the broader political objective of refusing to trade in goods produced by slaves would require that we be able to set different trade terms for slave-shirts and non-slave-shirts. The same logic would apply to prohibitions on imports of goods produced by child labor, or to goods whose production requires incidental devastation of the local environment. Oddly, the WTO treaty includes a specific allowance in Article XX(e) that countries can refuse to allow imports of goods produced by prison labor (as long as the prohibition is enforced in a non-discriminatory manner). This implies that there has always been some opening in the like-products regime for the idea that production methods may be considered in determining "likeness."

What is as yet unknown is the size of that opening. Could we say that steel produced with renewable energy is a different product than steel produced with fossil-fuel energy? Could we say that products exported from democratic countries are not like-products with those from non-democratic countries? If brass chandeliers are not "like-products" with non-brass chandeliers, who is to say that union-made brass chandeliers are "like-products" with non-union-made chandeliers (or red chandeliers with blue chandeliers)? The possibility for intense political fights over "likeness" is readily apparent. The more that production methods are allowed to figure into setting the categories of the HTS, the more one's trade partners must pay attention to the internal workings of one's industries; and yet the prison labor exception and the Shrimp–Turtle case both suggest that the WTO is already heading down this path. Future disputes are likely to center on questions of these kinds, with the result that future panel and Appellate reports will likely clarify (or create) the scope of the production-methods exceptions.

Conclusion

The World Trade Organization is founded on a set of commitments that states make to each other and to the organization, which creates a structure of rules for international trade. Abiding by these rules means that states give up their freedom to make unilateral decisions about tariffs, trade, and policies that affect the pattern of their imports and exports. In exchange, they get predictability and regularity in the trade policies of their partners. The ambition of the WTO is to maximize the extent to which trade patterns reflect economic and market factors rather than political factors and the parochial interests of policy-makers. The underlying assumption is that market-driven trade maximizes the growth and prosperity of all trade partners, whereas politically motivated trade laws enrich one sector or country at the expense of others.

The enormous growth in world trade since the signing of the GATT has undoubtedly contributed to the concomitant growth in global wealth. It may also have contributed to the growth in wealth inequality, and its possible contribution to the absolute decline in wealth in the world's poorest regions remains unclear and concerning. The WTO's rules standardize trade and reduce tariffs mainly for those goods in which the industrialized countries are already highly productive, and they generally exclude those goods of greatest export interest to the poorest countries, such as agriculture, textiles, and raw materials. These generally remain outside the WTO, or are subject to fewer and weaker rules, and politically motivated trade patterns tend to dominate at the expense of the poorer countries. The WTO itself often notes that problems such as rich-country agricultural subsidies, which do so much to discourage production in poor countries, are the fault of the subsidizing countries and not really the responsibility of the WTO itself. However, we cannot absolve the WTO of blame for its part in sustaining a structure of international trade that reinforces these inequalities, though the extent of its contribution is the subject of much debate.

The WTO's contribution to a stable regime of international trade policy is a result of the combination of its legal rules and the power politics that shape and enact them. This chapter has focused on three of the most fundamental legal rules in the WTO system: most-favored nation, national treatment, and bound tariffs. These place significant constraints on the policy choices of WTO members, and the dispute-settlement system exists to authorize countervailing tariffs in cases where members are found to have transgressed against them. The effects of these decisions and rules in the real world of trade policy and international politics depend on how the rules interact with the political power of those who would use them, and on the subtle qualifications and loopholes created by other aspects of the GATT treaty. Such complexity suggests that a legal approach to the WTO is a necessary beginning but not sufficient; a fuller understanding of the effects of the organization requires close attention to the details of the particular cases, products, and disputes in which these rules are put to work.

Further Reading

The WTO website is excellent for the legal agreements that make up the international trade regime and for the archive of cases and disputes. See www.wto.int. For discussion and commentary on WTO law and politics, see Mitsuo Matsushita and colleagues' *The World Trade Organization: Law, Practice, and Policy* (Oxford University Press, 2015) and the excellent book by Bernard M. Hoekman and Michel M. Kostecki, *The Political Economy of the World Trading System: The WTO and Beyond* (Oxford University Press, 3rd edn., 2010). See also Michael Tebilcock, Robert L. Howse, and Antonia Eliason, *The Regulation of International Trade* (Routledge, 4th edn., 2010).

An excellent book by Mark Pollack and Gregory Shaffer traces the case of genetically modified foods as it weaves in and out of the WTO, the EU, the US, and international politics. See Pollack and Shaffer, *When Cooperation Fails: The International Law and Politics of Genetically Modified Foods* (Oxford University Press, 2009). Up-to-date cases and commentary can be found at the International Economic Law and Policy blog, at worldtradelaw.net.

APPENDIX 5
Key GATT Clauses

www.wto.org/english/docs_e/legal_e/gatt47_02_e.htm

Article I: General most-favoured-nation treatment

1. With respect to customs duties and charges of any kind imposed on or in connection with importation or exportation or imposed on the international transfer of payments for imports or exports, and with respect to the method of levying such duties and charges, and with respect to all rules and formalities in connection with importation and exportation, and with respect to all matters referred to in paragraphs 2 and 4 of Article III, any advantage, favour, privilege or immunity granted by any contracting party to any product originating in or destined for any other country shall be accorded immediately and unconditionally to the like product originating in or destined for the territories of all other contracting parties.

Article II: Schedules of concessions

1. (a) Each contracting party shall accord to the commerce of the other contracting parties treatment no less favourable than that provided for in the appropriate Part of the appropriate Schedule annexed to this Agreement.

Article III: National treatment on internal taxation and regulation

2. The products of the territory of any contracting party imported into the territory of any other contracting party shall not be subject, directly or indirectly, to internal taxes or other internal charges of any kind in excess of those applied, directly or indirectly, to like domestic products. Moreover, no contracting party shall otherwise apply internal taxes or other internal charges to imported or domestic products in a manner contrary to the principles set forth in paragraph 1.

Article VI: Anti-dumping and countervailing duties

1. The contracting parties recognize that dumping, by which products of one country are introduced into the commerce of another country at less than the normal value of the products, is to be condemned if it causes or threatens material injury to an established industry in the territory of a contracting party or materially retards the establishment of a domestic industry ...

2. In order to offset or prevent dumping, a contracting party may levy on any dumped product an anti-dumping duty not greater in amount than the margin of dumping in respect of such product. For the purposes of this Article, the margin of dumping is the price difference determined in accordance with the provisions of paragraph 1.

Article XVI: Subsidies

2. The contracting parties recognize that the granting by a contracting party of a subsidy on the export of any product may have harmful effects for other contracting parties, both importing and exporting, may cause undue disturbance to their normal commercial interests, and may hinder the achievement of the objectives of this Agreement.

3. Accordingly, contracting parties should seek to avoid the use of subsidies on the export of primary products. If, however, a contracting party grants directly or indirectly any form of subsidy which operates to increase the export of any primary product from its territory, such subsidy shall not be applied in a manner which results in that contracting party having more than an equitable share of world export trade in that product, account being taken of the shares of the contracting parties in such trade in the product during a previous representative period, and any special factors which may have affected or may be affecting such trade in the product.

Article XIX: Emergency action on imports of particular products

1. (a) If, as a result of unforeseen developments and of the effect of the obligations incurred by a contracting party under this Agreement, including tariff concessions, any product is being imported into the territory of that contracting party in such increased quantities and under such conditions as to cause or threaten serious injury to domestic producers in that territory of like or directly competitive products, the contracting party shall be free, in respect of such product, and to the extent and for such time as may be necessary to prevent or remedy such injury, to suspend the obligation in whole or in part or to withdraw or modify the concession.

Article XX: General exceptions

Subject to the requirement that such measures are not applied in a manner which would constitute a means of arbitrary or unjustifiable discrimination between countries where the same conditions prevail, or a disguised restriction on international trade, nothing in this Agreement shall be construed to prevent the adoption or enforcement by any contracting party of measures:

(a) necessary to protect public morals;

(b) necessary to protect human, animal or plant life or health;

(c) relating to the importations or exportations of gold or silver;

(d) necessary to secure compliance with laws or regulations which are not inconsistent with the provisions of this Agreement, including those relating to customs enforcement, the enforcement of monopolies operated under paragraph 4 of Article II and Article XVII, the protection of patents, trade marks and copyrights, and the prevention of deceptive practices;

(e) relating to the products of prison labour;

(f) imposed for the protection of national treasures of artistic, historic or archaeological value;

(g) relating to the conservation of exhaustible natural resources if such measures are made effective in conjunction with restrictions on domestic production or consumption.

6　The International Monetary Fund and the World Bank

The two international financial institutions created after World War II provide a similar service to countries but in very different contexts and for different purposes. Both pool the resources of their members and use that capital to fund lending to members in need. The IMF can only lend to countries with immediate balance-of-payments problems. It makes short-term loans of foreign currencies that the borrowing country must use to finance the stabilization of its own currency or monetary system. As a precondition to the loan, the Fund generally requires that the borrower change its policies in ways that enable future monetary stability. The World Bank makes longer-term loans to pay for specific projects related to development or poverty reduction. Most Bank loans are tied to a particular project undertaken by the borrowing government.

The World Bank and the International Monetary Fund are twinned institutions with a common origin and many shared structural features. Their practices and their purposes are, however, very different, and the contrast that they display helps to show how very different outcomes can arise out of similar legal structures. The two organizations originate in the explosion of institution-making at the end of World War II, where the Bretton Woods conference of 1944 was used as a forum for negotiating among the capitalist powers of the day a new institutional architecture for international economics. They were both founded by inter-state treaties, known as the Articles of Agreement of each respective institution, agreed on at Bretton Woods.

The International Monetary Fund (IMF) was intended to be a central coordinating mechanism for exchange rates among countries. It was normal at that time for currency values to be fixed relative to each other and to the price of gold, and managed by national governments. The Fund was given authority over exchange-rate changes. Much like the Security Council centralized the decision to go to war and took away from governments a measure of independence, the IMF became the central authority on currency values. Governments had to request permission to change their currency value, and the Fund would assess whether the underlying economic conditions merited the change. To avoid frequent or dramatic changes, it was also given control over the pool of foreign currency that countries could borrow to stabilize extreme balance-of-payments deficits. The first half of this authority (over exchange-rate changes) became obsolete in the 1970s when the main countries in the international economy shifted to market-driven exchange rates instead of giving their currencies a fixed value relative to that of an ounce of gold, but as we shall see below the Fund continues to collect and loan out the foreign-exchange resources contributed by its members.

The World Bank was also intended to pool and lend its members' money but it was created with an explicit mandate to finance development and reconstruction. In 1944, this was taken to mean the redevelopment of Europe and Asia after World War II, but by the 1960s it had been reinterpreted with reference to development as a strategy against poverty in poor countries around the world. It uses the money contributed to it by its members as collateral with which to borrow many times more money on international markets which it then packages as loans to governments to support specific development projects.

This chapter examines the Articles of Agreement for each in order to show the legal framework within which they operate and to see the formal obligations demanded of their members. But perhaps more than any other organizations in this book, the Bank and the Fund have a practical, political life in the international system which cannot be understood by looking at their legal charters. In considering how and why states comply with either institution, and how the institutions strive to enforce their decisions on states, the chapter therefore turns away from the Articles of Agreement and joins with discussions from international politics and international economics. It ends with a case study of Argentina, which has been a steady borrower from both institutions and whose recent relationship with the IMF in particular helps to understand the powers, limits, and politics of these international organizations.

Member states have relationships with the Fund and the Bank at two very different levels. There are first of all the general commitments that states make as signatories of the treaties and as members of the organizations. These include the standard obligations of international organizations, such as to contribute resources to the common pool and to support the organization, as well as the standard rights such as participation in the plenary bodies. They also include, for the Fund, commitments regarding how the country will manage its exchange rate. A second level of commitment arises when a member borrows from either the Fund or the Bank. The substance of these lending-specific commitments is framed in a general way by the legal terms of the organizations but their real content is the result of negotiations between the borrowing state and the international organization – the obligations that they entail are therefore highly particular. The general obligations of membership are relatively slight compared to very detailed political and legal relationships that can develop through specific loans.

Over non-borrowing members, the IMF and the Bank have almost no authority at all. To non-borrowers, the organizations may appear similar to the International Labor Organization: a member must pay its dues as required by the treaty, and allow certain kinds of surveillance of its domestic conditions (this is much more intrusive in the IMF than in the World Bank or the ILO), but beyond that the organizations have very little opportunity to become involved in the policy choices of their members. This chapter has therefore separated the relatively thin obligations that members owe to the organizations themselves from the very involved relationships that arise in the context of the specific loan agreements between states and the Fund or the Bank.

key facts

International Monetary Fund

Headquarters: Washington, DC

Members: 189 countries

Website: www.imf.org

Mandate: to ensure the stability of the international monetary system by offering technical assistance and loans to avoid crises in balance of payments.

Key structure: a pool of $325 billion available for members to borrow.

Key obligations: to accept periodic surveillance of the domestic monetary position and to abide by any conditions attached to a borrowing arrangement.

Enforcement: loans are disbursed in stages, and future stages (as well as future loans) are in theory dependent on compliance with past conditions.

key facts

Key clauses:

Article I describes the goals of the organization

Article IV describes exchange-rate obligations, including to

- collaborate with the Fund and other members to ensure orderly exchange arrangements (Art. IV(1)).
- avoid manipulating exchange rates (Art. IV(1)iii).
- accept Fund "surveillance over the exchange rate policies of members" (Art. IV(3)b).

Article V on the mechanics of borrowing

Article VIII on general obligations of members

The International Monetary Fund came into being in 1945, after its Articles of Agreement had been ratified by 29 states. It is governed by a Board of Governors made up of the finance ministers or central bankers of all 189 member states. This very senior group delegates most of its power to the 24-member group known as the Directors of the Executive Board, which includes permanent seats for eight large "quota" holders in the Fund (i.e. its biggest contributors) along with 16 other members who speak (and vote) on behalf of groups of states. All IMF members are thus represented among the Executive Directors, in some form, though for most states this is very indirect. It is the Directors who decide on loan requests and other operational decisions of the Fund while the Board of Governors decides on the highest-level policy questions. As with the World Bank below, formal voting in the Fund takes place under a weighted system that apportions votes according to countries' size and economic influence in the international system. The top five IMF members (the US, Japan, Germany, France, and the UK) have approximately 17, 6.12, 6, 5, and 4.9 percent of the total votes respectively. Decisions generally require 85 percent majorities, though in practice the Fund tries to operate by consensus and so formal votes are less important than behind-the-scenes machinations.[1] The practice of consensus decision-making may, depending on one's view, make the Fund more democratic by neutralizing the unequal distribution of votes or less democratic by reintroducing a political system in place of a voting system. Such divergent

---

[1] James Raymond Vreeland, *The International Monetary Fund: Politics of Conditional Lending.* Routledge, 2007, ch. 1.

interpretations play a large part in debates about the governance of the Fund, and of the World Bank as well.

The Fund is striking among international organizations for having survived, and even thrived, despite radical changes in its operating environment. The original IMF treaty largely forbade countries from allowing their exchange rates to float, and forbade the IMF from having any authority over mobile capital, but since the 1970s most major economies have abandoned the fixed exchange rates that were required by the Bretton Woods system and adopted floating rates. These were violations of the IMF Articles of Agreement at the time, but in order to accommodate the change the Fund reinvented itself and its rules at a series of meetings through the 1970s. Rather than try to force its members back into compliance with the Articles of Agreement, it amended the Articles so that what the countries were doing was now permitted, indeed required, and what had formerly been allowed, indeed required, was now outlawed. More recently, as the flows of international capital grew exponentially through the 1990s and 2000s as a result of government deregulation of the movement of capital, the dynamics of international finance have again come to challenge the Fund. Its capital reserves have been outpaced by the incredible growth in mobile capital, and the Fund has had to figure out how to remain relevant in its new environment. Today's international financial regime is premised on free trade in capital, floating exchange rates, and massive private capital flows – the kinds of crises that are possible in the system today are very different than those of the 1940s, and the IMF's contribution to international stability must come, if it is to come at all, in this new setting. However, rather than disband, the IMF has repeatedly redefined its authority and its members' obligations in the effort to fulfill its purpose as a lender of last resort for governments.

Despite the change in its environment, the IMF's overarching and central purpose remains as it was at its founding at the Bretton Woods meetings in 1944: to contribute to the broader public good of international financial stability. At the time of its inception, this meant monitoring fixed exchange rates and providing emergency funding of foreign reserves to help maintain those fixed rates. In today's world, this means helping countries maintain relatively stable exchange rates in a world of floating rates and unregulated flows of private capital. Its key function now is providing emergency lending when capital is fleeing the country so quickly and in such large quantities that it threatens financial and social stability. The following sections examine the macroeconomic features of balance-of-payments problems and look at the IMF's role in the collective response to financial crises.

Obligations

The IMF Articles of Agreement must surely rank among the least interesting international treaties to read. It is long and highly technical, heavy with jargon from the fields of international law and international finance, and yet somehow manages to give relatively little insight into what the organization actually does. It describes an institution whose goal is to facilitate stability in the exchange rates of the world's currencies and to manage the interdependencies that arise as a consequence of national monetary policies in a global context. The general obligations of members include: to "collaborate with the Fund and other members to assure orderly exchange arrangements and to promote a stable system of exchange rates" (Art. IV(1)), and to "avoid manipulating exchange rates or the international monetary system ... to gain an unfair advantage over other members" (Art. IV(1)iv). Because the international financial system (both for states and for private actors) changes so much over time, the content of these obligations depends on the prevailing systems of national exchange rate policies at any given time, and so the general commitment of members to "stable exchange rates" (for instance) is not particularly illuminating of the organization's practical impact.

A more specific set of obligations is described in Article IV of the Articles of Agreement, under the heading of the Fund's "surveillance" function. While this function gets less attention than does Fund lending, surveillance makes up the bulk of the Fund's regular workload because it mandates an annual review of all members. Surveillance is an ongoing project, and exists independently of the IMF's involvement in countries facing a crisis. The object of surveillance is to identify potential macroeconomic tension in countries before it becomes so unstable that it precipitates a national or systemic crisis. The surveillance function reflects the core reasoning behind the existence of the Fund, which is that since a monetary crisis in one member state could potentially undermine others or even the entire system, each member has a duty to the collective regarding its circumstances and policies. The Fund is the institutional expression of that duty and its surveillance is designed to alert the collective as well as the country itself of impending crises. Article IV(3) says "The Fund shall oversee the international monetary system in order to ensure its effective operation" and "the Fund shall exercise firm surveillance over the exchange rate policies of members ... Each member shall provide the Fund with the information necessary for such surveillance." This is a formal grant of authority to the Fund by its members and as such its precise language becomes important when there are disagreements between states and the Fund, which is frequent ... Most importantly, surveillance is limited by Article IV(3) to "exchange rate policies" and "the information necessary for such surveillance." States frequently chafe over requests for information that they feel go beyond what is related to exchange mechanisms, and the Fund frequently argues that a country's monetary stability is a function of a broader set of policies which might include non-monetary issues such as trade barriers, fiscal subsidies, and market regulations. As we will see below, after 2006 Argentina for a time refused to allow Article IV surveillance in reaction to what it felt had been the Fund's overly invasive behaviors.[2] This reflects the deeper fact that it is impossible to neatly separate a country's monetary policy from the broader economic and policy environment in which it is set; the boundaries of monetary policy are neither self-evident nor fixed.

Along with these obligations, members of the IMF also get an important right: they are allowed to request loans from the IMF's pool of cash reserves. This lending inserts the Fund directly into an active role in managing economic crises in its members and gives it a highly politicized and controversial character. The most important choices that IMF members make arise with respect to negotiating and then complying with the terms of these loans, and so I treat the IMF's system of loan conditionality next under the heading of "compliance."

Compliance

To speak of "compliance" with the Fund is largely to speak of compliance with the terms of the loans that the Fund makes to members that request them.[3]

---

[2] *Wall Street Journal*, "IMF: Argentina Refusal to Allow IMF Surveillance 'Odd'." October, 4, 2009, http://online.wsj.com/article/BT-CO-20091004–701798.html. Accessed November 13, 2009.

[3] Though compliance questions have also been addressed to Article IV surveillance and Article VIII current-account restrictions. See for instance Beth A. Simmons, "The Legalization of International Monetary Affairs," *International Organization*, 2000, 54: 573–602, and Stephen C. Nelson, "Does Compliance Matter? Assessing the Relationship between Sovereign Risk and Compliance with International Law," *Review of International Organizations*, 2010, 5(2): 107–139.

Each time the Fund lends money to a member, the two parties engage in negotiations that define the terms of the loan and then come to what the IMF calls an "arrangement" that allows the use of its funds. The legal basis of this practice is in Article I of the Articles of Agreement, which says in part that the Fund should work "by making the general resources of the Fund temporarily available to [members] under adequate safeguards." By "general resources" this means the aggregated subscriptions of all members, though in recent times the Fund has also acted as a facilitator for organizing even larger loans directly from the richest governments to IMF borrowers. By "adequate safeguards" it means there should be an agreement with the government over how it will change its policies to ensure that the conditions that caused the crisis are improved so that the loan is paid back and the system protected. Every loan agreement includes the amount of the loan, its expected repayment date or dates, and a set of criteria by which to judge the country's performance in improving its balance-of-payments position. Loans are usually disbursed in installments, and the later payments are in theory conditional on good performance according to these criteria. (In practice, as we shall see below, the Fund has a habit of continuing to disburse loans even without good performance.)

The lending of the Fund is limited under the Articles of Agreement to situations where it is necessary to remedy a balance-of-payments problem for the member. This is described in Article V(3)b(ii) as the requirement that "the member represents that it has a need to make the purchase [i.e. to borrow from the Fund] because of its balance of payments or its reserve position or developments in its reserves." The paradigmatic case in which this arises is the situation of a country that is continually paying more to foreigners (for imports, foreign remittances, and other elements of the "current account") than foreigners are sending to it. This is unsustainable over the long run since outflows indicate that the local currency is being exchanged for foreign currencies in order to complete the transactions. If the exchange rates are floating, these sales into the open market will depress the value of the currency; if the exchange rates are fixed, the local government must be working to absorb the excess supply of its currency.

At some point, the local government will be either unable to continue absorbing that supply or will be unhappy with the continuing decline in the value of its currency. Where foreign investors lose confidence in the stability of a local currency, this process can unfold in a matter of days, with hundreds of millions of dollars leaving the country, forcing a crisis in public policy. This was the situation that precipitated the Asian financial crisis in 1997 as first the Thai baht collapsed, followed by the Indonesian rupiah and the South Korean won, and beyond. The IMF's lending program is intended to greatly increase a government's access to foreign currency, which the government then uses to buy the local currency being sold by fleeing investors. This is essentially what the IMF did in response to the Asian financial crisis. As a rule, therefore, loans are made in response to an unsustainable situation in the government's balance of payments or foreign exchange positions. They are not made to cover general spending or to assist with development. A budget deficit or other crisis in the government is not sufficient justification to borrow from the IMF.

The Fund expects its loan to be repaid, and to earn a profit from it. It therefore insists that the government make policy changes that will remedy the underlying economic problems that led to the crisis. This is the essence of "conditionality" in Fund lending, and the source of high controversy. The conditions are restricted to those that are relevant to solving the underlying problem. Article V(3)a says "The Fund shall adopt policies on the use of its general resources ... that will assist members to solve their balance-of-payments problems in a manner consistent with this Agreement and that will establish adequate safeguards for the temporary use of the general resources of the Fund." This is not very revealing. In practice, the conditions attached to IMF loans are often of the kind illustrated by the agreement with Argentina in 2003, which is reproduced below as Appendix 6.A. These include changes in the country's tax policies to reduce "distortions," a target for a budget surplus, changes in monetary policy and banking regulations, the restructuring of its sovereign debt, changes in its policies on utility companies so that prices could be raised to reflect market conditions, and so on.

The Fund is frequently accused of imposing conditions that are unrelated to its mandate regarding stability in monetary relations and more generally of using its loans as leverage to force countries to adopt a neoliberal model of government–market relations. The Fund's critics make two important points: first, that it is not clear that the set of policies which the Fund proposes actually improves the economic condition of the country and its people, and second, that the burdens imposed by the policies are borne disproportionately by the most vulnerable classes in society while the benefits accrue to the rich and powerful.

By understanding the rules that govern Fund loans, it is easier to see both sides of these controversies. The Fund does indeed expect its borrowing countries to adhere to a particular set of policies, and these are indeed modeled on a theory of economics that privileges private markets in relation to a very limited government. It argues that in an internationally, interdependent economy many government policies might have some impact on its balance of payments and so be within the purview of IMF conditionality.

It is a separate question whether the Fund's recommendations do indeed help the situation. Joseph Stiglitz, once the chief economist at the World Bank, has come to the view that they do not. He says that "the billions of dollars which it [the Fund] provides are used to maintain exchange rates at unsustainable levels for a short period, during which the foreigners and rich are able to get their money out of the country at more favorable rates."[4]

If the policies favored by the Fund are in fact counterproductive to the welfare of the citizens, then there would be good reason to suspect that the "market rationality" that governs much of the IMF's conditionality is an ideological agenda rather than a body of proven, technocratic expertise. This concern should be assessed with case-by-case research on the content of specific loan agreements and their actual effects, measured against a realistic counterfactual scenario, that is: what would have happened had the IMF loan not happened.

Enforcement

The capacity for the direct enforcement of the Fund's rules is extremely limited. The Fund is given no authority to order states to change their policies and it has no legal power to punish those who fail in their commitments.

The only formal measures in the Article of Agreement regarding non-compliance and enforcement arise in Article XXVI, which says that "if a member fails to fulfill any of its obligations under this Agreement, the Fund may declare the member ineligible to use the general resources of the Fund." It goes on to say "if, after the expiration of a reasonable period following a declaration of ineligibility ... the member persists in its failure to fulfill any of its obligations under this Agreement, the Fund may ... suspend the voting power of the member" and eventually "that member may be required to

---

[4] Joseph E. Stiglitz, *Globalization and its Discontents*. Norton, 2002, p. 209.

withdraw from membership in the Fund." This procedure has never been carried out, and the enforcement of obligations to the Fund in practice takes place largely outside the terms of Article XXVI.

For non-compliance with the conditions of a single loan, the Fund uses the threat of withholding future disbursements of the loan. For non-compliance in repayment, as with Argentina's threat to default on its IMF loans discussed below, the Fund relies on a combination of institutional and informal pressures, put together out of the assorted currencies of power in the international political economy: political influence, the threat to reputation and credit rating, and above all the suggestion that access to future loans is contingent on correct behavior with respect to present loans. These devices are only loosely indicated in the Articles of Agreement but they can be very hard to resist for many governments.

However, political power does not rest only with the IMF in these relationships, and borrowers find "agency" relative to the Fund in interesting ways. As we will see below with respect to Argentina, borrowers are often able to use the threat of default as an instrument of leverage with which to force the IMF to renegotiate the terms of an existing loan. By one set of measures, only about a half of IMF loans qualify as compliant in their own terms – the other half have some serious deficiency, either in repayment or in meeting the agreed performance criteria.[5] For non-compliant loans, the IMF very frequently grants a "waiver" from the performance criteria (essentially, an admission that the country cannot meet the requirement and so will be exempted from it), and in many others non-compliance is tolerated in informal ways or overlooked on the grounds that the positive effects of the loan outweigh the problems of non-performance. When borrowers force the Fund to renegotiate a loan, or to accept significant deviation from the agreed performance criteria, they display a measure of effective political power that is not often discussed by those who are interested in the inequalities of power between the Fund and its "clients." The Fund's informal enforcement devices do clearly reach a limit with respect to some borrowers who have the capacity to turn the tables on the Fund. However, it is certainly true that the poorest and most needy borrowers are the least likely to have this capacity.

---

[5] James Vreeland surveys a range of measures of "compliance" to arrive at an estimate of between 40 to 60 percent compliance. James Raymond Vreeland, *The International Monetary Fund: Politics of Conditionality.* Routledge, 2007.

World Bank

Headquarters: Washington, DC

Members: 189 countries (in the International Bank for Reconstruction and Development)

Website: www.worldbank.org

Mandate: to reduce poverty by lending the money of the rich countries to the poor countries for specific development projects, and by providing technical assistance to poor countries.

Key structures:
- assets of $275 billion based on contributions of members.
- $59 billion in loans and credits in the 2009 financial year by the institutions of the World Bank group.
- the Bank issues bonds backed by its capital in order to raise money for lending.

Key obligations: all members contribute to the common pool of resources. Those who borrow agree to the terms of the loan, which may include policy changes.

Enforcement: borrowings become part of the sovereign debt of the borrower and must be repaid according to the rules of sovereign debt payments.

Key clauses of the IBRD Articles of Agreement:
- Article II(3)a: Each member shall subscribe shares of the capital stock of the Bank.
- Article III(1)a: Resources and facilities of the Bank shall be used exclusively for the benefit of members with equitable consideration for projects of development and projects for reconstruction alike.
- Article III(2): Each member shall deal with the Bank only through its Treasury, central bank, stabilization fund or similar fiscal agency.
- Article III(4)i: When the member in whose territories the project is located is not itself the borrower, the member or the central bank or some comparable agency of the member which is acceptable to the Bank, fully guarantees the repayment of the principal and the payment of interest and other charges on the loan.
- Article V(3): Each member shall have two hundred and fifty votes plus one additional vote for each share of stock held.

The World Bank operates on very similar principles to the IMF: it is an inter-state organization that pools its members' resources and considers requests for loans. The organizational structure of the Bank is also similar to that of the Fund, with a Board of Governors, an Executive Board, and a President. The members contribute a "subscription" of funds to the Bank, and as with the Fund the amount is both relative to the size of its economy and the determinant of the country's quota of votes in the organization. The compliance and enforcement logics of the Bank are also akin to those of the Fund, where the primary incentive for compliance comes from the country's interest in maintaining a good credit rating with the Bank and with private financial institutions.

The Bank and Fund differ because they were established with very different purposes at Bretton Woods in 1944: the Bank's mandate is to finance development projects, while the Fund is concerned with the stability of exchange rates. Despite the structural similarities, therefore, the two engage in distinct practices and generate distinct controversies.

The World Bank Group, as it is formally known, makes several financial instruments available to the states that join as members. These instruments are largely variations on the theme of opportunities for the member government to borrow money from the institutions of the World Bank Group. These are managed by separate entities within the Group, and under distinct legal arrangements. The core institution in the Group is the International Bank for Reconstruction and Development (IBRD, also known generically as the World Bank), and this is the main focus of the remainder of this chapter. The other bodies were added over the years to expand the ways that the Bank can become involved in national development strategies. For instance, the International Finance Corporation (IFC) was created in 1956 to organize financing for private (rather than government-led) development programs, a type of loan that is expressly forbidden to the IBRD. The International Development Agency (IDA), created in 1960, raises its own money from rich members and lends it at highly favorable rates to the poorest and most indebted countries.

The World Bank Group is directed by the Boards of Governors, who are typically the finance or development ministers of the member states. Each member has a representative on the Board of Governors and it meets in a large regular session once per year. In between these formal meetings, the operative decisions on loans and other financing, as well as interpreting the Articles of Agreement and setting Bank policies, are made by a body known as the Executive Directors. This is a body of twenty-five members. The five largest shareholders in the bank each have an automatic seat. These are the United States, Germany, Japan, the United Kingdom, and France. The remaining seats are allocated among quasi-regional groupings of member states such that every member is represented by an Executive Director, though likely not one of their own citizens. The Executive Directors (known collectively as the Board of Executive Directors, or the Board) strive to operate by consensus, but when formal votes are taken they are weighted by countries' subscriptions to the organization. In the IBRD, for instance, the Executive Director from Canada has approximately 62,217 votes, which include the 45,045 votes assigned to Canada by virtue of its own shares in the Bank plus 17,172 votes from the twelve other countries on whose behalf it votes as the chair of its "representation" group. The United States has approximately 265,219 votes, or about 16 percent of the total, and is the largest. The smallest member is Palau, with 0.03 percent of the total votes.

Obligations

The Bank draws its legal mandate from its Articles of Agreement. This section of the chapter examines members' obligations under that treaty, and the following section looks at compliance with the terms of its lending to member countries.

The Articles of Agreement define the Bank as a kind of corporate partnership, owned through a system of shares held by the members in proportion to their investments in the joint enterprise. These investments include the original subscription made upon joining the organization as well as periodic increases in its capitalization. Members are obligated to purchase shares upon joining the organization and this stock of investment funds the Bank's lending, akin to the contributed capital of a firm. There are about 1.5 million shares in existence, of which the US owns the most (about 265,000 shares, producing its bloc of votes) followed by Japan, Germany, France, and the UK. The shares are not tradable on any market, and the Articles of Agreement forbid countries from selling their shares to anyone other than the Bank itself or from using them as collateral for any sovereign borrowing. Shares in the Bank are therefore not useful as an asset in any of the ways that shares of a private firm are valuable. They are only relevant for the country's position within the Bank itself.

Twenty percent of the value of a country's shares must be paid up front in gold or in US dollars upon joining – this is the initial subscription. The rest must be made available to the Bank in various currencies upon request by the Bank. Since it deals across currencies, fluctuations in the relative values of these currencies produce interesting effects in the life of the Bank. Most of its assets are held in US dollars or in dollar-denominated securities, and so declines in the US dollar manifest themselves as automatic reductions in the wealth of the Bank and perhaps in its ability to lend. Declines in other currencies may mean that the subscriptions of those countries are worth much less to the Bank than previously, though perhaps with a consequent rise in the relative value of its dollar holdings. Article 2(9) of the Articles of Agreement describes the possibility of a mandatory infusion of cash by a country whose currency has declined greatly, somewhat like a margin call for an investor.

This money provides the capitalization of the Bank and the Bank uses it as collateral for its own borrowing from international financial markets. The funds that the Bank lends to its members are sourced in these markets. It does not lend out of the subscriptions of capital that its members contribute (this is different than the IMF which does lend its own money). The strength of the Bank comes from its ownership structure: the richest and most powerful states are the main shareholders, and it is ultimately their wealth behind the Bank that makes the Bank's international borrowing a good risk for investors.

The mechanics behind the Bank's lending show that the Bank takes advantage of the workings of the international credit rating system. The Bank has advantages in borrowing due to its size, stability, and consequent credit worthiness, which it uses when approaching large international investors (both private funds and sovereign states). The Bank has a long history of on-time repayment of its bonds, and has both a stock of capital and the implicit backing of the richest states. It is seen by international markets as a highly reliable borrower. As a result the Bank can borrow more cheaply than almost any country, and in 2004 it raised $13 billion in this way on about $1.5 billion of capitalization. Because its costs for borrowing are much lower than those faced by its own member states, it can lend to its members at much lower rates of interest than they would pay if they raised the money themselves. The Bank adds fees to each loan on top of its own costs of borrowing, and so the Bank makes a profit on its regular operations – but even with this premium over the market rate, its lending terms are far more favorable than most of its members could generate themselves on the international market.

Compliance

The core of the Bank's lending happens through the IBRD, and its operations are limited by the Articles of Agreement to loans "for the purpose of specific projects of reconstruction or development" (Article 3(4)vii). This is crucial to understanding the Bank's role in international development, and its distinction from the International Monetary Fund. The Bank is engaged in *project-specific lending*, and those projects must fit under the heading of "reconstruction or development."

Projects are initiated when a state approaches the Bank with a proposal regarding a development project for which it seeks funding. From there a negotiation takes place between the government and Bank officials over the nature of the project, the terms of the loan, and other details. Other parts of the World Bank Group may lend to private actors, but the IBRD lends only to states and to borrowers for whom a state is willing to provide guaranteed backing. IBRD loans generally have long maturities, often thirty years, and the Bank usually insists that the borrower find other funding partners to supplement the Bank's contribution so that the risk is diversified. Appendix 6.B shows one agreement between Argentina and the Bank that led to a $70 million loan in 2005 to fund flood-management construction in Buenos Aires.

The Bank's political controversies arise both over the way it grants its loans and over the terms of the loans. The Bank has operated under a number of overarching concepts since 1947 and these define distinct periods in its history. These are usually the result of the president's worldview regarding how best to work toward the organization's goals. The period under Robert McNamara, from the late 1960s through the 1980s, is generally thought of as characterized by attention to meeting the basic needs of poor people, and contrasts with the previous period where the Bank favored very large construction projects with a more openly anti-communist agenda. In the 1980s, this shifted to a concern with funding the "structural adjustment" of borrowing countries' economies to integrate with the international market and an emphasis on the private sector. The current period is defined by the Millennium Development Goals set at the 2000 UN Summit, including sustainability, basic health care, and partnership with other international organizations. Each of these approaches rests on an ideological model which is subject to controversy, and the World Bank has frequently been criticized for adopting a narrowly market-oriented attitude toward its work and for being easily swayed by demands from Washington.

However, the Bank should properly be judged by the content of its specific loans, and so a more informed assessment of its work must rest on a close reading of specific loans, their terms, and their consequences. This requires certain expertise, and so such an assessment is less common than are examples of highly generalized and poorly founded defense or critique of the Bank. To make a serious assessment of the impact of the Bank in any particular case requires a detailed knowledge of the terms of the specific loan in question, a knowledge of the broader project to which it is attached, and a strong background in the local political and economic conditions. It may also require some technical knowledge of civil engineering, biology, sociology, or other field in order to understand the implications of the project. The best critiques of the Bank's activities, such as James Ferguson's excellent study of Lesotho, are informed by immersion in the local setting.[6]

Enforcement

Like the IMF, the World Bank relies on states' concerns with their future borrowing as the lever to induce them to repay their loans. It has no capacity, legal or otherwise, to access government accounts to force them to repay their loans. Indeed, the Articles of Agreement do not give the Bank any enforcement powers at all, save for the threat to cut off future lending. This may sometimes be an extremely influential threat, especially to the extent that other lenders may look to the Bank for signals about the credit-worthiness of a borrowing country. The structural power of the lender is an important instrument of influence, as we saw with the IMF.

The Bank's technique of enforcing its rules by limiting future lending may, however, sometimes amount to an idle threat, and there are many ways that the power relationship between borrower and lender might become inverted. For instance, a half-funded project may be difficult to cancel, even if the borrower shows signs of reneging on its promises – half a bridge contributes little to local welfare, and the Bank may be inclined to press on to a finished project even if the borrowing country has made unilateral changes that displease the Bank. In

---

[6] James Ferguson, *The Anti-Politics Machine: "Development," Depoliticization, and Bureaucratic Power in Lesotho.* University of Minnesota Press, 1994.

other cases, the borrower may have a powerful patron at the Bank such that it is unlikely that future loans really are dependent on past performance. The US government has often used its influence over the Bank to ensure a flow of loans to governments that it favors. In this vein, there are often disagreements between the Board of Directors and the Bank's staff over the wisdom of a loan, and the Board may push for a loan that serves the broader foreign policy interests of powerful states despite concerns from the staff that it does not satisfy the Bank's technical criteria.

Enforcement is not therefore straightforward. This reflects the reality that the Bank is engaged in highly consequential social and political engineering that is inherently controversial, with both winners and losers and with the geopolitical interests of powerful states at stake. By supporting some projects rather than others, and by responding to requests from local governments, the Bank is directly involved in decisions about what should be done in society. It is unavoidably political and controversial whether it is supporting mega-projects or micro-politics or anything else, as Daniel Immerwahr has pointed out.[7]

The dynamics of enforcement become even more interesting when one considers the implications of corruption. This is an important concern of the Bank, and one to which the Bank is increasingly attuned. The Bank has recently placed itself at the heart of the international anti-corruption regime, and has said that "corruption is the greatest obstacle to reducing poverty."[8] Among international organizations, the Bank is a leader in assessing the effects of corruption on governance and it devotes a good deal of attention to designing mechanisms both in its loans and more generally to minimize opportunities for losses due to corruption.

Based on his experience in Indonesia, Jeffrey Winters has estimated that perhaps one-third of the $30 billion borrowed by the Suharto regime from 1967 to 1998 was diverted for the personal enrichment of members of the regime. This appears to be about the "normal" rate of corruption of World Bank loans, meaning that over $100 billion of the Bank's approximately $400 billion in loans since 1946 has been stolen.[9] Even this margin likely understates the impact of corruption on World Bank programs since it refers to the amount

---

[7] "Thinking Small Won't End Poverty," *The Jacobin*, 2015, www.jacobinmag.com/2015/11/capitalism-small-is-beautiful-world-bank-imf-free-trade.

[8] http://go.worldbank.org/QYRWVXVH40. Accessed March 1, 2010.

[9] Jeffrey A. Winters, "Criminal Debt," in Jonathan R. Pincus and Jeffrey A. Winters (eds.), *Reinventing the World Bank*, Cornell University Press, 2002, pp. 128–184. IBRD, "How IBRD is Financed," http://go.worldbank.org/LAG4BZ1VD1. Accessed March 1, 2010.

taken "off the top," as it were, as the money enters the governments' hands, and does not include corruption further down the line, as when subcontractors deliver below-quality goods and services. This is an astonishingly large amount of money, and the consequences of such corruption may well spell failure for many projects.

Benjamin Olken, an economist at MIT, found an innovative way to measure the scale of corruption in some development projects. He visited a set of roads that had been built in Indonesia with development funding from the World Bank and others and had engineers take core samples of the finished roads. By comparing these samples with the original contracts, he could gauge whether the materials that had been contracted for actually ended up being used in the roads.[10] Olken found an average rate of skimping of about 24 percent by value – that is, one-quarter of the budget allocated to materials was stolen. He also found this rate was significantly reduced for roads where the construction company was led to believe it would be audited after the fact.

Jeffrey Winters makes a further point in the case of Indonesia: he argues that much of this corruption was easily predictable in advance to the World Bank and the Bank chose to ignore it. By his estimate, about $10 billion of missing money lost in Indonesian loans was stolen with the full knowledge of the Bank, largely because the Bank was directed by the US to continue lending to the Suharto government despite these losses. This reflects in part the way the Bank has been used (during the Cold War as well as after) as an instrument to sustain governments which Washington favored, but it raises an important legal question: should the people of Indonesia be legally liable for funds lent by the Bank and stolen by its leaders? The sovereign debts of the country are the responsibility of the country as a corporate actor and persist regardless of changes of government. They are taken on by leaders but must be repaid by the country and its population, according to the agreement between the Bank and the country.

Corruption by the government amounts to a violation of the terms of that agreement, and Winters calls this "criminal debt." Who should be responsible for the missing money? The primary responsibility is obviously held by the individuals who stole the money, but assuming they have escaped with the payoff, the question arises as to whether the country can be said to have legally borrowed that money from the Bank in the first place. Winters suggests that there are good reasons to treat such corruption as losses of the Bank rather than of the

[10] Benjamin A. Olken, "Monitoring Corruption: Evidence from a Field Experiment in Indonesia," *Journal of Political Economy*, 2007, 115(2): 200–249.

borrowing country. Changing the location of responsibility in this way would have several useful effects: first, it relieves the population from the burden of repaying money the benefit of which they never received in the first place, and so would significantly reduce the debt burden of countries already suffering under corrupt leaders; second, it would situate moral accountability more clearly at the intersection between the Bank and the borrowers, where it rightly belongs, rather than at the intersection between the public and their corrupt officials; and third, it would create an incentive for the Bank to be more careful in its lending since it would now be responsible for the share of losses due to corruption – too much corruption could well ruin the Bank. The value of these changes is premised on the assumption that the Bank is not doing everything it can to track the money it lends or to protect against corruption, and this no doubt varies greatly among cases.

CASE: Argentina

Argentina has borrowed significantly from both the IMF and the World Bank and provides a good example of those relationships in "normal" times as well as their potential for crisis. Its relationship with the Bank has been relatively quiet, at least in comparison with the intensely contentious and fraught relations with the Fund. The Argentina–IMF controversies since the 1990s provide a window into power politics in international political economy, crossing seamlessly between public players and private actors and between international relations and domestic conditions. It is an ideal case study of the lived experience of the contemporary global political economy.

By way of contrast, consider first the World Bank. The Bank has made hundreds of loans to Argentina, with several dozen projects active at a time. These have included local construction projects, as seen in Appendix 6.B, as well as projects situated in the larger region, such as one aimed at controlling the H1-N1 flu pandemic in Argentina and across its borders. The Bank has also contributed to more "conceptual" projects that address the long-term bases for economic growth. One ongoing project, for instance, combines science, education, and trade under the heading of "Unleashing Productive Innovation." It is designed to facilitate an environment in which high-tech start-up companies can develop and involves both investments in hardware, laboratories, and education, and changes in government policies relating to "innovation." Such broad combinations show that the Bank's mandate on development and poverty reduction can often bring it very close to domestic policy decision-making, though of course always with the formal consent of the state. Argentina has never defaulted on a World Bank loan.

By contrast, its relationship with the IMF has been a high-stakes drama for several decades.[11] It involves huge sums of money, high-level brinksmanship, repeated defaults, subsequent reconciliations, the threat of economic and social collapse, and most recently a solution held hostage by some New York hedge funds. The case even makes transnational contract law seem interesting.

Argentina adopted a neoliberal economic model in the 1990s under IMF guidance and with IMF funding. It opened the economy to foreign trade and transnational finance and privatized industries that had previously been government-owned. The revenue from these privatizations was used to fund the government's fiscal deficit and in the mid-1990s Argentina was noted for its low inflation, decent growth, and workable social services. But as it ran out of assets to sell-off, the government found itself in an unsustainable position: it could not meet the payments on the debt that it had accumulated, could not raise taxes any further, could not afford the domestic social services on which people depended. International banks hiked the interest rate on new loans to Argentina, reflecting the risks they saw in the situation. The IMF continued lending to Argentina throughout, waiving formal limits and requirements.[12] A recession in the late 1990s exposed the underlying inconsistency in the economy, and as the unemployment rate approached 20 percent in late 2001, public protest forced a change in government and a change in policy priorities.[13]

The proximate cause of the crisis with the IMF was the tension between Argentina's fixed exchange rate and its enormous foreign debts. This combination defined the Argentine position in the international financial system for many years. In response to years of extreme inflation, by the 1990s the Argentine government kept the currency pegged to the US dollar and, as a sign of credibility, committed to convert to dollars any amount of local currency brought in to a bank. This required that the central bank maintain reserves of dollars equal to the amount of local currency in circulation, and it also meant that as the US dollar increased in value there was an equal and automatic

[11] Stephen C. Nelson, *The Currency of Confidence: How Economic Beliefs Shape the IMF's Relationship with its Borrowers*. Cornell University Press, 2017 gives an account of the years leading up to the events leading up to the 1990s.

[12] ibid.

[13] Carolyn Thomas and Nicolas Cachanosky, "Argentina's post 2001 Economy and the 2014 Default," *The Quarterly Review of Economics and Finance*, 2016, **60**.

increase in the value of the Argentine currency. A rising currency makes a country's exports more expensive and encourages locals to buy imports rather than domestically produced goods, and so causes a net outflow of currency. With its reserves of dollars pinned down to support the pegged currency, Argentina was borrowing repeatedly from the IMF loans to pay its obligations to the foreigners who had previously lent it money.

This increased its debt in a manner that entrenched the vicious cycle, made worse by the apparent disappearance through corruption of much of the new IMF loans. By 2001 it was evident that the country could not simultaneously meet its two main goals of maintaining its fixed currency value and continuing to repay its international debts in dollars. Sensing an impending rupture, many of those who controlled mobile capital (both wealthy locals and foreign investors) traded their Argentine currency for dollars and invested it elsewhere. This created a run on the local banks, wiped out the government's dollar reserves, and caused the government to strictly regulate how much money people could withdraw from their bank accounts. Rioting ensued. After a change in government, the new president halted repayments on the country's foreign debt to private banks in late 2001, then worth close to $100 billion. This new government lasted only a few weeks before resigning. Its replacement made the second half of the change when it abandoned the fixed exchange rate in early 2002.

Rather than default on its IMF debt, the government negotiated new terms for repayment with the Fund. This is a common practice for the Fund in cases of imminent default and Argentina's position was no doubt strengthened by the resolve it had shown in stopping payments to its private creditors. Its willingness to default in the commercial debt markets of the international economy made clear to the Fund that it could not induce compliance by threatening Argentina's credit rating; Argentina's good name among investors had already been destroyed by its private default. The dynamics of power in renegotiations such as these are very interesting, as it is not clear whether the IMF or the debtor is the one in charge. The perceived danger to the international financial system of an Argentine default on its IMF debt meant that the normally strong international actors were in this case quite at the mercy of the borrower, though the local costs of the crisis were immense.[14] By the time the immediate monetary crisis subsided in 2003, the country had gained a stable exchange rate system but at the

---

[14] On the dynamics of the Argentine crisis, from the point of view of the IMF, see the excellent report by the Fund's Independent Evaluation Office "Report on the Evaluation of the Role of the IMF in Argentina 1991–2001," www.imf.org/External/NP/ieo/2004/arg/eng/index.htm. Accessed March 2, 2010.

cost of a massively devalued currency, 25 percent unemployment, and greatly reduced wealth in society. Half the population was living below the poverty line. With the help of the Venezuelan government, Argentina repaid the last of its debts to the IMF early in January 2006. This was seen as an assertion of independence from the Fund and from neoliberal global economic governance.[15]

A new chapter in the drama then opened as Argentina negotiated with its private creditors. In 2005 it offered to pay 30 cents on the dollar to the holders of the debt on which it had defaulted and it ultimately got the assent of 93 percent of those creditors. The remaining bondholders, known as the "holdouts" (led by two hedge funds that had bought some of the debt for pennies on the dollar when it looked unlikely to be repaid at all – the so-called "vulture" funds) refused to accept the "haircut" and instead sued Argentina in New York courts demanding repayment in full. The cases hinged on small-print questions of contract law and the terms of the debt bonds but they raised enormous questions about the liability of sovereign states, the jurisdiction of New York courts, the equal treatment of bond holders, and more. The drama was multiplied when the court sided with the holdouts and insisted that they were due the full value of the bonds. By the rules of *pari passu* in the bonds, all holders needed to be treated equally and so the implication was that now Argentina was on the hook again to pay 100 percent of this debt, this time enforced by a domestic court in the United States. Unwilling to accept this ruling, Argentina simply defaulted again on the debt in 2014, leaving holdins and holdouts without payment. More negotiations followed. A new government eventually agreed to a version of the court's ruling and in 2016 finished the repayment to all parties.

The involvement of these New York hedge funds does not centrally involve the IMF but it helps to show the tight connection between the public and private sides of global finance, and also highlights political consequences to private market contract laws when sovereign parties are involved.

The relationship between Argentina and the credit markets, including the IMF, helps reveal the legal and political ambiguities that lie just below the surface of international political economy. What look like unbreakable commitments between the government and its lenders turn out, in the context of a deep crisis, to be entirely negotiable. What looks like a political relationship of

---

[15] Reuters, "IMF has no Specific Plans for Argentina Review," www.reuters.com/article/idUSN0511538120091105, November 5, 2009. Accessed March 2, 2010.

dependence on the part of the borrower turns out to be reversed when, again in a crisis context, the borrower is willing to use default as an instrument of power against the creditors. The system of rules and structures that the Bretton Woods institutions created for the international political economy can be quickly transformed into an open-ended arena of fluid political negotiation where the rules have very little influence. There are real costs to these transformations, and they are largely borne by people who had no influence over the choices made by either the government or the lenders, but they reveal how precariously the rules-based system rests on top of more powerful forces in political economy.

Conclusion

The World Bank and the IMF are both designed to help avoid the situation in which the economic problems of one country lead to a generalized crisis in the international system. This goal reflects the intellectual origins of the organizations, rooted in a time that was very much concerned with understanding the dynamics of the Great Depression. Both institutions are therefore built on the recognition that extreme poverty and extreme financial instability are potentially dangerous to the stability of the system as a whole, are potentially contagious, and have negative externalities that are easier to remedy early in the development of a crisis rather than later, at a point of all-out crisis. The political function of the two organizations can be seen in terms akin to the domestic welfare state: they are concessions or investments by the rich to avoid instability in the social system as a whole.

The IMF makes loans to countries that are in balance-of-payments crises. It makes short-term loans to governments which are used to finance buying local currency on international markets or in other ways that help to stabilize a falling exchange rate. It also requires that the local government guarantee that it is making policy changes that will ameliorate the political or economic conditions that produced the crisis in the first place. This is seen as crucial in the Fund for ensuring that the loan will be repaid and that it will contribute to a long-term solution.

The World Bank makes long-term loans to support specific development projects. Its core mission is to lend to governments through the International

Bank for Reconstruction and Development, though it also gives loans, grants, and loan guarantees to a wide range of actors through its other institutions. It supports specific projects, and the terms of the loan require that the Bank's money be put toward that project in ways that are negotiated between the country and the Bank in advance.

As lenders, the Bank and the Fund have leverage over their members that is distinctively different than the power of the other international organizations in this book. Countries approach the Fund only when they are in extreme crisis, and as a result the political relationship between the two is usually characterized by a kind of structural imbalance between a desperate government and a wealthy Fund. This is despite the fact that the country is formally sovereign and therefore free to choose whether or not to ask for the loan or to agree to its terms. The Bank generally deals with longer-term development and so does not conduct most of its business in the context of a fast-unfolding crisis, and yet the structural inequality that it manifests (with thousands of staff and "experts" advising poor governments on how things should be done) is similar to that of the Fund. Both also have leverage in the sense that they can control countries' access to future capital through the mechanism of the credit rating, and more generally by signaling either positive or negative information to world markets. This is an important source of power over the borrowing states. However, states also retain some measure of agency relative to the institutions and may find leverage over the Bank or Fund, most dramatically by threatening to default.

Further Reading

The Fund and the Bank are each the subject of excellent volumes in the excellent Routledge series of books on "global institutions." They are Katherine Marshall, *The World Bank: From Reconstruction to Development to Equity* (Routledge, 2008), and James Raymond Vreeland, *The International Monetary Fund: Politics of Conditional Lending* (Routledge, 2007). Mark S. Copelvitch gives a comprehensive account of the Fund's role and politics in *The International Monetary Fund in the Global Economy* (Cambridge, 2010). The international financial architecture is explored in Manuela Moschella, "International Finance," in Jacob Katz Cogan, Ian Hurd, and Ian Johnstone (eds.), *Oxford Handbook of International Organizations* (Oxford University Press, 2016).

The Fund and the Bank also maintain very good websites that provide details of their operations in every country along with supporting documents on their loans, programs, and assistance. See www.worldbank.org and www.imf.com. Both include a wealth of material on their relationships with Argentina. In addition, the World Bank has published a very useful introduction to its operation and structure: *Guide to the World Bank* (World Bank, 2007). For a similar account of the Fund's self-description see *What is the International Monetary Fund?* (IMF, 2006).

It is also important to step outside the perspectives of the organizations themselves. Among the excellent works on how the two interact with their borrowers and with the wider world are Ngaire Woods, *The Globalizers: The IMF, World Bank, and Their Borrowers* (Cornell University Press, 2014), Valerie Sperling, *Altered States: The Globalization of Accountability* (Cambridge University Press, 2009), Grigore Pop-Eleches, *From Economic Crisis to Reform: IMF Programs in Latin America and Eastern Europe* (Princeton University Press, 2009), and Catherine Weaver, *The Hypocrisy Trap: The World Bank and the Reform of Poverty* (Princeton University Press, 2008).

The IMF–Argentina case is expertly set out by Stephen C. Nelson in *Currency of Confidence: How Economic Beliefs Shape the IMF's Relationship with its Borrowers* (Cornell University Press, 2017). The 'holdouts' issue in the 2010s is at the center of Carolyn Thomas and Nicolás Cachanosky, "Argentina's Post-2001 Economy and the 2014 Default," *The Quarterly Review of Economics and Finance*, 2016, **60**: 70–80.

APPENDIX 6.A
IMF Loan to Argentina (excerpt)

(www.imf.org/external/np/sec/pr/2003/pr03160.htm) Press Release No. 03/160

September 20, 2003
Corrected: October 15, 2003
International Monetary Fund 700 19th Street, NW
Washington, DC 20431 USA

IMF Approves US$12.55 Billion Three-year Stand-by Credit for Argentina

The Executive Board of the International Monetary Fund (IMF) today approved a three-year, SDR 8.98 billion (about US$12.55 billion) Stand-By Credit Arrangement for Argentina to succeed the arrangement that expired on August 31, 2003 (see Press Release No. 03/09). In addition, the Executive Board approved the authorities' request for an extension of repayment expectations to an obligations schedule in an aggregate amount equivalent to SDR 1.74 billion (about US$2.43 billion).

Program Summary

The Argentine authorities have prepared a three-year economic program aimed at establishing sustained growth, reducing widespread poverty and addressing a number of vulnerabilities – including from a massive debt overhang in the public and private sectors, an undercapitalized banking system stressed by crisis, and a weakened investment environment.

Growth and inflation: GDP growth is targeted to reach 5.5 percent in 2003 and stay at around 4 percent in 2004–06. Core inflation is expected to be maintained in single digits.

Fiscal policy will aim to raise the consolidated primary surplus from 2V2 percent of GDP in 2003 to 3 percent in 2004. Beyond 2004, the authorities have committed to primary surpluses at levels sufficient to cover net payments on performing debt and obligations that may result under a debt restructuring agreement.

Structural fiscal reforms are envisaged to underpin the programmed fiscal consolidation and facilitate the phasing out of tax distortions. The reforms are sequenced to give time to build consensus. The authorities have committed to submit tax reform and intergovernmental reform legislation to Congress during 2004, with a view to their being introduced in the context of the 2005 budget.

Monetary policy will continue to aim at entrenching low inflation expectations, with base money growth driven mainly by the accumulation of international reserves. The authorities are considering moving to an inflation targeting regime by end-2004, and implementing supportive reforms aimed at increasing the autonomy of the central bank.

Banking reforms: The program aims at strengthening the soundness of the overall system and putting public banks on a sound financial footing. By end-2003, the authorities plan to eliminate temporary forbearance on the classification and provisioning of private loans and compensate banks for asymmetric pesoization and asymmetric indexation. As regards losses experienced by banks because of the legal injunctions (*amparos*), the authorities have committed to assess their impact and to identify measures to strengthen the system by end of 2003.

Debt restructuring: The authorities have also committed to advance negotiations with external creditors that is consistent with medium-term sustainability. They aim to conclude negotiations by mid-2004.

Utility companies: The authorities aim to obtain congressional approval by end-2003 of new legislation that delegates powers to the executive branch to renegotiate public concessions and effect interim tariff increases.

Predictable legal framework: The authorities will commit to review the effectiveness of the insolvency system with a view to putting in place a legal and regulatory framework conducive to progress in private corporate debt restructuring.

APPENDIX 6.B

World Bank Project Loan to Argentina: Urban Flood Prevention and Drainage APL 2, P093491

The Urban Flood Prevention and Drainage Project will help reduce the vulnerability of Argentina to flooding, through a mix of structural and non-structural measures. The project consists of the following components: Component 1) aims at providing provincial institutions with flood risk management instruments that can assist with the implementation of specific institutional development activities. Component 2) will provide housing in safe areas for those families that may be resettled from the lands required for the works and for lower income families living in flood prone areas in their immediate proximity. Component 3) will finance works to protect important urban areas against flood effects. It will contain minor rehabilitation of existing schemes and would include fortification of flood defenses in geographic areas with strong economic activity and the greatest vulnerability to serious repeated flood damage. Component 4) Technical assistance would be provided for US$2.39 million (or 3.4 percent of project loan) to help implement the project.

Project information document (PID) appraisal stage	
Report No.: AB1823	
Project Name	Argentina – Urban Flood Prevention and Drainage APL 2
Region	LATIN AMERICA AND CARIBBEAN
Sector	General water, sanitation and flood protection sector (100%)
Project ID	P093491
Borrower(s)	REPUBLIC OF ARGENTINA
Implementing Agency	
	Argentine Republic
	Argentina
	UCP&PFE-SUCCE
	Hipolito Yrigoyen 250

(*cont.*)

Project information document (PID) appraisal stage	
	Buenos Aires
	Argentina
	Tel: 541143498445
	ptrind@miv.gov.ar
Environment Category	[X] A [] B [] C [] FI [] TBD (to be determined)
Date PID Prepared	September 13, 2005
Date of Appraisal Authorization	September 28, 2005
Date of Board Approval	December 1, 2005

1. Country and Sector Background

Argentina's Exposure to Flood Risk. Flooding is the major natural hazard in Argentina, where the phenomenon poses a major challenge to development. Since 1957, Argentina has had 11 major floods. The floodplains in the country cover over a third of Argentina. That area contains the most developed agricultural and industrial zones in the country, an extensive transportation network and two major hydroelectric dams. Of the 11 major floods in Argentina, three have caused direct damage in excess of US$ 1 billion each: the 1983 flood, US$ 1.5 billion; the 1985 flood, US$ 2 billion; and the 1998 flood, US$ 2.5 billion. According to the statistics of Swiss-Re (1998), Argentina ranks 18th in the world in potential flood losses, in excess of A$ 3 billion a year (US$ 3 billion in 1998). Argentina is also one of 14 countries whose potential flood losses are greater than 1 percent of GDP. In Latin America, only Ecuador has a higher GDP exposure from flood risk. In pure potential economic loss terms, Argentina has the highest risk in Latin America.

2. Objectives

The program will develop a risk management framework to increase economic resilience to flooding. The APL is horizontal and will assist the City of Buenos Aires (phase 1) and provinces subject to flooding (phase 2).

The phase 1 of the proposed project, approved on April 5, 2005, will be executed over a period of six years. The City of Buenos Aires will benefit from a direct loan from the Bank with a sovereign guarantee from the Argentinean government. The project will help develop a risk management program for the City, through the improvement of the level of protection of its drainage system and the implementation of a risk management program. The project is implemented within the framework of the Buenos Aires

Hydraulic Master Plan, involving the whole city for non structural measures and the Maldonado Basin for the first stage of the structural measures. The risk management scheme will aim at providing assistance to the city government to promote a prevention, mitigation and emergency response to floods. In addition, the scheme will strengthen the City Agencies so that the transfer of responsibilities from the implementation unit to the Agencies will be fully carried out during project implementation.

Phase 2 would target the provinces matching the trigger indicators agreed upon and would strengthen the country's risk management scheme through geographical expansion of sustainable institutions and infrastructure investments. Phase 2 would be prepared in the framework of the Federal Water Agreement and in close coordination with the Federal Hydraulic Committee (COHIFE), which developed a nationwide water management strategy. Priority would be given in phase 2 to provinces located along the two main rivers, the Paraná and Paraguay, which are, with the City of Buenos Aires, highly vulnerable to flooding. Phase 2 will build on priority activities identified by the Water Basin Management study carried out in the preparation stage of the ongoing project . . .

3. Description

The proposed project will have 4 components:

Component [US$ million]	Total	IBRD	Counterpart
1. Institutional strengthening	3.13	3.13	0.00
2. Improving flood preparedness	13.22	12.56	0.66
3. Development of key defense facilities (including contingency amounts)	67.08	48.30	18.78
4. Project implementation and administration	2.67	2.67	0.00
	86.10	66.66	19.44
Unallocated		3.34	
Total		70.00	

7 The International Labor Organization

key facts

Headquarters: Geneva

Members: 187 countries

Mandate: to recommend to members regulations for the safety and health of workers.

Key structure: plenary organization includes representatives of government, unions, and employers and issues recommendations ("conventions") to states.

Key obligations: member states must consider ILO conventions for adoption, but are not required to adopt them.

Enforcement: the Governing Body can recommend punishments against countries that fail in their obligations under the conventions.

Key legal clauses of the ILO Constitution:
Article 19(2) on voting for new conventions and recommendations.
Article 19(5) on states' obligations to consider ratifying a convention.
Article 19(6) on states' obligations toward recommendations.
Article 22 on states' obligations to report each year on each convention it has ratified.
Article 33 on enforcement.

It is a perpetual dilemma in market capitalism that firms face a never-ending incentive to reduce costs in order to increase profits. For workers, this is experienced as downward pressure on both wages and working conditions. A global market economy seems to amplify these pressures. The International Labor Organization was created during an earlier period of "globalization" to limit the damage this does to the working conditions of citizens in the international economy. The organization produces labor regulations which member governments are encouraged to adopt as domestic laws. Its structure and authority are highly peculiar, reflecting the highly political nature of its subject matter. It includes representatives of labor and employer groups from each member country alongside representatives of their governments. It also has no authority to impose rules on members, relying instead on the process of deliberation to generate rules that will be appealing to states' self-interests.

At the end of World War I, the architects of the Treaty of Versailles believed that future wars could arise from economic inequalities between states or from a hyper-competitive race-to-the-bottom among national labor regulations. They felt there was a connection between the mistreatment of workers domestically and the tendency for international conflict, via either domestic social unrest or friction with trading partners. This link between labor standards and international peace and prosperity was widely accepted as conventional wisdom in 1919 and it has returned to the forefront of thinking about the effects of globalization in recent years. The issues at the heart of the International Labor Organization are very relevant again today. Both the contemporary and historical versions of this thinking are based on the same insight: that global capitalism produces an incentive for exporting countries to lower their labor standards to gain a competitive advantage in international trade, and this incentive (when allowed to operate unchecked) is bad for workers, bad for social stability, and bad for international peace and order.

This chapter examines the structure of the ILO, which includes non-state actors in an unprecedented way, and the unique system it creates by which members can choose on a case-by-case basis which decisions of the organization they will accept as binding. The chapter uses the rules against forced labor to present a case study of Myanmar/Burma that illustrates both the power of and the gaps in this enforcement system.

The International Labor Organization was created at the Versailles peace conference in 1919 and was given the mandate of coordinating labor standards across countries. This was thought at the time to be an important contribution both to the dignity and rights of working people around the world and to the long-term peace and stability of the post-war order. Despite, or perhaps because of, the dramatic process of the globalization of production, the ILO's goals and operation remain largely the same today as they were almost 100 years ago, and so do the concerns regarding the destabilizing possibilities of unlimited competition.

There are several reasons to study the International Labor Organization in comparison with other international organizations. First, it remains the central international body responsible for encouraging labor standards through law across a nearly global membership. It is therefore a potentially useful instrument to be used by the advocates of internationally mandated labor standards. That it has received little attention by those looking to institutionalize common standards suggests it may be an underutilized resource. Second, it contains a unique and interesting means of reconciling organizational authority with state sovereignty. It makes rules that only become binding on states when the states explicitly consent to each rule. In the terms of this book, therefore, it is a very revealing case. It uses a very different method to achieve compliance than any of our other institutions because it makes a significant sacrifice in the ambition of its legal rules in order to gain a high rate of compliance. Finally, it is unique among international organizations in allowing non-state actors such as business groups and labor unions to participate as official members of national delegations. This unusual structure was designed in 1919 and today it looks prescient given the dramatic shift in global power from government to firms, non-governmental organizations (NGOs), and other kinds of non-state actors. Many international organizations are seeking ways to incorporate these players into their processes, and to manage the results in ways that serve the organization's interests, and the ILO shows one way that it can be done. Thus, in both its structure and its substantive work, the ILO straddles the line between state power and globalization to a degree impossible to imagine for the strictly state-centric organizations in this book such as the United Nations and the International Court of Justice.

The ILO is composed of three parts: an assembly of delegates from all member states, known as the International Labor Conference (ILC); a smaller assembly of fifty-six of those delegates, known as the Governing Body, which operates as the executive committee of the ILO; and a secretariat, known as the International Labor Office (the Office), to provide bureaucratic support to the other two bodies. The ILC meets once a year to draft new labor standards, set the organization's budget and finances, admit new member states, and provide a general forum for the discussion of labor issues. The Governing Body meets more frequently and provides much of the monitoring of existing labor conventions. The delegates to both the ILC and the Governing Body include representatives of governments as well as representatives from labor and employer groups. Each national delegation in the ILC has four people in it, two from the national government and one each from labor and employer groups. Most of the fifty-six members of the Governing Body are elected for three-year terms from out of the ILC, fourteen from among the labor delegates, fourteen from the employers, and the rest from the governments. Ten seats in the Body are not elected, and are instead reserved for the government delegates of the ten states "of chief industrial importance" in the world (Art. 7(2)).[1] One of the Governing Body's functions is to figure out which are the ten states of chief industrial importance. The flexibility that this gives is in marked contrast to the rigid definition in the United Nations Charter of the five permanent members of the UN Security Council. Where the UN Charter codified the "Big Five" from 1945, leading to intense institutional problems as international power has shifted since then, the ILO Constitution avoids assigning seats over these ten permanent seats on its executive body. The political fighting over seats at the ILO is therefore structured around the Governing Body's formula for deciding which economies should be included, while the fights over the UN Security Council take place in diplomatic campaigns to revise the Charter.

The tripartite (national government, labor group, employer group) delegations of the ILO are not copied in any other major international organization, and indeed even within the ILO their existence is limited to the deliberative processes in the ILC and the Governing Body. This opens up an intriguing potential for tension in the organization: while labor and employer representatives have a voice and a vote in formulating new labor standards, those standards create obligations only on the governments of member states. In cases where the labor or employer groups are really independent of the government, their interests can shape the outputs of the ILO. In general, though, governments exert a great deal of influence over which labor and employer groups are allowed to participate in the ILO.

Despite this innovative representation structure, the ILO's legal powers are in fact quite conventional in the sense that the obligations that it monitors and enforces are obligations of states and states alone. The organization's Conventions are standard instruments of public international law, binding only

---

[1] Today these are Brazil, China, France, Germany, India, Italy, Japan, Russia, the United Kingdom, and the United States.

on the nation-states that sign them; they break no new legal or conceptual ground in terms of creating obligations for non-state actors. As we consider those obligations in this chapter, as well as the practice of compliance and the ILO's powers of enforcement, it is interesting to see how the tripartism of the organization is absent from the substantive legal outputs that it produces, and the opening this creates for a possible future where international law might impinge directly on firms' treatment of their workers.

Obligations

The substantive work of the ILO comes when it adopts new labor standards. These come in the form of "Conventions" and "Recommendations" and must be approved by a two-thirds majority vote in the ILC. The former include legally binding policy changes (upon domestic ratification) that must be made by states and the latter are merely hortatory. Excerpts of one convention are included below in Appendix 7.B (C.105 on forced labor). On its own, a newly passed convention (or recommendation) has no authority or power. It exists in a form that is just like any new international legal treaty which can be signed and ratified by any country that chooses to adopt it, but also can be left aside by any state that chooses not to adopt it. To become legally binding on a state, a new convention must be adopted and ratified through the normal treaty-ratifying process in the state's domestic political institutions.

   This second stage in the legal life of the document is crucial: only once it has been ratified by a state is the convention legally binding on it. States therefore have an entirely legal way to avoid taking on new obligations as the ILC passes new conventions. The existing corpus of ILO conventions makes up a global web of labor standards but it applies to states only in a piecemeal fashion, depending on which conventions have been formally adopted by which states. There are 189 conventions in force today, of which eight are considered by the ILO to be of fundamental importance.[2] About two-thirds of the ILO's member states have adopted all eight fundamental conventions.

---

[2] These are two each on forced labor (C.29 and C.105), freedom of association and the right to organize (C.87 and C.98), the elimination of discrimination (C.100 and C.111), and the abolition of child labor (C.138 and C.182).

As a result, member states take on two distinct kinds of obligations by joining the International Labor Organization: general obligations to the Constitution of the ILO and specific obligations to conventions and recommendations. On the one hand, the Constitution of the ILO includes the general requirements that states make various kinds of reports to the organization about their labor policies and that they consider adopting the labor conventions and recommendations passed by the International Labor Conference. On the other hand, each of those conventions and recommendations might include specific commitments and obligations which are binding on states. The procedures, applicability, and consequences of these two sets of obligations are entirely different from each other. In what follows, I first examine the general obligations of ILO members and then turn to consider the specific obligations that arise under one particularly interesting convention, that on forced labor (C.105). For a full picture of the obligations that come from the ILO, one would have to examine each convention in close detail, and consider which countries have accepted the obligations that it contains.

The primary general commitment of ILO member states is to consider for ratification all conventions and recommendations adopted by the International Labor Conference. This is set out in Article 19(5) of the ILO Constitution, where the language is clear and forceful: "each of the Members undertakes that it will, within the period of one year at most ... or if it is impossible ... in no case later than 18 months ... bring the Convention before the authority or authorities within whose competence the matter lies, for the enactment of legislation or other action." (The procedure is the same, in Article 19(7), for "recommendations.") The relevant authorities might be the domestic legislature or executive, or (in a federal system) a sub-national government such as a province or canton.

Therefore, the primary obligation of members is to consider ratifying the rules proposed in the conventions. Once the matter has been considered by the relevant national authorities, one of two things can happen: either the rule is adopted by these authorities, in which case the state will ratify the convention, or the authorities will decline to adopt it, in which case the country incurs no further obligations. To make perfectly clear the limits of these obligations, Article 19 goes on to say that, apart from bringing the matter to the attention of the relevant authorities for their consideration, "no further obligation shall rest upon the Member" if those authorities decline to adopt the convention.

Thus, whether rejecting or adopting a convention, the ILO Constitution requires that the state report back to the organization on its decision, along with either the reasons for declining or the measures it plans to take to

implement it. This is the source of the second component of members' obligations: to periodically report to the ILO Director-General on their domestic labor
regulations and practices. These reporting requirements appear in Articles 19(5)
and 19(6) of the ILO Constitution, which were added in an amendment to the
Constitution in 1948. These clauses give the Governing Body the authority to
require that states report to it about their laws and practices in the area covered
by the convention. This power is intriguing because it arises even with respect to
conventions that the state has declined to adopt, and as such it represents a form
of power of the ILO over states who have refused to consent to the convention.
Clearly, the power is only to require reports and information from the state; the
ILO does not compel non-ratifying countries to follow the rules of conventions
that they do not adopt. However, it does mean that with each convention that
the organization creates, it expands the realm of obligation of states by increasing the reporting that it could require of its members, even those who exercise
their ILO rights to decline to ratify the convention. It is therefore not quite true
to say that by declining to ratify a convention a state avoids all obligation
toward the ILO with respect to that convention.

It is easy to criticize the reporting system on the grounds that there is nothing
in it to discourage platitudes or cheap talk from states. States can, of course,
produce all manner of whitewash to make it look like they are being responsible
citizens of the ILO through their labor laws and practices, and there are few
institutional checks by which their statements might be challenged. While this
may sometimes be a problem, in general such a criticism underestimates the
political importance of states' public statements. Even whitewash requires effort
on the part of officials, and the bureaucratic investment that goes into making
reports can be useful from the ILO's perspective if it means the state is acknowledging that it has responsibilities to the organization on the subject.

Also, states may find themselves held to account down the road for statements that they had not thought at the time were particularly serious. Part of the
insight of Margaret Keck and Kathryn Sikkink's work on the politics of human
rights is that official statements are never cost-free: in the hands of activists,
they can often take on political significance which governments had not
intended and may become tools against the state.[3] The potential for what Frank
Schimmelfennig and others have called "rhetorical entrapment" raises a key
question about the ILO's place in world politics: should we interpret a state's

---

[3] Margaret Keck and Kathryn Sikkink, *Activists Beyond Borders: Advocacy Networks in
International Politics*. Cornell University Press, 1998.

refusal to be bound by a convention as evidence of an obligation to give a public and legal rationale for that refusal, or is refusal simply the absence of obligation? To the extent that one believes that reasoned public discourse makes up an important aspect of world politics, these reporting requirements may themselves be influential levers by which the ILO shapes state policy and the broader international environment.[4]

Aside from the general obligations set out in the Constitution, the ILO then creates new legal obligations by passing conventions that contain specific requirements for public policy. The convention on forced labor, for instance, requires that states "take effective measures to secure the immediate and complete abolition of forced or compulsory labor" (C.105, reproduced in Appendix 7.B). The convention defines the key term ("forced labor") and then invites ILO member states to ratify the convention through their domestic legal systems. The convention on discrimination in employment (C.111) says that states must "pursue a national policy designed to promote, by methods appropriate to national conditions and practice, equality of opportunity and treatment in respect of employment and occupation." Similar to C.105, C.111 defines the term "discrimination" and attempts to specify what is and is not a forbidden form of discrimination in employment. It says, for instance, that the claim of "discrimination" is not available to individuals who are "justifiably suspected of, or engaged in, activities prejudicial to the security of the State," thus carving out a large space for states to use national security as a justification for what might otherwise look like discrimination. The convention on forced labor also includes language common to many ILO conventions regarding their entry into force (Articles 3 and 4), denunciation (Article 5), and the possibility of a superseding convention (Article 9). These are now included in all new conventions.

There is some flexibility built in so that states with more strict rules on a subject are not required by an ILO convention to weaken them. Article 19(8) says that conventions and recommendations cannot be used to lessen existing labor regulations that "ensure more favorable conditions to the workers concerned than those provided for in the Convention or Recommendation." In opening this

---

[4] See for instance Frank Schimmelfennig, *The EU, NATO, and the Integration of Europe.* Cambridge University Press, 2003, and Thomas Risse and Kathryn Sikkink, "The Socialization of International Human Rights Norms into Domestic Politics: Introduction," in Thomas Risse, Stephen C. Ropp, and Kathryn Sikkink, *The Power of Human Rights: International Norms and Domestic Change.* Cambridge University Press, 1999, pp. 1–38.

possibility, the ILO system acknowledges the reality that these are subjects of great national variation, and it is in essence conceding that it does not provide the last word when it comes to labor regulation. Rather than insist on uniformity across its membership, it aims to encourage countries whose standards are considered insufficient to bring them to a broadly agreed upon minimum, while allowing those that are already higher to remain as they choose.

Compliance

The International Labor Organization is built around two institutional devices to encourage compliance by member states: tripartism and voluntarism. These both represent institutional innovations as compared to all of the other organizations in this book, and so they merit some attention both for understanding the ILO and for comparison with how other international organizations aim for compliance. The ILO is consciously striving for maximum compliance by states, and so as a general rule whenever there is a trade-off between stronger substantive regulations on labor conditions and higher rates of compliance, it chooses to maximize the rate of compliance at the expense of the substantive content of the laws. This is evident in both the design of tripartism and the extreme voluntarism of the convention process.

Tripartism: The inclusion of non-governmental delegates should be seen as an attempt to ensure that when conventions are passed by the ILC they have already been vetted by important domestic constituencies in each state. They should therefore be less controversial and more likely to be adopted and implemented once they are brought back to domestic political institutions for approval. By building in a formal role for labor and employer representatives, the ILO internalizes both advocates and potential opponents of new conventions. It is bargaining that their inclusion will help uncover those new labor standards that can successfully pass through the various sectoral interests in domestic politics and emerge as rules that states will actually comply with.

Voluntarism: The second device is the two-stage approval process for new conventions, described above. Because states must explicitly consent to each convention for it to be binding on them, those that are consented to are presumably likely to be acceptable to the governments. This is a process of self-selection. The ILO's internal logic rests on the assumption that states which strongly disagree with a given standard are free to declare themselves to be not governed by it. Those who oppose it drop out, and the overall measured rate of compliance with ILO conventions will be higher than it would otherwise be. Of course, this relies on measuring only compliance by states with those conventions they have ratified, and sets aside the behavior of all those states that refused to accept the obligation in the first place. In strictly legal terms, this is a reasonable move because states that do not ratify a treaty are under no obligation to comply with it and therefore cannot be said to be in violation. But from the broader perspective of spreading labor standards as widely as possible, this trade-off shows one way in which the ILO aims low in the pursuit of its objectives. It will accept a lower rate of adoption by states in order to get a higher rate of compliance by those that do adopt.

That said, to the extent that there is a "peer pressure" effect motivating states to adopt conventions that they otherwise do not agree with, this logic of self-selection for compliance may not work very well. Do states feel social pressure to adopt labor standards which they have no intention of implementing? The ILO clearly believes that inter-state peer pressure is powerful in some settings, since it is at the heart of the effort to promote the eight "core" human rights conventions as basic standards of legitimate conduct. In branding these as something like the markers of civilized statehood, the ILO hopes that states will see signing them as valuable signals to others about their legitimacy. If this induces cynical states to ratify these conventions for public relations reasons without a genuine commitment to following them, then self-motivated compliance is unlikely to follow. The enforcement regime in the ILO Constitution, discussed below, would then become more relevant.

Enforcement

The ILO has some capacity to enforce its conventions against states that have ratified but not complied with them. These rules are primarily described in Articles 24, 26, and 33 of the ILO Constitution. The system works on the basis of complaints about the failure of a member to fulfill its obligations under a convention. These can be investigated by a committee of member states from the ILO and may lead to censure or expulsion from the organization.

Complaints about non-compliance on the part of a state can be submitted to the ILO by a variety of agents, including worker or employer groups, member states of the ILO, or the Governing Body itself. This range of sources for complaints is unusual among international organizations. The WTO, by contrast, will in general only consider disputes that originate with states that can claim to have been harmed by another member's failure to fulfill its obligations, and the ICJ generally only accepts cases referred to it by two (or more) states who are party to the dispute. Allowing non-state actors to submit complaints, and allowing the Governing Body to initiate complaints, makes the ILO akin to the ICC where the Prosecutor's Office has the authority to initiate investigations on its own, relying in some cases on information supplied by non-governmental organizations or others.

A complaint in the ILO context takes the form of what the ILO calls a "representation" that a member state has failed to implement an ILO Convention which that member has accepted. This is defined in Articles 24 and 26. Once such a claim is made, the state in question is usually given an opportunity to respond (though in Article 26 it is not mandatory that the target be given a chance to answer the charges) and then the Governing Body makes a judgment about whether the matter should be further investigated by a committee of the ILC known as a "Commission of Inquiry."

These investigations are governed by Article 28, which says that the Commission "shall prepare a report embodying its findings on all questions of fact ... and containing such recommendations as it may think proper as to the steps which should be taken" and the report is then made public and the parties to the dispute are asked to respond (Art. 29). If the report substantiates a complaint against a member, that state can be asked to change its policies, and its behavior is then monitored by the Governing Body and ultimately by the general membership of the ILO sitting in the International Labor Conference. The Governing Body can "recommend to the Conference such action as it may deem wise and expedient to secure compliance" with the report's recommendations. This process has been used only once, as we shall see in the Myanmar case below.

Despite this enforcement structure, the logic of the ILO in general rests on encouraging self-motivated compliance rather than centralized coercive enforcement. The ILO's history of enforcement is thin. The working premise behind the organization is that states can be induced to improve their conditions for workers by recognizing their self-interests and by the subtle play of international norms and adverse publicity to sway those who fall below the standards. This is entirely different than a coercive model in which an international organization strives to force recalcitrant states to adopt positions to which they object. The coercive model sets up a power struggle between the organization and its members and presumes that progress will come through the process of confrontation. International organizations are, in general, poorly equipped to win such direct contests of political power with their members, and the ILO has tried it only once in its history (Myanmar), with limited success.

Power struggles between international organizations and their members are not unheard of, and it is far from certain that the states, even powerful ones, always win these contests – each organization in this book has had some measure of success forcing its members to change their policies. But the ILO helps to show that compliance and enforcement are only loosely connected for international organizations: compliance often comes without enforcement, and enforcement tools are not often put to use. The ILO is designed from the start to avoid direct confrontations with members, and so most of its useful work takes place away from the spotlight of hot disputes between its rules and its members.

As a result, finding empirical evidence that the ILO improves labor standards is not easy. This is not because it is necessarily ineffectual, but largely because the process through which it influences states is mixed with so many other political influences that it is very difficult to trace the independent effect of the ILO. It is true, for instance, that countries that have ratified the ILO conventions on occupational safety have lower rates of accidental death in the workplace.[5] But this correlation can only form the beginning, rather than the end, of a discussion about the ILO's contribution. Is the correlation because signing ILO conventions leads states to enact stricter workplace safety rules? Or is it because those with strict workplace safety rules are happy to accept ILO standards that they already meet? More generally, do states actually change their policies as a result of new ILO standards, in ways that they would not have done without the standard? This is, ultimately, a more concrete version of a big question: (how) does the ILO matter in the world?

CASE: Myanmar

The long-running dispute between the ILO and Myanmar shows the working of its enforcement system, in both its strengths and weaknesses. The military government of Myanmar has been the target of repeated ILO enforcement action

---

[5] Donald Wilson et al., "The Ratification Status of ILO Conventions Related to Occupational Safety and Health and Its Relationship with Reported Occupational Fatality Rates," *Journal of Occupational Health*, 2007, 49(1): 72–79.

since the mid-1990s.[6] The issue stems from the government's widespread practice of forcing civilians to work as unwilling labor in construction projects and in support of military operations against what the government sees as "unrest" and "insurgencies" throughout the country. Despite being a signatory to ILO Convention 29 which outlaws "the use of forced or compulsory labor in all its forms," the government in the 1980s and 1990s relied heavily on forced labor to prop itself up.[7] It also used forced labor as a means of individual and collective punishment.

The Forced Labor Convention (C.29) is one of the eight conventions which the ILO considers to make up the set of fundamental human rights. It was adopted in 1930 and was signed by Myanmar in 1955. Myanmar at the time was known as the Union of Burma, a newly founded parliamentary democracy after separating from British colonial control since 1948. After a coup in 1962, Myanmar spent decades governed by variations on the theme of oppressive military dictatorship, characterized by extreme poverty. However, under the international law of state succession, the treaties and other obligations entered into by a predecessor state remain in force for the successor state, and so the Union of Burma's commitment to suppressing forced labor in 1955 remains as a treaty obligation of the current military government. Myanmar has never adopted Convention 105 (1957, Appendix 7.B below), which includes a ban on forced labor as a political tool, and so it is not bound by the more recent rules contained in that convention.

However, Myanmar continues to be obligated to follow the earlier Convention that it did adopt, Convention 29, and therefore the exact language of the Convention is therefore crucial to identifying its obligations and assessing its compliance and any enforcement action by the ILO. The 1930 Convention on Forced Labor says:

> Art. 1(1) Each member of the International Labor Organization which ratifies this Convention undertakes to suppress the use of forced or compulsory labor in all its forms within the shortest possible period.
> Art. 2(1) For the purposes of this Convention the term forced or compulsory labor shall mean all work or service which is exacted from any person under the menace of any penalty and for which the said person has not offered himself voluntarily.

---

[6] I follow UN convention with the name "Myanmar" rather than the pre-1989 name Burma.
[7] Richard Horsey, *Ending Forced Labour in Myanmar: Engaging a Pariah Regime.* Routledge, 2011. Kay Seok and David Scott Mathieson, "Allies in Paranoia and Repression," *Far Eastern Economic Review*, July 3, 2009. Also at: www.hrw.org/en/news/2009/07/02/allies-paranoia-and-repression. Accessed August 4, 2009.

Art. 2(2) Nevertheless, for the purposes of this Convention, the term forced or compulsory labor shall not include-

(a) any work or service exacted in virtue of compulsory military service laws for work of a purely military character;

(b) any work or service which forms part of the normal civic obligations of the citizens of a fully self-governing country;

(c) any work or service exacted from any person as a consequence of a conviction in a court of law, provided that the said work or service is carried out under the supervision and control of a public authority and that the said person is not hired to or placed at the disposal of private individuals, companies or associations;

(d) any work or service exacted in cases of emergency, that is to say, in the event of war or of a calamity or threatened calamity . . .;

(e) minor communal services of a kind which, being performed by the members of the community in the direct interest of the said community, can therefore be considered as normal civic obligations incumbent upon the members of the community, provided that the members of the community or their direct representatives shall have the right to be consulted in regard to the need for such services.

The enforcement action against Myanmar began in 1996 when a group of delegates in the ILO representing workers submitted a complaint about Myanmar's compliance with the Convention. Their complaint was built on many years' worth of criticism of Myanmar's practices by ILO groups and others. It was the first use of the formal complaints procedure in relation to Myanmar. Article 26(1) of the ILO Constitution allows any country that is a member to complain "if it is not satisfied that any other Member is securing the effective observance of any Convention which both have ratified." Article 26 allows the Governing Body to create a Commission of Inquiry to investigate the complaint if it feels there are grounds to do so, and the Commission is charged with completing a report that may include recommendations for changes to the country's policies or practices.

This process was carried out vis-à-vis Myanmar in the 1990s, and the Commission of Inquiry issued a report in 1998 that found that there was "widespread and systematic" use of forced labor in the country in violation of Convention 29.[8] It said that "Myanmar authorities, including the local and regional

---

[8] www.ilo.org/public/english/standards/relm/gb/docs/gb273/myanmar.htm.

administration, the military and various militias, forced the population of Myanmar to carry out a wide range of tasks. Labor was extracted from men, women and children, some of a very young age. Workers were not paid or compensated in any way for providing their labor, other than in exceptional circumstances, and were commonly subjected to various forms of verbal and physical abuse including rape, torture and killing."[9] It found that this forced labor was widely used across all aspects of society controlled by the government, including to support the military, for infrastructure projects, and to manufacture goods for export. It estimated that between 1992 and 1995 alone, two million people had been forced to work on road, bridge, and railway construction projects without pay.[10] The military work included walking in minefields to ensure a path for soldiers.[11] Village leaders were required to maintain information about all villagers to make it easier to find people to put to work, and each household would generally be required to send a member, even where it meant sending children, the elderly, and pregnant women. The village leader would be the first to be punished if recruits failed to appear, though recruits and their families were often terrorized as well with torture, rape, and murder. People with money could generally pay a bribe to avoid being recruited. The basic legal question for the Commission of Inquiry was whether the government had lived up to its specific commitments under Convention 29.

The Commission explored both the laws of Myanmar and its practices. Two laws, from 1908 and 1909, required that citizens be available to assist the military as porters, guides, and general labor, without their consent and without pay. These clearly violated the obligations under the Convention. Moreover, the practice of forced labor was far more extensive and systematic than even these laws allowed. The Commission found a series of government memos from 1995 that prohibited unpaid labor in national development projects, but the Commission appears to have given them little credence, in part because they were labeled "secret" and so had never been communicated with local officials and in part because there was no evidence that they had been applied in practice.[12] They also found that forced labor had been made illegal under Myanmar's national laws, which is an important part of the state's obligations in Article 1 of the Forced Labor Convention, but again the Commission saw no evidence that this was ever followed in practice. All of this information came at

---

[9] 1998 Commission of Inquiry, para. 274.   [10] Ibid., para. 285.   [11] Ibid., para. 300.
[12] Ibid., para. 473.

the initiative of the Commission as the government of Myanmar never chose to participate in the Commission's work. Overall, the final report amounted to a detailed indictment of the national practices of Myanmar, and a wholesale critique of its underperformance with respect to Convention 29 in particular and human rights in general. It therefore provides a usefully extreme case of non-compliance with which to assess the enforcement capacity of the ILO and of international organizations more broadly.

The Commission's report presented several demands to the Myanmar government. These included changing the 1908 and 1909 laws so that they complied with the Convention, ending the practice of forced labor, and fully enforcing the existing laws against forced labor. Under the terms of a Commission of Inquiry, as set out in Article 29 of the ILO Constitution, the Commission has the power to issue "recommendations as it may think proper" to remedy any non-compliance that it finds. The formal authority of the Commission is therefore ultimately to recommend, rather than to decide or demand. It cannot directly compel states to change their practices. However, the language of the Myanmar report was surprisingly forceful and blurred the distinction between a demand and a recommendation: it said "the recommendations made by the Commission require action by the Government of Myanmar without delay." It also made a more general critique of Myanmar's system of government, not typical of language used in inter-state organizations. It said "The Commission considers that the impunity with which government officials, in particular the military, treat the civilian population as an unlimited pool of unpaid forced laborers and servants at their disposal is part of a political system built on the use of force and intimidation to deny the people of Myanmar democracy and the rule of law ... The establishment of a government freely chosen by the people and the submission of all public authorities to the rule of law are, in practice, indispensable prerequisites for the suppression of forced labor in Myanmar."[13] In other words, the Commission seemed to believe that the government was unlikely to change its practices, and that the people of Myanmar would not be spared further forced labor until their military dictators were overthrown. It is strikingly unusual for an international organization to criticize a member's system of government in such a pointed and forceful manner.

Article 33 of the ILO Constitution says that the Governing Body can recommend "such action as it may deem wise and expedient to secure compliance" with the recommendations of a Commission of Inquiry. The Myanmar case has been

---

[13] Ibid., para. 542.

tangled up in Article 33 since the Commission issued its report in 1998. Looking for an effective strategy to change the government's practice, and with the open-ended language of Article 33 in hand, the ILO has chosen to negotiate with the Myanmar government over the forced labor issue, rather than to punish or expel it. After another scathing ILO report in 2001, the two parties agreed in 2002 that the ILO should install a "liaison officer" in the country to "assist the government to ensure the prompt and effective elimination of forced labor." When this person found themselves marginalized in the country and learned that citizens lodging complaints were being arrested, a new agreement was negotiated that was meant to guarantee the safety of people making complaints. By 2008, the situation had not improved.[14] A new "joint strategy for the elimination of forced labor" was agreed to between the ILO and the government in 2011 after the regime began a series of quite fundamental changes in its mode of governance. Amid indications that the changing political coalition running Myanmar was serious about restraining forced labor, the relationship between the ILO and Myanmar grew less antagonistic and in 2012 the organization allowed Myanmar to return to some of the regular business of the ILC from which it had long been suspended. The ILO has characterized the government since 2012 as a 'reluctant' partner in ending forced labor.[15] Richard Horsey, the ILO's representative in Myanmar for many of these events, sees a qualified success for the ILO: "while there have been a number of problems, the fact that the regime has been pushed to take a number of significant steps – including agreeing to an incredible intrusive complaints mechanism – is striking. It is very unusual for any diplomatic strategy to be successful in securing progress on human rights by a regime such as Myanmar's."[16]

The episode highlights the power, limits, and contradictions of the ILO's attempts to influence member states. When faced with intransigent non-compliance, it is not clear what the ILO's options are. Its authority under Article 33 is extremely broad but unfocused in the sense that there are few valued goods or privileges granted to members by the ILO Constitution that could be taken away as punishment. As the ILO has no power over trade policy or tariffs or sanctions, there is no channel by which it could directly impose economic or

---

[14] US Department of State, 2008 Human Rights Report: Burma, www.state.gov/g/drl/rls/hrrpt/2008/eap/119035.htm. Accessed September 9, 2009.

[15] Nyein Nyien, "ILO: Current Govt 'Reluctant Partners' in Fight Against Forced Labour," *The Irrawaddy*, February 12, 2016, citing ILO liaison officer Piyamal Pichaiwongse.

[16] Richard Horsey, *Ending Forced Labour in Myanmar: Engaging a Pariah Regime*. Routledge, 2011, p. 2.

military sanctions against a recalcitrant member state. The most it could do is expel the country from the organization. Short of that, it has generally opted to continue to negotiate with governments such as Myanmar while working to publicize its non-compliance in the hopes that other states, other IOs, and NGOs might add their influence in the direction of compliance.

The Myanmar case shows the limits – but also some capacity – of an international organization when faced with a member that reveals itself to be entirely unwilling to fulfill its obligations. It is often impossible to code the results as unambiguous "success" or "failure." Having exhausted its instruments of enforcement, the ILO is left struggling to find a means by which it can continue to include Myanmar among its members while maintaining the integrity of its core mission.

Conclusion

The ILO is an important player in the world of international labor standards, even though it has never been constituted in such a way that it can enforce standards on recalcitrant states. Rather, it has two somewhat more subtle roles to play. First, it helps to create and define an international consensus on the baseline regulations for aspects of labor and employment. Second, it provides a forum in which complaints against states can resonate and be amplified. Together, these two mean that the ILO provides an opportunity for states to make public and legal commitments regarding their labor laws and a mechanism by which they might be held to account for them.

The obligations that the ILO imposes on members are relatively strong and unambiguous compared with those of many other international organizations. There are few ways to dodge out of the duties imposed by the ILO and, in the sense of having a clear mandate of legal authority that trumps the sovereignty of its members, the organization is among the most authoritative in world politics. However, its authority extends only to the procedural matters of requiring that members consider adopting certain labor standards; it does not require that they actually adopt anything. The net result is either a very strong or a very weak organization depending on whether one is looking at the legal superiority of the organization above its members or at the organization's substantive power over actual labor conditions – at legal authority or policy effects. Said differently, the ILO is in absolute control of a set of legal instruments which are detached from the actual machinery of governance.

The peculiar strong-yet-weak legal and political make-up of the ILO reappears in various ways, as when it comes to deciding what goes into a convention in the first place. This reflects the fact that the ILO operates in highly politicized terrain and deals in matters of great domestic importance to states. Few states are seriously willing to delegate to an international agency the power to legislate domestic policies relating to industrial or labor policy. These are subjects which governments have shown a strong interest in managing autonomously. They have, however, been willing to promise to consider changes to their policies, and the ILO's role in practice has come to be as a centralized location for the discussion and suggestion of these changes. Rather than directly challenge members' sovereignty over domestic policies, the ILO has chosen a path in which it codifies policies which members already want to adopt. This greatly reduces the potential for conflict between the organization and its members, but at the cost of greatly reducing the ambition of the organization with respect to labor policies. Whether this trade-off is worth it is a matter of judgment.

Most studies of international labor standards focus on the worst failings of and abuses by states, and are motivated by revealing how governments use their power to deny basic rights to their citizens. This attention is important, but it should also be complemented by attention to how those rights and minimum standards have come into being. Here, the ILO is a very important actor. Through its process of deliberation and tripartite voting, the ILO provides a mechanism for sifting through a range of possible labor standards and model laws and identifying those that can carry something close to an international consensus. This consensus need not be total, as we have seen that the peculiar system of obligations that the ILO creates for states allows for individual states to opt out of any proposed convention, but conventions do not proceed through the organization unless they have broad support that extends beyond the most activist states. Its products are therefore rarely at the leading edge of high standards, but they often represent a "reasonable middle" below which state policies attract a natural suspicion.

The process of deliberation, ratification, and reporting provides states with many moments where they are expected to make official public statements about their own labor regulation. These statements may be in favor of a new convention or opposed to it, but either way they add up to a body of public commitments that the government may have a hard time disavowing in the future. By requiring that states make public defense of their labor standards, the processes in and around the ILO give other governments, NGOs, and even private citizens political resources when disputes arise. Governments are generally highly averse to being seen as hypocrites, and one of the important functions of the ILO is to provide a place in which government practice can be publicly compared to government rhetoric, at least with respect to the matters specifically contained in conventions. This accountability rarely rises to the level seen in the Myanmar case, but the intuition behind the ILO is that states will in general be better behaved with respect to their labor practices because they know that extreme mistreatment and extreme hypocrisy could be exposed in the ILO process.

Further Reading

The Constitution of the ILO is clear and accessible (at: www.ilo.org), and the ILO's companion booklet called *International Labor Standards: A Workers' Education Manual* (ILO, 4th edn., 1998) is a useful introduction to the organization. Alfred Wisskirchen, a long-time member of the International Labor Conference, has a detailed article on his practical experiences at the ILO ("The Standard-Setting and Monitoring Activity of the ILO: Legal Questions and Practical Experience," *International Labor Review*, fall 2005, **144**(4): 253–290). On labor standards more broadly, see *Rules of the Game: A Brief Introduction to International Labor Standards* (ILO, 2005), and Kaushik Basu et al., *International Labor Standards: History, Theory, and Policy Options* (Wiley-Blackwell, 2003). For the ILO's relationship with individual countries, including Myanmar, the ILO's website includes country reports (at: www.ilo.org/global/Regions/lang-en/index.htm). The US State Department's Bureau of Democracy, Human Rights, and Labor publishes a useful annual report of human rights and labor standards with a chapter on every country (other than the US).

Brian Langille gives a helpful introduction to labor issues in international organization in Langille "Labor," in Jacob Katz Cogan, Ian Hurd, and Ian Johnstone (eds.), *The Oxford Handbook of International Organizations* (Oxford University Press, 2016).

On Myanmar, see the first-hand account of an ILO official in Richard Horsey, *Ending Forced Labour in Myanmar: Engaging a Pariah Regime* (Routledge, 2011).

APPENDIX 7.A

Constitution of the International Labor Organization (excerpts)

Article 19

1. When the Conference has decided on the adoption of proposals with regard to an item on the agenda, it will rest with the Conference to determine whether these

proposals should take the form: (a) of an international Convention, or (b) of a Recommendation to meet circumstances where the subject, or aspect of it, dealt with is not considered suitable or appropriate at that time for a Convention.

2. In either case a majority of two-thirds of the votes cast by the delegates present shall be necessary on the final vote for the adoption of the Convention or Recommendation, as the case may be, by the Conference.

3. In framing any Convention or Recommendation of general application the Conference shall have due regard to those countries in which climatic conditions, the imperfect development of industrial organization, or other special circumstances make the industrial conditions substantially different and shall suggest the modifications, if any, which it considers may be required to meet the case of such countries.

. . .

5. In the case of a Convention:

    (a) the Convention will be communicated to all Members for ratification;

    (b) each of the Members undertakes that it will, within the period of one year at most from the closing of the session of the Conference, or if it is impossible owing to exceptional circumstances to do so within the period of one year, then at the earliest practicable moment and in no case later than 18 months from the closing of the session of the Conference, bring the Convention before the authority or authorities within whose competence the matter lies, for the enactment of legislation or other action;

    (c) Members shall inform the Director-General of the International Labour Office of the measures taken in accordance with this article to bring the Convention before the said competent authority or authorities, with particulars of the authority or authorities regarded as competent, and of the action taken by them;

. . .

6. In the case of a Recommendation:

    (a) the Recommendation will be communicated to all Members for their consideration with a view to effect being given to it by national legislation or otherwise;

    (b) each of the Members undertakes that it will, within a period of one year at most from the closing of the session of the Conference or if it is impossible owing to exceptional circumstances to do so within the period of one year, then at the earliest practicable moment and in no case later than 18 months after the closing of the Conference, bring the Recommendation before the authority or authorities within whose competence the matter lies for the enactment of legislation or other action;

    (c) the Members shall inform the Director-General of the International Labour Office of the measures taken in accordance with this article to bring the Recommendation before the said competent authority or authorities with particulars of the authority or authorities regarded as competent, and of the action taken by them;

(d) apart from bringing the Recommendation before the said competent authority or authorities, no further obligation shall rest upon the Members, except that they shall report to the Director-General of the International Labour Office, at appropriate intervals as requested by the Governing Body, the position of the law and practice in their country in regard to the matters dealt with in the Recommendation, showing the extent to which effect has been given, or is proposed to be given, to the provisions of the Recommendation and such modifications of these provisions as it has been found or maybe found necessary to make in adopting or applying them.

Article 20

Any Convention so ratified shall be communicated by the Director-General of the International Labour Office to the Secretary-General of the United Nations for registration in accordance with the provisions of Article 102 of the Charter of the United Nations but shall only be binding upon the Members which ratify it.

. . .

Article 22

Each of the Members agrees to make an annual report to the International Labour Office on the measures which it has taken to give effect to the provisions of Conventions to which it is a party. These reports shall be made in such form and shall contain such particulars as the Governing Body may request.

Article 33

In the event of any Member failing to carry out within the time specified the recommendations, if any, contained in the report of the Commission of Inquiry, or in the decision of the International Court of Justice, as the case may be, the Governing Body may recommend to the Conference such action as it may deem wise and expedient to secure compliance therewith.

APPENDIX 7.B

ILO Convention 105, Abolition of Forced Labor, 1957 (excerpts)

Article 1

Each Member of the International Labor Organization which ratifies this Convention undertakes to suppress and not to make use of any form of forced or compulsory labor –

(a) as a means of political coercion or education or as a punishment for holding or expressing political views or views ideologically opposed to the established political, social or economic system;

(b) as a method of mobilising and using labor for purposes of economic development;

(c) as a means of labor discipline;

(d) as a punishment for having participated in strikes;

(e) as a means of racial, social, national or religious discrimination.

Article 2

Each Member of the International Labor Organization which ratifies this Convention undertakes to take effective measures to secure the immediate and complete abolition of forced or compulsory labor as specified in Article 1 of this Convention.

Article 3

The formal ratifications of this Convention shall be communicated to the Director-General of the International Labor Office for registration.

Article 4

1. This Convention shall be binding only upon those Members of the International Labor Organization whose ratifications have been registered with the Director-General.

2. It shall come into force twelve months after the date on which the ratifications of two Members have been registered with the Director-General.

3. Thereafter, this Convention shall come into force for any Member twelve months after the date on which its ratification has been registered.

Article 5

1. A Member which has ratified this Convention may denounce it after the expiration of ten years from the date on which the Convention first comes into force, by an act communicated to the Director-General of the International Labor Office for registration. Such denunciation shall not take effect until one year after the date on which it is registered.

. . .

Article 6

1. The Director-General of the International Labor Office shall notify all Members of the International Labor Organization of the registration of all ratifications and denunciations communicated to him by the Members of the Organization.

. . .

Article 9

1. Should the Conference adopt a new Convention revising this Convention in whole or in part, then, unless the new Convention otherwise provides:
   (a) the ratification by a Member of the new revising Convention shall ipso jure involve the immediate denunciation of this Convention, notwithstanding the provisions of Article 5 above, if and when the new revising Convention shall have come into force;
   (b) as from the date when the new revising Convention comes into force this Convention shall cease to be open to ratification by the Members.
2. This Convention shall in any case remain in force in its actual form and content for those Members which have ratified it but have not ratified the revising Convention.

Article 10

The English and French versions of the text of this Convention are equally authoritative.

8 The International Court of Justice

key facts

Headquarters: The Hague

Members: 193 states parties

Mandate: to settle inter-state legal disputes with the consent of both parties.

Key structure: fifteen international judges provide definitive legal judgments when requested by states.

Key obligations: states agree to follow the decisions of the Court in cases to which they are a party, and to carry out provisional measures as requested by the Court.

Enforcement: a party that is unsatisfied with the performance of the losing party in a case may refer the matter to the UN Security Council.

Key clauses in the ICJ Statute:
Articles 2, 3, and 4 on the composition of the Court.
Article 34 on states as parties.
Article 36 on jurisdiction.
Article 38 on the sources of law.
Article 41 on provisional measures.
Article 59 on the absence of precedent.
UN Charter Article 94 on the obligation to comply with the ICJ.
UN Charter Article 96 on advisory opinions.

When countries find themselves in a dispute over their international legal obligations with one another, the International Court of Justice can provide a decisive and binding judgment. The Court is an international juridical body that hears cases involving legal complaints between consenting states. Its jurisdiction is carefully defined to preserve the sovereignty of the states involved, and much controversy comes out of the complicated relationship between state sovereignty and the binding nature of international law. For instance, it expressly forbids its decisions from serving as precedents for future cases. The Court provides two important functions in world politics: first, its decisions constitute formal and explicit legal judgments regarding who is right and wrong in a given dispute; and second, these decisions enter into the political discourse of states, despite the absence of precedent, and may have substantial influence beyond their legal terms.

This chapter examines the law and politics of the International Court of Justice. The ICJ is the preeminent judicial body for disputes between states, with a history going back to the aftermath of World War I. The Court's decisions are final and binding on states but its jurisdiction is carefully crafted around the political realities of state sovereignty. The chapter explores one ICJ case in depth, dealing with genocide and sovereign immunity, to show some of the key features of the Court, including its composition, its jurisdiction, and the sources of law. It also shows the legal and political complications that accompany any effort to subsume sovereign states under the principle of the rule of law among states.

The tension between the concepts of international organization and of state sovereignty is most forcefully apparent in the case of international courts. It is unavoidable in the very definition of a court that it should have the power to impose its decisions on the losing party, and yet the rules of state sovereignty have been developed over centuries precisely to insulate countries from such outside and overarching influence. In the extreme, one might say that there is an absolute trade-off between an international court's ability to act like a court and a state's ability to remain sovereign when faced with that court. It is perhaps surprising therefore that there is a growing tendency in world politics to create new courts to deal with a variety of international problems, including trade and investment disputes, war crimes and genocide, and human rights, and in each case the design of the Court necessarily finds some mechanism to manage the tension between legal obligation and state sovereignty. These new courts reflect a general desire to extend to inter-state affairs the idea of the rule of law that is commonly found in models of domestic governance. The rule of law is a complicated and interesting device when those whom the rules are meant to bind are also those who created the rules and who decide how to interpret and to enforce them. Thus, the life of international courts is built out of tension, paradox, and compromise.

The International Court of Justice (also called the World Court) hears cases that arise out of legal disputes between states. Its architecture is set by the Statute of the ICJ, an international treaty that is an annex to the UN Charter and that is a revised version of the Statute of the Permanent Court of International Justice (PCIJ) from 1920. The PCIJ was the legal body of the old League of Nations, and the ICJ is the legal body of the United Nations. All states that join the UN automatically become members of the ICJ, as required by Article 93(1) of the UN Charter. This chapter examines the obligations of UN members toward the ICJ, as well as the Court's compliance tools and enforcement power.

As we shall see, while the Court is strictly a legal institution, its practice and its place in the world are so thoroughly connected to the political concerns and strategies of states that any analysis of the Court's role necessarily helps to make the point that in international relations the legal and political domains are entirely interwoven. The two cases at the end of this chapter make this clear, though in different ways: in the *Yerodia* case, the dispute between the Democratic Republic of Congo (hereafter "Congo") and Belgium was over whether a Congolese government minister suspected of inciting genocide could be prosecuted by Belgian courts; the question in *Australia v. Japan* was whether Japan's whale hunting was "scientific" enough to satisfy the permissive rules of the treaty on whaling. In both instances, the motivations behind the case and payoffs from them are inescapably political but framed in legal terms appropriate for a legal institution. They show the political content and shape of international juridification.

The Court hears cases in a process of written submissions and oral arguments. States are represented by their lawyers, generally led by their foreign ministry legal staffs and often involving lawyers from private law firms and university law faculties. The Court is composed of fifteen international judges, who are assigned to the Court full time. The Statute describes them as "independent judges, elected regardless of their nationality from among persons of high moral character, who possess the qualifications required in their respective countries for appointment to the highest judicial offices, or are jurists of recognized competence in international law" (Article 2). They are elected to the Court by the UN General Assembly and the Security Council, where each body must approve each judge by a majority vote (and the Security Council operates here without the veto).

Collectively, the judges are meant to represent "the main forms of civilization and of the principal legal systems of the world" (Article 9). The Court is therefore legally required to consider geographic and "civilizational" diversity but it is not required to pay attention to the gender of its judges. There is no rule similar to Article 36 8(a)iii of the ICC Rome Statute to require the equitable representation of women and men among the judges, and the very eminent Rosalyn Higgins was the first female judge in the history of the Court. She served as an ICJ justice from 1995 to 2009. (A very small number of women have been ad hoc judges.) Three of the fifteen judges today are women.

The judges are meant to be international civil servants and not representatives of their home governments, reflecting the fact that their decisions are supposed to be independent of the positions taken by their national governments. The phrase in Article 2 that judges are to be chosen "regardless of their nationality" reinforces the idea of the rule of law at the ICJ, as opposed the operation of national interest and diplomacy. Yet at other points the Statute undermines itself in this respect by acknowledging the expected influence of national bias among the judges. For instance, there cannot be more than one judge of the same nationality on the Court at a time (Art. 3(1)), a rule which seems to indicate an implicit belief that judges of the same nationality are likely to reason similarly. Additionally, parties to a case who do not have a judge of their nationality among the fifteen are entitled to appoint a temporary ad hoc judge of their choosing (Art. 31). This guarantees that parties always have a judge from their country among those hearing their cases, or at least a friendly judge of another nationality (as states do not always appoint their own citizens as ad hoc judges).

In the Yerodia case discussed below, neither party had a judge among the fifteen regular justices when the case reached the Court and so Belgium appointed Christine Van den Wyengaert and Congo appointed Saye-man Bula-Bula. Bula-Bula is an international lawyer in Kinshasa, Congo, and Van den Wyengaert is a Belgian criminal lawyer who was subsequently appointed as a judge at the International Criminal Court.

In practice, ad hoc judges tend to decide in favor of the governments that appointed them, and so the votes of the two ad hoc judges tend to cancel each other out. One might say therefore that the substantive outcome of the case is not affected. However, providing explicitly for a judge from each "home team" does serious damage to the idea that ICJ cases are decided entirely on legal rather than political terms. In fact, law and politics cannot be so easily separated and the ICJ provides good evidence of the inescapable politics within the judicialization of international politics.

Obligations of States and Powers of the Court

Only a tiny fraction of international legal questions are within the jurisdiction of the International Court of Justice, and of these only a tiny fraction involve governments that are willing to see them litigated at the Court. The authority of the Court, and states' obligations toward it, are defined in the technical terms of the Statute of the ICJ.

Three elements are necessary for an international dispute to come within the jurisdiction of the ICJ. The case must involve: (i) a legal dispute which is (ii) between states who (iii) consent to the jurisdiction of the Court to that case. All three conditions must be satisfied for the Court to be allowed to hear the case. Article 34 of the ICJ Statute says that "only states may be parties in cases before the Court" and Article 36(2) says that the Court can only hear cases involving "legal disputes" regarding "the interpretation of a treaty ... [or] any question of international law ... [or] a breach of an international obligation." Military disputes, economic disputes, and political questions are not within the purview of the Court, and the Court often works hard to show that it is avoiding taking a position on any issue that comes before it that might be rightly called a "political" rather than a legal matter.

When it does take up a case that satisfies these three requirements, the ICJ has the legal authority to make final and binding interpretations of international law and therefore to issue decisions that are dispositive on states. Under the UN Charter, states commit in advance that they will accept the decisions of the Court. Article 94(1) of the Charter says "Each Member of the United Nations undertakes to comply with the decision of the International Court of Justice in any case to which it is a party." The ICJ Statute says "the judgment [of the Court] is final and without appeal" (Art. 60).

It is therefore a key legal obligation of UN members to comply with the Court's rulings in cases in which they are parties.

The Court's decisions are legally binding only on the parties to the case and only with respect to the case in question. They are not binding on other states or on the Court itself, and as a result ICJ cases do not create precedents. This is explicitly stated in Article 59 of the Statute: "The decision of the Court has no binding force except between the parties and in respect of that particular case." This is logically necessary if states are to remain sovereign and the modern system is to retain state sovereignty as its legal foundation, for if decisions of the ICJ were able to create precedents then states would find themselves bound by rules that arose from cases in which they had no part. This would contradict state sovereignty. Since cases cannot go forward without the consent of the parties then it follows that decisions cannot be binding on non-parties who never had a chance to choose whether to consent or object. More generally, the concept of consent is central to the status of the Court, and it is equally central to the larger problem of being a court among sovereign states.

States can consent to a case at the ICJ in three different ways, all defined in Article 36 of the ICJ Statute. This Article says, in part, "The jurisdiction of the Court comprises all cases which the parties might refer to it and all matters specifically provided for in the Charter of the United Nations or in treaties and conventions in force" (Art. 36(1)), and also that "states ... may ... declare that they recognize as compulsory ... the jurisdiction of the Court" (Art. 36(2)). The three paths to jurisdiction are therefore: case-by-case referral, treaty-based consent, and prior declarations of consent. Each is worth some examination.

The first path to consent is when the parties to a case explicitly refer a particular dispute to the Court for a decision. In such an instance, both (or all) parties make an explicit statement of their consent to the case going forward, usually by a letter from the foreign ministry to the registrar of the Court. This was the procedure that was followed in a boundary dispute case between Benin and Niger that began in 2002.[1] The two countries had been negotiating for years to determine the precise boundary between them, complicated by two rivers and several islands. To finally settle the matter, they agreed to request a binding decision of the Court, and this was set in motion by their joint communiqué to the registrar requesting that the Court consider the matter. This is the most "traditional" model of consent at the Court as it does the most to preserve an old-style, state-centric image of sovereignty. It guarantees that cases only exist when both sides expressly consent to it, and so it tends to minimize the number of cases that arise and the volume of controversy they contain. The substance of the case remains contentious but its path to the Court depends on this consensus between the parties.

---

[1] Frontier Dispute (Benin/Niger), ICJ July 12, 2005, www.icj-cij.org/docket/files/125/8228.pdf. Accessed January 20, 2010.

The second path to consent, also described in Article 36(1), arises when an international treaty includes a clause to the effect that disputes over the interpretation of the treaty shall automatically be heard by the ICJ. In this case, signing the treaty indicates consenting to the jurisdiction of the ICJ in future disputes over the legal meaning of the treaty. For instance, this is the case in the Vienna Convention on Consular Relations, which includes an "optional protocol" that says "Disputes arising out of the interpretation of application of the Convention shall lie within the compulsory jurisdiction of the International Court of Justice." Such clauses are common in international treaties. They are sometimes integral to the treaty (as with the 1971 Montreal Convention on air terrorism) and sometimes attached as annexes that states have the option of not signing even as they sign the main treaty (as with the Convention on Consular Relations).

It is common for states to sign treaties that include automatic ICJ jurisdiction without fully imagining the situations that this might land them in later. The treaty-based path to jurisdiction opens the possibility that cases might proceed against the wishes of one of the parties and it tends to produce cases where the respondents are at their most bitter. For instance, in the 1990s the US and UK were most unhappy to find themselves as respondents to a case in which Libya complained that its rights under the Montreal Convention on air terrorism were being violated by UN Security Council sanctions over the Lockerbie bombing.[2] Similarly, after losing a series of cases under the Consular Relations treaty (which the US was unable to stop because it had signed its optional protocol on ICJ jurisdiction), the US went so far as to withdraw its signature from the protocol in 2005 and thus shut off any future cases that might follow the same path.

The third path to consent is described in Article 36(2), and it involves making a general declaration that the state accepts the Court's jurisdiction for all future legal disputes with other states. These are called "optional clause declarations" and they create a kind of compulsory jurisdiction of the Court among the subset of states that have so far been willing to do so.[3] As of November 2016, this included seventy-two states. These declarations are usually reciprocal; that is, they accept automatic jurisdiction only when the state is in a dispute with another state that has made a matching declaration.

---

[2] See Ian Hurd, "The Strategic Use of Liberal Internationalism: Libya and the UN Sanctions 1992–2003," *International Organization*, 2005, **59**(3): 495–526.

[3] For a list of Article 36(2) declarations see www.icj-cij.org/jurisdiction/index.php?p1=5&tp2=1&p3=3. Accessed January 22, 2013.

They also frequently come with exceptions or conditions. For instance, the US accepted compulsory jurisdiction in 1946 but it modified it with a statement to the effect that it did not accept that jurisdiction for any matter essentially within the domestic sovereignty of the United States as determined by the United States. This became known as the Connally Amendment. The first part of the US reservation is uncontroversial, and indeed is redundant since Article 2(7) of the UN Charter together with Articles 36 and 38 of the ICJ Statute ensure that neither the UN nor the ICJ has any authority over domestic matters. But the second part, about the US determining for itself what is "domestic," is a striking claim. The claim that the US can decide unilaterally what is in its domestic jurisdiction empties the declaration of its key component, that being the accept- ance of something compulsory. Reservations attached to treaty signatures are generally allowable under the international laws that govern treaties; the Vienna Convention on the Law of Treaties (1969), which is the governing document for the format and rules of inter-state treaties, says that states can add reservations to the treaties they sign as long as the substance of the reservation is not "incompatible with the object and purpose of the treaty."[4] In the US case, it is debatable whether the Connally Amendment was ever legally sound since it could well be interpreted as in conflict with the "object and purpose" of the ICJ Statute. The point is now moot; the US revoked its entire optional clause declaration, including the Connally Amendment, in 1986 in the midst of the Nicaragua cases at the Court, and so it can no longer be brought before the Court under this process.[5]

Many states have made similarly self-serving reservations to their optional clause declarations. A Canadian move with respect to fishing in the North Atlantic in the 1990s is instructive in how far states might go to carefully refine their legal obligations to the Court. After decades of overfishing, the populations of groundfish in the waters off the coast of Newfoundland collapsed in the late 1980s with devastating consequences for the welfare of communities dependent on fishing. The Canadian government greatly reduced catch limits for Canadian trawlers but it could not control foreign vessels (mostly from Europe) fishing just outside the 200-mile Exclusive Economic Zone off the shore. These, it suspected, were likely to undermine any gains made by limiting Canadian fishing but since they were in international waters the Canadians could not legally control them.

---

[4] Vienna Convention on the Law of Treaties, Article 19.
[5] See US Department of State Bulletin, "US Terminates Acceptance of ICJ Compulsory Jurisdiction," January 1986.

Anticipating action against these ships, the Canadian government in 1994 unilaterally amended its Article 36(2) declaration to add a reservation excluding "disputes arising out of or concerning conservation and management measures taken by Canada with respect to vessels fishing in the NAFO [Northwest Atlantic Fisheries Organization] Regulatory Area]."[6] This limited the exposure of the Canadian government to ICJ cases.

The reservation became salient in March 1995 when Canadian officials arrested a Spanish trawler in international waters for fishing with an illegal fine-meshed net. The Spanish government complained, and sent its navy to protect its fishing fleet in the North Atlantic. The Canadians responded by authorizing its warships and air force to fire on the Spanish, in what became known as the Turbot War. In the midst of this military posturing Spain argued to the ICJ that Canada had violated international law by interfering with Spanish ships on the high seas, and used the fact that both countries had Article 36(2) declarations in effect to prove that the Court had jurisdiction.

The case might well have proceeded under Canada's original optional clause declaration, but its new and more limited revised statement caused the Court to reject the case. With its reservation, Canada effectively and unilaterally redrew the boundaries of the ICJ's jurisdiction and ensured that it could not be found to be violating international law.[7] The progress of this dispute shows how it is possible in international relations to micromanage one's legal obligations and unilaterally redefine the content of one's commitments. The double nature of international commitments is also revealed here: while the flexibility of state commitments to compulsory jurisdiction means it is relatively easy for states to avoid being found to be violating international law, the lengths to which states go to avoid such a finding shows how seriously they take their reputations as law-abiding state-citizens in the international community.

The three paths by which the Court can establish jurisdiction over a dispute between states mean that the Court's authority is limited to that subset of world politics which states are willing to grant it. In other words, there is no way that a case can go forward in the ICJ without some act of consent on the part of all the

---

[6] Canadian Optional Clause Declaration, May 1994, www.icj-cij.org/jurisdiction/index.php?p1=5&p2=1&p3=3&code=CA. Accessed July 17, 2009.

[7] Spain pressed the issue anyway, arguing that the dispute was not about fishing but about the rights of flag-states of vessels on the high seas. It lost, and the Court described itself as effectively barred from the case by the Canadian optional-clause reservation. This is the Estai case of 1995. See Terry D. Gill, *Rosenne's The World Court: What it is and How it Works*. Martinus Nijhoff, 2003.

states involved, either in advance through a treaty or an optional clause declaration or at the outset of the specific case itself. Countries can, if they wish, completely remove themselves from all ICJ jurisdiction by carefully managing their treaty obligations and other paths to consent. This is entirely acceptable under international law. The limits on Court jurisdiction represent a compromise between two views of the relationship between international organizations and state sovereignty. The compulsory jurisdiction model described in Article 36(2) reflects what might be called a "world-law" view in which states should be held to account by the community for their failures to abide by the commitments they have made to other states. The fact that this model is made optional for states reflects the competing view that states are sovereign over their affairs and that their consent to international proceedings must be freely given and can be freely withheld. The two models are contradictory ideologies of world politics and arise in different forms whenever new international organizations are debated. For the ICJ, the Statute makes clear that consent rather than obligation is the dominant theme.

There is a second vehicle for Court activity, known as "advisory opinions," for which the the legal path and impact are entirely different than the contentious cases described above. These opinions are described in Article 96 of the UN Charter and in the Statute of the ICJ in Articles 65–68. The Court can be asked its opinion "on any legal question" by the UN General Assembly or the Security Council (Art. 96(1) UN Charter).[8] The opinion that the Court then returns is "advisory" in the sense that it does not create any legally binding obligations on any state or organization, and yet it has some legal and perhaps political impact because it represents the considered judgment of the Court on that question of international law. Notice that advisory opinions are not "cases" in any legal sense and they do not have "parties" to them; the difference in language is important. Advisory opinions are not addressed to particular disputes between any states and they do not result in "decisions" or "judgments" of the Court. They are instead responses to factual questions about the content of legal obligations. A classic example is the opinion in Certain Expenses of the United Nations from 1962. This opinion was requested by the General Assembly in the midst of the Congo crisis when France and the Soviet Union objected to paying their UN dues that would support the UN peace operation in Congo, which they

[8] Other agencies can ask for advisory opinions if the General Assembly authorizes them to do so. See Terry D. Gill, *Rosenne's The World Court: What it is and How it Works.* Martinus Nijhoff, 2003, pp. 86–89.

opposed. The Assembly asked the Court whether the costs of a military mission approved by the General Assembly "constitute 'expenses of the Organization' within the meaning of Article 17, paragraph 2."[9] The context of the question was that if these were expenses of the organization then the French and Soviet objections to paying their dues would presumably be illegal under the Charter. This was therefore a legal question with a clear political subtext. In finding that these were legitimate expenses of the organization as a whole, the Court therefore implied that the objection to paying them was legally unsustainable, and it led to the political compromise in which the UN peacekeeping budget was separated from the "regular" budget.

Terry Gill has noted that it is always a political choice for a state to accept being a party to a legal case at the ICJ.[10] It is equally true that advisory opinions are as much political moves as they are legal ones. The Certain Expenses opinion shows this, and the recent advisory opinion on the Israeli wall takes it to a new extreme.

The opinion in Legal Implications of the Construction of a Wall in the Occupied Palestinian Territory followed a request by the General Assembly that the ICJ explain "the legal consequences arising from the construction of the wall being built by Israel, the Occupying Power, in the Occupied Palestinian Territory." Notwithstanding the breadth of the question and the political context in which it appeared the Court accepted the request by framing it as a specific legal question, which was: "whether that construction is or is not in breach of certain rules of international law."[11] This is the legal question that the Court identified within the broader political agenda behind the request – that a large majority of the states in the Assembly were looking for tools with which to continue their objections to the Israeli wall, and an advisory opinion looked to them like a useful resource. In the end, the Court found that the wall violated international law in several ways, including by denying basic human rights to individuals and by impeding the collective rights of the Palestinian people to self-determination. It concluded by making several forceful statements about the legal obligations that rest on Israel (inter alia, to desist from its illegal actions), on other states (to refuse to cooperate with those illegal actions), and

---

[9] Certain Expenses of the United Nations, ICJ July 20, 1962, www.icj-cij.org/docket/files/49/5259.pdf. Accessed January 20, 2010.

[10] Terry D. Gill, *Rosenne's The World Court: What it is and How it Works*. Martinus Nijhoff, 2003, p. 68.

[11] ICJ advisory opinion 2004, p. 4. www.icj-cij.org/docket/files/131/1677.pdf. Accessed September 1, 2009.

on the Security Council and General Assembly at the UN (to consider what actions to take to remedy the violations).

These conclusions make the opinion very interesting in the history of ICJ law, since advisory opinions are generally understood as vehicles for clarifying the law; they are not contentious cases and cannot create new legal obligations. The wording of the Israeli wall opinion is careful not to overstep this line, but by finding that a state is clearly violating the law and by recommending remedies against it, the opinion has legal and political consequences for all states that go beyond what is traditionally expected of an advisory opinion.

States may therefore find themselves with obligations to the ICJ that are subtle and more political than might be obvious from the basic legal structure of the Statute. This is, of course, also true of all other international organizations: an international treaty is successful only when its legal obligations change the context for the political decisions of states. States are formally obligated under the ICJ Statute only in very limited ways, notably to carry out ICJ decisions to which they are parties and to consent to cases when they so choose. And yet this does not exhaust the means by which the Court has influence in world politics, and states may feel a social or political obligation to respond to matters that arise at the Court even if these do not rise to the level of a formal legal obligation.

Compliance

The Court's decisions in contentious cases have a good record of compliance.[12] In most instances where the Court makes demands of a losing party in a case that party does indeed change its behavior in line with the demand. In the Yerodia case discussed below, for instance, Belgium voluntarily changed its domestic laws in ways that satisfied the Court that the policies which had violated Congo's rights were rectified. This is the typical result in contentious cases.

In many ways, the rate of compliance may be less interesting than the reasons for compliance, and of course the reasons are much harder to discern. We might

---

[12] See Nagendra Singh, *The Role and Record of the International Court of Justice*. Springer, 1989. Also, Constanze Schulte, *Compliance with the Decisions of the International Court of Justice*. Oxford University Press, 2004.

expect a high rate of compliance because we know that every case that reaches the point of having a decision rendered has been consented to by both parties, and so we can probably assume that the states have decided in advance that they are reconciled to the possibility of an adverse judgment. In this case, the act of compliance reflects a prior decision by the state that it would not particularly mind changing its behavior. However, as states invest heavily in arguing their sides before the Court, they are clearly not indifferent between winning and losing, and so the decisions of the losing side are worth investigating. It is often difficult to interpret state behavior with respect to ICJ cases, and so deciding whether a state has complied or not with a judgment is sometimes a matter of interpretation. For instance, losing states may change their policies in line with the judgment of the Court but deny that the Court decision had any bearing on their decision; the ICJ found that Iran's seizure of the US embassy in 1979 violated international laws on diplomatic and consular relations, but the subsequent release of the embassy and hostages cannot count unambiguously as "compliance" with the judgment – it is impossible to assess the contribution of the Court's decision on the ultimate resolution of the crisis, even though the outcome was generally consistent with the decision. In another case, Constanze Schulte discusses the Corfu Channel dispute of 1949, where compliance is equally hard to measure but for different reasons: the case arose in 1946 when Albanian mines sank two British ships which had traveled uninvited into Albanian waters. The ICJ found, in 1949, that Albania was responsible for the damage and ordered it to pay reparations. Albania refused, and the matter remained open until a deal was worked out in 1992 under which Albania paid a sum to the UK in 1996. The case can be coded as "compliance," but with fifty years passing between judgment and compliance it is difficult to see it as an unmitigated success for the Court.[13] The ICJ's effectiveness is very hard to assess in a rigorous fashion but this does not mean it can be generally dismissed: it must be understood in the broader context of each case that it takes on.

In assessing compliance, it is worth repeating that contentious cases do not create obligations on states that are not parties to the dispute, and so compliance exists only for the states directly involved. From the point of view of state compliance with the ICJ, this leads to the important corollary that states do not have any obligation to comply with decisions in cases to which they were not parties, no matter how relevant the case might seem to their own situation. This

---

[13] The case is well told in Constanze Schulte, *Compliance with Decisions of the International Court of Justice.* Oxford University Press, 2004, pp. 91–99.

rule is essential to preserving state sovereignty at the Court since it ensures that states do not take on new legal obligations based on decisions in cases in which they did not participate. It does create an odd situation, however, as the Court looks into the international legal environment for clues as to what the law is on a given question. It can be informed by its own past decisions but it cannot refer to them as precedents. Each case is meant to be its own self-contained bundle of law containing a legal dispute, two parties, a set of laws, and a decision that creates obligations on the parties.

Compliance with the ICJ raises a further puzzle for students of international relations: since the Court has essentially no coercive tools to enforce its decisions (as we shall see below), and by definition the losing state would prefer to continue with its status quo policy rather than change it, it is not clear why a Court decision has sufficient compelling power to cause a change in state behavior. The tension between sovereignty and compliance, which is inherent in the effort to apply the rule of law to relations among sovereign states, motivates the search for the causal mechanism that brings losing states to modify their policies in line with the Court. This tension is both conceptual and empirical – that is, it is evident both in trying to explain the distribution of powers and authority between the ICJ and states, and in trying to account for the ICJ's practical effects in world politics. On both fronts, the question remains: What does the ICJ add to inter-state disputes that causes states to be willing to change their policies after losing the case when they were so unwilling before that they fought against it at the Court? This is a big question that deserves much more research.

States are generally worse at complying with "provisional measures" of the Court than they are at complying with its final judgments in cases. These are demands made by the Court ahead of deciding the case, which the Court issues in order to stop the parties from making the situation worse as the case proceeds. They are akin to interim orders and restraining orders in some domestic legal systems. States are obligated to comply with provisional orders of the Court under Article 41 of the Statute, though there is some controversy over this. The Article says "the Court shall have the power to indicate ... any provisional measures which ought to be taken to preserve the respective rights of either party" (Art. 41).[14] To do so, the Court issues an order indicating what the state

---

[14] The Law of the Sea treaty (1982) contains a much stronger regime of provisional measures than that in the ICJ Statute. See Shabtai Rosenne, *Provisional Measures in International Law: The International Court of Justice and the International Tribunal for the Law of the Sea.* Oxford University Press, 2005.

must do, or refrain from doing, in order to preserve the rights of the parties as the case makes its way through the ICJ process. In making such an order, the Court is responding to the request of one of the parties for protection against further deterioration in the situation during the course of the case. For instance, in a series of cases in the 1990s and 2000s in which countries complained that their citizens were being sent to death row in the US without being informed of their rights to assistance from their consulates, the complaining countries requested that the ICJ order that the US not execute those people until the cases had been fully heard. The Court agreed, and indicated provisional measures orders under Article 41 that the US refrain from carrying out the executions. The US, in the Breard and LaGrand cases, did not comply with these measures, and the individuals were executed by state authorities while the cases were still at the ICJ. The US federal government did issue formal apologies to the countries involved after these cases, even though the US states involved maintained that they were not bound by the commitments that the federal government had made under the ICJ statute and the Vienna Convention on Consular Relations.[15]

In addition to illustrating non-compliance with provisional measures, these death penalty cases are interesting for showing both the power and the limits of ICJ authority relative to member states. They show, among other things, the problems posed in international law by federal constitutions, in which federal governments are generally empowered to make all decisions regarding what treaties to sign and what international agreements to undertake on all subjects, but state governments are often sovereign over many of these subjects with respect to domestic law and policy. Thus, in the Vienna Convention on Consular Relations, the US federal government commits itself to certain treatment of foreigners arrested in the US, but most of the cases where these rules apply are entirely within the jurisdiction of US states and the federal government is expressly excluded by the US Constitution. While international law clearly forbids states from using their domestic laws to overrule their international obligations, the complications of federal systems give plenty of room for controversy in practice over how states take on and comply with legal obligations to other states.

The LaGrand case raises the question of whether orders of provisional measures are binding. This is important when assessing compliance with the

---

[15] On the controversies over provisional measures in these cases, see Jörg Kammerhofer, "The Binding Nature of Provisional Measures of the International Court of Justice: The 'Settlement' of the Issue in the LaGrand Case," *Leiden Journal of International Law*, 2003 **16**: 67–83.

Court, since only if these orders are compulsory can ignoring them be considered an act of non-compliance. Article 41 says nothing about the legal status of provisional measures but it would seem logically necessary that they be legally binding or else they would be irrelevant to the progress of the case. International practice has always treated them as binding, including with respect to the US hostages in Iran in 1979 and a 1951 dispute in which the Security Council considered Iran's non-compliance with provisional measures.[16] However, the US in 1998 argued that the words of Article 41 were "precatory rather than mandatory" in a US Supreme Court case related to the execution of foreign nationals, and other states have from time to time made similar claims.[17] This position has not been widely accepted, and so the general practice seems to suggest that states believe that they are obligated to comply with ICJ orders for provisional measures.

Enforcement

The beginning and the end of formal enforcement powers of the ICJ are contained in Article 94(2) of the United Nations Charter. This article has only been invoked once in the history of the Court, but its existence is interesting for both legal and political reasons.

Article 94(2) says that "If any party to a case fails to perform the obligations incumbent upon it under a judgment rendered by the Court, the other party may have recourse to the Security Council, which may, if it deems necessary, make recommendations or decide upon measures to be taken to give effect to the judgment." This piggy-backing of the ICJ on the Security Council reflects the fact that in the drafting of the United Nations in 1945 its framers saw the Council as the enforcement arm of the UN's legal complex, where the ICJ would decide on the legal merits of a dispute and the Council might use force to ensure compliance. However, there is a huge gulf between asking the Council to look into a matter and seeing real enforcement action, a gulf that is legal, conceptual, and political all at once. A request to the Council does not imply any obligation

[16] Jeremy B. Elkind, *Interim Protection: A Functional Approach*. Kluwer Law, 1981, p. 160.
[17] US Amicus Curiae, in *Breard v. Greene*, US Supreme Court 523 US 371, p. 51. Cited in Robert D. Sloane, "Measures Necessary to Ensure: The ICJ's Provisional Measures Order in Avena and Other Mexican Nationals," *Leiden Journal of International Law*, 2004, 17: 678.

on the Council to give the matter serious consideration, let alone take any action, and so whatever problem goes to the Council via Article 94 simply joins all the other issues that the Council might take up, and the decision to do anything about it becomes a question of the political priorities of the Council's members – perhaps they want to take it up, but perhaps not, and the ICJ has no special power to influence that decision.

The Article 94(2) procedure has been used only once. This was in the aftermath of the 1986 case by Nicaragua against the United States. Nicaragua won the judgment against the US on the grounds that American support for the anti-government Contra militia was an illegal form of aggression, in contravention of customary international law and a specific US–Nicaragua treaty of friendship. The US boycotted the substantive portion of the case after it failed to convince the justices that the Court lacked jurisdiction. The US did however get some of its arguments in defense in front of the judges in the form of memos and papers from the US State Department which the Court considered.[18] The Court ordered that the US cease the behavior at issue in the case and left for a future decision the question of reparations for damages as sought by Nicaragua. Despite its continued belief that the case should not have proceeded beyond the jurisdiction phase, the US found itself legally obligated to comply with the decision of the Court because of the obligation on all UN members to comply with ICJ decisions of which they are a part (Art. 94(1) of the UN Charter). When it failed to do so to the satisfaction of Nicaragua, Nicaragua invoked Article 94(2) and requested that the Security Council demand American compliance with its obligations. A draft resolution was circulated in the Council which called "for full and immediate compliance with the judgment of the ICJ." The US used its veto in the Council to defeat it.[19] Nicaragua went on to the UN General Assembly, using Article 10 of the Charter, and the GA passed a series of resolutions urging the US to comply. The US maneuver at the Council relied on its veto power to avoid a resolution that would enforce the ICJ's decision. This ended the international legal process for Nicaragua at an unhappy point. However, the ICJ's decision by itself was sufficient to establish the fact of law-breaking by the US, and this may carry some implications in the more informal processes of international politics, where reputation, face-saving, and diplomacy work in unknowable ways.

[18] Constanze Schulte, *Compliance with Decisions of the International Court of Justice*. Oxford University Press, 2004, p. 193.

[19] Cited in Bruno Simma et al., *The Charter of the United Nations: A Commentary*. Oxford University Press, 1994, p. 1006.

The case therefore represents an instance of the clash between the power politics interests of a strong state and the obligations of the rule of law in international affairs. These instances arise less often than is sometimes supposed, but this episode is one glaring example.

In the absence of stronger enforcement power, the Court relies for its effect on either (or both) (i) the losing party recognizing that self-motivated compliance is in its long-term interest, or (ii) other states and institutions finding ways to pressure the state into complying. Both are motivations that go far beyond the Court's own effort to deal only in international legal matters and to avoid international politics, and they reflect how the distinction between international law and international politics is unsustainable in practice. The Court is a player in the games of international political legitimation, whether one likes it or not, and its capacity to confer and withhold legitimation on states and their behavior may be its real source of power and influence.

CASE I: *Yerodia* or *Belgium v. Congo*

The mechanics of the ICJ are well illustrated by the case of *Belgium v. Congo*, which began in 2000. This case, also known as the Yerodia case, rested on a complaint by Congo that a Belgian attempt to arrest the former Congolese foreign minister for genocide amounted to a violation of Congo's sovereignty.

The Yerodia case was part of the long and still-continuing echo of the Rwandan genocide, in the same sense that the Genocide Convention of 1948 and all its subsequent applications are part of the long echo of the Nazi Holocaust. In Rwanda in 1994, before the genocide, Belgium was a significant troop-contributing country to the UN mission known as the UN Mission in Rwanda (UNAMIR). This was a peacekeeping mission in the sense described in Chapter 4, and its legal mandate was to monitor compliance with a reconciliation plan between the Rwandan government and an anti-government rebel army. When the genocide began, the Belgian soldiers and the rest of the UN mission were legally and logistically barred from intervening directly to save civilians, and when the genocidaires killed ten Belgian soldiers, the Belgian government reacted by removing all its troops from the country. The logic behind the decision was this: since these remaining soldiers were not allowed to intervene to help stop the genocide, they were serving no useful function that would justify their presence in the face of such great personal danger. The practical effect of the decision, however, was to further abandon the people of

Rwanda to the killers, and to signal to killers and victims alike that in response to the genocide the international community was moving out of the country rather than moving in. Belgium was far from alone among troop-contributing countries in making this choice, but it became later a source of national shame in Belgian politics and led to a serious effort to rework national law and practice in order to ensure that the country was supporting, rather than undermining, international human rights for future cases.

One result was a renewed effort to use Belgian courts to pursue war criminals and genocidists from around the world, taking advantage of a 1993 Belgian law that allowed Belgium to prosecute people suspected of the worst crimes regardless of whether there was any connection to Belgium. This law was at the time the broadest application in any country of the principle of "universal jurisdiction," that is, the idea that some crimes are so serious that every country has automatic jurisdiction over them. The Belgian law provided a useful vehicle for a legal and political rehabilitation of Belgium's tarnished international reputation after the fiasco of the Rwandan withdrawal. A series of cases were begun against perpetrators of the Rwandan genocide, marking a milestone in the history of international human rights law, filling the institutional gap that had always existed for international crimes by inserting Belgian courts into the breach. The cases resulted in convictions of four Rwandan genocidaires in 2001.

The Yerodia case centered on this law, and its application in another African genocide. Abdoulaye Yerodia Ndombasi, Congo's foreign minister, was thought to have encouraged people to commit genocide in speeches he made in 1998. He called on his audiences to massacre Tutsi people in Congo. Because of his position within the government of Congo, it was unlikely that this conduct would generate criminal investigation in Congo. A group of Belgian citizens took up the issue and presented it to Belgian courts under the 1993 law on universal jurisdiction. Following a judicial investigation, a Belgian judge was convinced there was sufficient evidence of crimes by Yerodia, and he issued a warrant for his arrest.[20] The warrant was transmitted through Interpol, and in so being it became executable in all Interpol member countries.[21] If Yerodia were found in any of those countries, he must be arrested and subject to extradition for trial in Belgium.

---

[20] Alberto-Luis Zuppi, "Immunity vs. Universal Jurisdiction: The Yerodia Ndombasi Decision of the International Court of Justice," *Louisiana Law Review*, 2003, 63(2): 309–339.

[21] Interpol is the international organization that links the national police forces of member countries. Its formal name is the International Criminal Police Organization.

The government of Congo complained to the ICJ that Belgium had violated the rights of Congo as a sovereign state. The submission had two main elements: that Belgium's claim to prosecute crimes of universal jurisdiction was an illegal usurpation of authority, contravening the laws of sovereignty that protect countries from outside interference; and that Belgium was ignoring the rules of sovereign immunity by seeking to arrest someone for actions taken while serving as a member of the government. The first was a direct challenge to Belgium's drive to implement the idea of universal jurisdiction through its national judicial institutions. The second was a more traditional argument about the protections owed by one government to members and diplomats of other governments. In relation to both parts of Congo's claim, it is important to notice that the case had to do entirely with obligations owed by Belgium as a country to Congo as a country. It was not really a case about international human rights or genocide, nor was it about what Yerodia had or had not done. Indeed, Yerodia as an individual was quite irrelevant to the legal issues in the dispute; as a matter of law, he served as a vehicle by which Congo asserted that Belgium had harmed Congo's rights. Instead, the case was constructed out of arguments over how much Belgium could interfere with activities going on in Congo, or with the travels of Congolese officials (and former officials) in other countries. This is crucially important for the jurisdiction of the ICJ since, as we have seen above, the Court can only hear cases that involve legal disputes between states (under Articles 34 and 36). Congo's case was organized as a two-pronged complaint that its rights as a sovereign state were being violated by Belgium. As it happened, Congo eventually withdrew the section of its complaint dealing with universal jurisdiction, and so the final act of the drama centered entirely on the question of immunity for foreign ministers and other officials.

The decision of the Court in the Yerodia case is reproduced as Appendix 8.B at the end of this chapter. The judges, by large majorities, sustained the case presented by Congo and ruled that by issuing the arrest warrant Belgium had violated the rights of Congo by not respecting the traditional rule that gives foreign ministers immunity from criminal jurisdiction while traveling the world. They could not find a formal treaty that governed the subject, and so they made their judgment about the law based on the long-established practice of states in which this kind of jurisdictional immunity seemed to be recognized. The Court rejected Belgium's arguments that recent developments in international criminal law had changed this practice and taken away this official immunity for cases involving the most serious of international crimes such as genocide and crimes against humanity. Some of its reasoning can be seen in the excerpt in Appendix 8.B.

The decision helps to show how the Court approaches the job of interpreting international law. Article 38(1) says that in making its judgments, the Court "shall apply:

a) international conventions, whether general or particular, establishing rules expressly recognized by states;
b) international custom, as evidence of a general practice accepted as law;
c) the general principles of law recognized by civilized nations;
d) . . . judicial decisions and the teachings of the most highly qualified publicists of the various nations"

This list is often referred to as the "sources of law" for the ICJ, and it is organized hierarchically. In other words, in assessing what is the law on a particular question the Court begins with "a)" and moves down the list only if it cannot find a complete answer. Treaties, covered under "international conventions," are considered the strongest evidence for the existence of a rule of international law because they involve explicit consent by states to be bound by some explicit rule. Failing that, as happened in the Yerodia case, the Court can look to see if there is long-established practice that has the force of law. Where this exists, the Court decides that "customary law" exists and rules accordingly, as it did in *Yerodia*. Where neither treaty law nor customary law can be found, the Court can look for evidence of law by extrapolating from concepts that exist in the national legal systems of a range of member states (Art. 38(1)c) or by inquiring into the writings of legal scholars and others (Art. 38(1)d). These last two are not particularly compelling to the Court and they are not often used. The "general principles of law" in Article 38(1)c might include concepts such as equity (i.e. one cannot complain about behavior that one is also doing oneself) and estoppel (one cannot, among other things, present two contradictory interpretations of the same basic facts).

Several features of the Yerodia case illuminate important aspects of the power and authority of the ICJ. First, consider that the Belgian law on universal jurisdiction included an explicit provision that "[i]mmunity attaching to official capacity of a person shall not prevent the application of the present Law."[22] This

---

[22] Cited in ICJ case, p. 10.

was meant specifically to ensure that government officials would not be able to claim sovereign or diplomatic immunity in the way Congo did for Yerodia, and so it might be thought to be relevant to the ICJ's consideration of the matter. It was not. The authority of the ICJ, as we have seen, lies in interpreting international rather than domestic law. It found that there was a customary law among states that forbade the arrest of government ministers in this fashion, and the fact that Belgium had claimed to itself the right to do so was not compelling evidence of a general change in customary law more widely. Thus, Belgium could not unilaterally change the rules of international law simply by passing domestic laws that contradicted them.

A second interesting feature of the case is that it concerned whether a wrong had been done to Congo by Belgium. It did not concern Yerodia as a person, either in his alleged conduct or his rights as an individual. The case was about the rights and obligations owed by one country to another, as are all cases at the ICJ. The conclusion of the Court's judgment was that "the issue against Abdu-laye Yerodia Ndombasi of the arrest warrant of 11 April 2000, and its international circulation, constituted violations of a legal obligation of the Kingdom of Belgium towards the Democratic Republic of the Congo."[23] This language of inter-state obligations is important because it reflects the basic facts of the Court's jurisdiction in Articles 34 and 36: the Court is open only to cases of legal disputes between states. The Court must refuse to accept any case that does not fit this frame, no matter how important are the issues at stake in it. The Yerodia case was therefore not essentially about the law of international human rights, or with genocide and war crimes in Congo. It was understood by the ICJ to be about the rules of international diplomacy that states have agreed to, implicitly or explicitly, among themselves. The ruling is about where states have customarily drawn the line that divides the jurisdiction of one country's courts from that of another's courts. However, as a consequence of understanding where that line lies between Congo and Belgium, the Court's decisions had the substantive effect of broadening the privileged domain of immunity from accountability on which the organizers of mass killing depend. The Court rarely deals with human rights issues but in this case it may have dealt a setback to the development of institutional devices for defending human rights through national and international law.

---

[23] ICJ press release February 14, 2002.

CASE II: The Whaling Case – *Australia v. Japan*

A remarkable ICJ case ended in 2014 when the ICJ ordered that the Japanese government stop hunting whales in the Southern Ocean.

The case centered on the rules contained in the International Convention on the Regulation of Whaling (ICRW), the treaty that sets quotas on killing whales for commercial purposes in order to prevent their extinction. Both Australia and Japan are signatories to the ICRW. In the early 1980s anti-whaling activists convinced a majority of ICRW countries to set the quota at zero, so that in effect there would be a moratorium on the commercial whale hunt until the ICRW decided otherwise. Whale hunting was considerably reduced by this measure and many whale populations rebounded as a result. The ICRW, which had been essentially the charter for a club of like-minded whale-hunting countries, had been transformed into a document that pro-hibited whale hunting – at least for some species, in some places, and for some countries.[24]

Japan was among the minority of ICRW members that opposed the mora-torium in 1982 and opposed the Southern Ocean Whale Sanctuary that was created in 1994. It wanted to continue whale hunting: whale meat was widely available in Japan and whale hunting was the economic heart of several fishing communities. The whaling treaty contains several clauses designed to accommodate differences of opinion among the members. Japan made use of several of these. The first is a provision that allows members individually to refuse to accept amendments to the rules, including changes to the quota. Article V(3) states that changes to the rules will not apply to governments that formally protest within 90 days of the change, and that renew their objection every 90 days thereafter. As a kind of protection against the tyranny of the majority, it either enhances or detracts from the democratic decision-making of the organization depending on how one looks at it. It allows the majority to go ahead with changes that they collectively agree upon and prevents the minority from either preventing those changes or being bound by them. Japan, Norway, and Iceland made these objections in 1986, which allowed them to continue under the quotas that existed before the moratorium. The new rules did not apply to them. Under pressure from

---

[24] Not all whale species or whale hunts are covered by the ICRW so some whaling continued despite the moratorium.

the US government, Japan abandoned its objection in 1988. (Norway and Iceland continue their objection.)

The ICJ case however arose in light of what Japan did next. It reorganized its whaling fleet under the auspices of a government-sponsored research institute (the Institute for Cetacean Research) which was empowered to issue permits for scientific research involving whales – it had previously used this institution in a more limited way. This nominally ended "commercial" whaling and inaugurated "research" whaling. The motivation here was legal: Article 8 of the ICRW creates separate legal rules for commercial whaling, aboriginal subsistence whaling, and whaling for scientific research purposes. The first of these is governed by the quota system described above but the latter two are left up to individual governments. Article VIII(1) says in part "Notwithstanding anything contained in this Convention any Contracting Government may grant to any of its nationals a special permit authorizing that national to kill, take and treat whales for purposes of scientific research subject to such conditions as the Contracting Government thinks fit." By designating its whaling as "scientific" and requiring its whalers to apply for these permits, Japan asserted that it was complying with the ICRW while continuing to hunt whales in ways prohibited by the moratorium and the Southern Ocean sanctuary.

In 2010, the government of Australia sought to advance whale conversation and to that end it complained to the ICJ that Japan was violating its obligations under the ICRW. Since both countries had previously accepted the compulsory jurisdiction of the Court under Article 36(2), the case went forward despite Japan's objection.

The core question before the Court was whether Japan's scientific whaling program was permitted under the ICRW. The judges interpreted this in a broad way as a question about "science" itself and set about to determine whether Japan's program was genuinely about scientific research or whether it was a commercial program in disguise. The former would be unlawful while the latter would be lawful. Japan argued for a more limited interpretation of the question as being about whether Japan had satisfied the formal language of Article VIII that required the government to issue permits. It argued – and lost – that the *content* of those permits was up to the government to decide and not reviewable by the ICJ or other parties to the ICRW.

The ICJ judges therefore set an interestingly difficult task for themselves: to decide whether what Japan was doing was "science" or not. They found themselves therefore on terrain more commonly traveled by philosophers of science, wondering about the role of hypothesis testing, data gathering, peer review, replicability, and other endlessly contested concepts and practices that factor into debates about "science." They concluded that Japan's program was not genuine science as intended by Article VIII and that instead it was an illegal attempt to disguise commercial whaling behind scientific language. The decision, *Whaling in the Antarctic (Australia v. Japan: New Zealand Intervening)* (2014), was a victory for Australia and anti-whaling activists who had sought to use these legal instruments and institutions to raise the political costs to Japan of its support for whaling.

In the years after 2014, the government of Japan has continued to support whale hunting in the Antarctic with a redesigned scientific-permit system that applies higher standards for evidence, data, and other markers of "scientific" practice.

The Yerodia and whaling cases shows how hot disputes in international relations can be redefined as legal disputes for the purposes of ICJ jurisdiction. They also show how the Court searches the international system for relevant resources, both legal resources under Article 38(1) and also broader more overtly "political" or social resources with which to make its decisions. These are used to answer the specific legal question at hand in the dispute, and also contribute to wide-scope flow of international politics by shaping what people and states fight over, what resources they can use, and who can claim the legitimating power of international legality in defense of their own positions.

The legal mechanisms at work in the Court are easily understood from the Statute; what gives the Court its intriguing character is that these mechanisms and disputes are inevitably set within the broader political context of international affairs where the Court's informal influence can be, in different contexts, both greater and less than its "merely" formal legal authority.

Conclusion

The International Court of Justice is an important element in the legal architecture of international relations. It fulfills the role of an institution that gives definitive judgments in legal disputes among countries. It has considerable authority in that its decisions are final and binding on states: there are no means for appeal, and states commit in advance to accepting whatever result the Court produces. These give the decisions of the Court a status in international law that supersedes the choices of governments. But its authority is sharply limited by the fact that it only has jurisdiction over disputes in which all parties consent to its involvement. It is worth debating whether these two facts together make the Court very powerful or very weak as compared to states.

The decisions and advisory opinions of the Court are influential in world politics for both legal and political reasons. The legal reasons are evident in the formal powers discussed above. Its political influence is subtle but at least as important as its formal legal powers. States treat the ICJ as a powerful actor in world politics, and in so doing they help to give it that power. The Court's judgments are important sources of political legitimation and delegitimation, and states use them to reinforce their own positions and undermine those of their opponents. This capacity to legitimize state behavior means that the Court's influence cannot be entirely captured with a description of its formal, legal authority. The Court's position in world politics is broader than its position in international law. A full accounting of the influence of the Court must recognize both its considerable, though circumscribed, legal authority as defined in the Statute and also the subtle influence that comes from its political utility in the practice of foreign policy.

Further Reading

An excellent introduction to the ICJ is Terry D. Gill, *Rosenne's The World Court: What it is and How it Works* (Martinus Nijhoff, 2003). It describes the legal framework of the Court's authority and also provides useful short summaries of all the contentious cases to date. Also excellent is Constanze Schulte, *Compliance with Decisions of the International Court of Justice* (Oxford University Press, 2004). Nagendera Singh, who was a justice at the Court for many years, and its President, has written many works that combine a legal with an insider perspective. See for instance *The Role and Record of the International Court of Justice* (Springer, 1989).

The ICJ's excellent website (www.icj-cij-org) has a comprehensive database of cases, opinions, and materials. For analysis of international legal themes and cases, especially on current developments, see the excellent resources of the American Society of International Law (www.asil.org) and the European Society of International Law (www.esil-sedi.edu) and their many print and online publications.

APPENDIX 8.A
Statute of the International Court of Justice (1949)

Article 1

The International Court of Justice established by the Charter of the United Nations as the principal judicial organ of the United Nations shall be constituted and shall function in accordance with the provisions of the present Statute.

Chapter I: Organization of the Court

Article 2

The Court shall be composed of a body of independent judges, elected regardless of their nationality from among persons of high moral character, who possess the qualifications required in their respective countries for appointment to the highest judicial offices, or are jurisconsults of recognized competence in international law.

Article 3

1. The Court shall consist of fifteen members, no two of whom may be nationals of the same state.

. . .

Article 4

1. The members of the Court shall be elected by the General Assembly and by the Security Council from a list of persons nominated by the national groups in the Permanent Court of Arbitration, in accordance with the following provisions.

. . .

Article 9

At every election, the electors shall bear in mind not only that the persons to be elected should individually possess the qualifications required, but also that in the body as a whole the representation of the main forms of civilization and of the principal legal systems of the world should be assured.

. . .

Article 17

1. No member of the Court may act as agent, counsel, or advocate in any case.
2. No member may participate in the decision of any case in which he has previously taken part as agent, counsel, or advocate for one of the parties, or as a member of a national or international court, or of a commission of enquiry, or in any other capacity.

. . .

Article 18

1. No member of the Court can be dismissed unless, in the unanimous opinion of the other members, he has ceased to fulfill the required conditions.

. . .

Article 31

1. Judges of the nationality of each of the parties shall retain their right to sit in the case before the Court.
2. If the Court includes upon the Bench a judge of the nationality of one of the parties, any other party may choose a person to sit as judge. Such person shall be chosen preferably from among those persons who have been nominated as candidates as provided in Articles 4 and 5.
3. If the Court includes upon the Bench no judge of the nationality of the parties, each of these parties may proceed to choose a judge as provided in paragraph 2 of this Article.

. . .

Article 33

The expenses of the Court shall be borne by the United Nations in such a manner as shall be decided by the General Assembly.

Chapter II: Competence of the Court

Article 34

1. Only states may be parties in cases before the Court.

. . .

Article 35

1. The Court shall be open to the states parties to the present Statute.

. . .

Article 36

1. The jurisdiction of the Court comprises all cases which the parties refer to it and all matters specially provided for in the Charter of the United Nations or in treaties and conventions in force.
2. The states parties to the present Statute may at any time declare that they recognize as compulsory ipso facto and without special agreement, in relation to any other state accepting the same obligation, the jurisdiction of the Court in all legal disputes concerning:
   a. the interpretation of a treaty;
   b. any question of international law;
   c. the existence of any fact which, if established, would constitute a breach of an international obligation;
   d. the nature or extent of the reparation to be made for the breach of an international obligation.
3. The declarations referred to above may be made unconditionally or on condition of reciprocity on the part of several or certain states, or for a certain time.
4. Such declarations shall be deposited with the Secretary-General of the United Nations, who shall transmit copies thereof to the parties to the Statute and to the Registrar of the Court.

. . .

Article 38

1. The Court, whose function is to decide in accordance with international law such disputes as are submitted to it, shall apply:
   a. international conventions, whether general or particular, establishing rules expressly recognized by the contesting states;
   b. international custom, as evidence of a general practice accepted as law;
   c. the general principles of law recognized by civilized nations;
   d. subject to the provisions of Article 59, judicial decisions and the teachings of the most highly qualified publicists of the various nations, as subsidiary means for the determination of rules of law.
2. This provision shall not prejudice the power of the Court to decide a case ex aequo et bono, if the parties agree thereto.

Chapter III: Procedure

Article 39

1. The official languages of the Court shall be French and English. If the parties agree that the case shall be conducted in French, the judgment shall be delivered in French. If the parties agree that the case shall be conducted in English, the judgment shall be delivered in English.
2. In the absence of an agreement as to which language shall be employed, each party may, in the pleadings, use the language which it prefers; the decision of the Court shall be given in French and English. In this case the Court shall at the same time determine which of the two texts shall be considered as authoritative.
3. The Court shall, at the request of any party, authorize a language other than French or English to be used by that party.

. . .

Article 41

1. The Court shall have the power to indicate, if it considers that circumstances so require, any provisional measures which ought to be taken to preserve the respective rights of either party.
2. Pending the final decision, notice of the measures suggested shall forthwith be given to the parties and to the Security Council.

. . .

Article 53

1. Whenever one of the parties does not appear before the Court, or fails to defend its case, the other party may call upon the Court to decide in favour of its claim.
2. The Court must, before doing so, satisfy itself, not only that it has jurisdiction in accordance with Articles 36 and 37, but also that the claim is well founded in fact and law.

. . .

Article 55

1. All questions shall be decided by a majority of the judges present.
2. In the event of an equality of votes, the President or the judge who acts in his place shall have a casting vote.

Article 56

1. The judgment shall state the reasons on which it is based.
2. It shall contain the names of the judges who have taken part in the decision.

Article 57

If the judgment does not represent in whole or in part the unanimous opinion of the judges, any judge shall be entitled to deliver a separate opinion.

Article 58

The judgment shall be signed by the President and by the Registrar. It shall be read in open court, due notice having been given to the agents.

Article 59

The decision of the Court has no binding force except between the parties and in respect of that particular case.

Article 60

The judgment is final and without appeal. In the event of dispute as to the meaning or scope of the judgment, the Court shall construe it upon the request of any party.

Chapter IV: Advisory opinions

Article 65

1. The Court may give an advisory opinion on any legal question at the request of whatever body may be authorized by or in accordance with the Charter of the United Nations to make such a request.

   . . .

Article 67

The Court shall deliver its advisory opinions in open court, notice having been given to the Secretary-General and to the representatives of Members of the United Nations, of other states and of international organizations immediately concerned.

APPENDIX 8.B
ICJ Decision, press release (excerpts)

Arrest Warrant of 11 April 2000

(*Democratic Republic of the Congo v. Belgium*)

The Court finds that the issue and international circulation by Belgium of the arrest warrant of 11 April 2000 against Mr. Abdulaye Yerodia Ndombasi failed to respect the immunity from criminal jurisdiction and the inviolability which the incumbent Minister for Foreign Affairs of the Congo enjoyed under international law; and that Belgium must cancel the arrest warrant.

The Hague, 14 February 2002

Today the International Court of Justice (ICJ), principal judicial organ of the United Nations, delivered its Judgment in the case concerning the Arrest Warrant of 11 April 2000 (*Democratic Republic of the Congo v. Belgium*).

In its Judgment, which is final, without appeal and binding for the Parties, the Court found, by thirteen votes to three,

> "that the issue against Mr. Abdulaye Yerodia Ndombasi of the arrest warrant of 11 April 2000, and its international circulation, constituted violations of a legal obligation of the Kingdom of Belgium towards the Democratic Republic of the Congo, in that they failed to respect the immunity from criminal jurisdiction and the inviolability which the incumbent Minister for Foreign Affairs of the Democratic Republic of the Congo enjoyed under international law"

and, by ten votes to six,

> "that the Kingdom of Belgium must, by means of its own choosing, cancel the arrest warrant of 11 April 2000 and so inform the authorities to whom that warrant was circulated."

The Court reached these findings after having found, by 15 votes to 1, that it had jurisdiction, that the Application of the Democratic Republic of the Congo ("the Congo") was not without object (and the case accordingly not moot) and that the Application was admissible, thus rejecting the objections which the Kingdom of Belgium ("Belgium") had raised on those questions.

The Reasoning of the Court

Jurisdiction and Admissibility

The Court first rejects certain objections of Belgium based on the fact that Mr. Yerodia was no longer the Minister for Foreign Affairs, or even a member of the Government of the Congo, at the time that the Court was dealing with the case.

With regard to the Court's jurisdiction, Belgium argues that there no longer exists a "legal dispute" between the Parties within the meaning of the declarations filed by them pursuant to Article 36(2) of the Statute, and that, therefore, the Court lacks jurisdiction. On this point, the Court recalls that its jurisdiction must be determined at the time of the institution of the proceedings, and that at that time there was clearly "a legal dispute between . . . [the parties] concerning the international lawfulness of the arrest warrant of 11 April 2000 and the consequences to be drawn if the warrant was unlawful". The Court accordingly rejects the first Belgian objection.

Merits

The Court then observes that in the present case it is only the immunity from criminal jurisdiction and the inviolability of an incumbent Minister for Foreign Affairs which it has to consider. Having referred to certain treaties which were cited by the Parties in this regard, and having concluded that they do not define the immunities of Ministers for Foreign Affairs, the Court finds that it must decide the questions relating to these immunities on the basis of customary international law.

The Court states that, in customary international law, the immunities accorded to Ministers for Foreign Affairs are not granted for their personal benefit, but to ensure the effective performance of their functions on behalf of their respective States. In order to determine the extent of these immunities, the Court must therefore first consider the nature of the functions exercised by a Minister for Foreign Affairs. After an examination of the nature of those functions the Court concludes that they are such that, throughout the duration of his or her office, a Minister for Foreign Affairs when abroad enjoys full immunity from criminal jurisdiction and inviolability. That immunity and inviolability protect the individual concerned against any act of authority of another State which would hinder him or her in the performance of his or her duties. In this respect, no distinction can be drawn between acts performed by a Minister for Foreign Affairs in an "official" capacity and those claimed to have been performed in a "private capacity", or, for that matter, between acts performed before the person concerned assumed office as Minister for Foreign Affairs and acts committed during the period of office. Thus, if a Minister for Foreign Affairs is arrested in another State on a criminal charge, he or she is clearly thereby prevented from exercising the functions of his or her office.

The Court then turns to Belgium's arguments that Ministers for Foreign Affairs do not enjoy such immunity when they are suspected of having committed war crimes or crimes against humanity. It points out that, after having carefully examined State practice, including national legislation and those few existing decisions of national higher courts, such as the House of Lords or the French Court of Cassation, it has been unable to deduce from this practice that there exists under customary international law any form of exception to the rule according immunity from criminal jurisdiction and inviolability to incumbent Ministers for Foreign Affairs.

After examination of the terms of the arrest warrant of 11 April 2000, the Court states that the issuance, as such, of the disputed arrest warrant represents an act by the Belgian judicial authorities intended to enable the arrest on Belgian territory of an incumbent Minister for Foreign Affairs on charges of war crimes and crimes against humanity. It finds that, given the nature and purpose of the warrant, its mere issue constituted a violation of an obligation of Belgium towards the Congo, in that it failed to respect the immunity which Mr. Yerodia enjoyed as the Congo's incumbent Minister for Foreign Affairs and, more particularly, infringed the immunity from criminal jurisdiction and inviolability then enjoyed by him under international law. The Court also notes that Belgium admits that the purpose of the international circulation of the disputed arrest warrant was "to establish a legal basis for the arrest of Mr. Yerodia ... abroad and his subsequent extradition to Belgium." It finds that, as in the case of the warrant's issue, its international circulation from June 2000 by the Belgian authorities, given the nature and purpose of the warrant, constituted a violation of an obligation of Belgium towards the Congo, in that it failed to respect the immunity of the incumbent Minister for Foreign Affairs of the Congo and, more particularly, infringed the immunity from criminal jurisdiction and the inviolability then enjoyed by him under international law.

The Court finally considers that its finding that the arrest warrant was unlawful under international law, and that its issue and circulation engaged Belgium's international responsibility, constitute a form of satisfaction which will make good the moral injury complained of by the Congo. However, the Court also considers that, in order to re-establish "the situation which would, in all probability have existed if [the illegal act] had not been committed", Belgium must, by means of its own choosing, cancel the warrant in question and so inform the authorities to whom it was circulated.

9 The International Criminal Court

Headquarters: The Hague

Members: 124 countries

Mandate: "to put an end to impunity for the perpetrators of" war crimes, genocide, and crimes against humanity, "and thus to contribute to the prevention of such crimes" (ICC Preamble).

Key structure: an "assembly of states parties" to oversee the treaty; plus, a criminal court of eighteen judges with jurisdiction over the most serious crimes of international concern, supported by a prosecutor's office and a staff branch known as the "registry."

Key obligations: the Court may have jurisdiction over a crime if it occurred on the territory of a state party or was committed by a citizen of a state party, and if the domestic courts prove themselves unwilling or unable to genuinely carry out an investigation or prosecution.

Enforcement: the Court can impose prison sentences on those found guilty. It has no police or military capability and relies on national governments to capture and deliver to it suspects.

Key legal clauses of the Statute of the ICC:
Articles 5–9 defining the crimes relevant for the Court.
Article 12 on jurisdiction by territory or citizenship.
Article 13 on the three paths by which the Court may take up a case.

Articles 17 and 20 on "complementarity," the genuineness test, and relations to domestic courts.

Article 27 declaring that senior government officials have no special rights or immunities at the Court.

Article 28 on the responsibility of commanders for conduct of their subordinates.

Article 33 limiting the defense of "just following orders." Article 55 on the rights of accused persons.

The Nuremberg Tribunals after World War II institutionalized the notion that individual persons could have criminal obligations under international law. Previously, criminal law was understood as a relationship between a person and their government. By the end of the twentieth century, it became possible for a person to violate "international criminal law" and be prosecuted by a judicial institution at the international level. This is dramatically new, and the International Criminal Court is the capstone to this system. It prosecutes individuals for these crimes when there is no domestic legal system capable of doing so. Among its member states, the ICC has the authority to investigate and prosecute individuals for these "international" crimes and to imprison those convicted. Its jurisdiction is limited in important and interesting ways, and the application of its authority is highly controversial, but its legal status is unambiguous: the ICC has decisive legal authority over individuals for the worst types of crimes.

The International Criminal Court performs two separate functions. While these are intertwined in the fabric of the organization, their contribution to deterring gross abuses of human rights are distinct. First, the Court ensures that states standardize their domestic laws on war crimes, genocide, and crimes against humanity, and by so doing it helps spread the idea that these crimes will not go unpunished in the parts of the world controlled by countries that are ICC members. Second, it provides the institutional framework and the legal authority to prosecute these crimes in those cases where a state fails in its obligations to do so itself. The former is a piece of legal homogenization, spreading a set of common legal standards around the world, and is therefore one aspect of the broad process of globalization. The latter function creates a completely new international institution with autonomous legal powers and a powerful political role. Binding these two functions together is the concept of "complementarity," which specifies that the ICC shall be "complementary" to domestic courts rather than supersede them.

The Court was established in 2002, under the terms of the Rome Statute of 1998, and it stands as the primary international institution responsible for prosecuting the worst "international crimes" (that is, crimes with special status in international law). It conducts criminal prosecutions of individuals at the international level, and so contrasts clearly with the ICJ's power to adjudicate disputes between states. It has all the apparatus of a criminal court: prosecutors, defendants, judges, sentences, and appeals. It sees cases through from start to finish – that is, from identifying suspects, to investigating the facts of the case, to prosecution, and on through convictions, acquittals and jail sentences. Never before in the history of the inter-state system has there been an international institution with these kinds of powers. There are 124 countries that have signed and ratified the ICC Statute, making them the members of the ICC (known as the "states parties" of the Court). Within their territory, and over their citizens, the authority of the ICC is decisive for both individuals and governments.

The politics of the Court are as dramatic as its legal structure. When it acts, when it does not act, and what it does when it does act are all driven by the political interests of those actors that are able to make use of the Court. It makes use of legal modalities but these are put to use in the pursuit of political goals. The controversies around the ICC are the stuff of high-politics. Who gets prosecuted and who doesn't? Who is exempt and who decides? Why have all defendants so far been men from Africa? These and other questions emerge at the intersection of the institutional features of the Court defined by its legal instruments and practical interventions into local and global society. The Court's power to punish and its necessarily selective application of that power generates tremendous controversy. Supporters of the Court tend to see it as self-evidently good, and as serving the obviously desirable goal of deterring and punishing mass human rights violations. But this understates its contribution to shaping political outcomes – that is, who wins, who loses, who gets off scot free – in specific conflicts and fails to speak in the same terms as ICC critics. In 2016, South Africa, Burundi, and Gambia said they were considering withdrawing from the Court.

Obligations

The ICC Statute defines the powers of the new Court. Most of these are powers that relate to how the Court treats individuals who appear before it as accused. For example, they define over what kinds of crimes the Court has jurisdiction, what rights the accused have, and how trials can be conducted – in other words, obligations on individuals rather than on governments. However, there are also a small number of obligations in the Statute that bear directly on the states parties rather than on individuals, and these are gathered in Part 9 of the Statute.

The main obligation that the Statute imposes on its states parties is to "cooperate fully with the Court in its investigation and prosecution of crimes within the jurisdiction of the Court" (Art. 86). This is further developed in subsequent articles dealing with the obligation to arrest and surrender suspects to the Court, to assist with gathering evidence for the Court, and to help in collecting fines or providing prison space as needed based on the outcomes of cases. The Court therefore demands that its member states facilitate all aspects of investigation, prosecution, and incarceration. The Court itself has no prisons, no police force, and no detectives. The Statute also expressly forbids signatories from attaching reservations to their signatures (Art. 120), meaning that states must be prepared to accept all of the treaty at the time they become members.

However, the most distinctive contribution of the Court is not contained in these obligations but rather in the new set of rules it establishes which allow international law to reach down to the level of individual persons. This thoroughly transforms the conventional understanding of the relationship between people and the institutions at the international level because it does away with the idea that the national government is the sole conduit for legal rights and obligations between the international system and individual citizens. In legal terms, these could be cast as obligations owed by individuals to the international community in the sense that among ICC countries the behaviors listed as crimes in the Statute create a compelling connection between international law and "natural" persons (i.e. human beings). Traditionally in international law such connections exist only as mediated through states and citizenship – that is, international law was relevant to individuals (and individuals were relevant to international law) only to the extent that the person's state of citizenship was involved. The ICC embodies this novel development of the late twentieth century: a channel of authority that runs directly from international institutions to individual human beings.

The most important part of the Statute is that which defines when the Court can have jurisdiction over a person and when it cannot. There are three tests which a claim of jurisdiction must pass. First, the Court can have jurisdiction over an individual only if the person is suspected of one of the crimes listed in Article 5 (war crimes, genocide, or crimes against humanity). No other crimes are relevant. Second, there must be a connection between the individual or the crime and an ICC state: as set out in Article 12(2), either the crime must have been committed on the territory of a state party or the accused must be a citizen of a state party. Third, the courts of the domestic jurisdiction must have failed to genuinely investigate and (if warranted) prosecute the matter (Art. 17). All three of these must be true for a case to qualify for consideration by the Court.

The crimes over which the Court has jurisdiction are described in Articles 5 to 8 and in a related document called "The Elements of Crimes." The Elements text is a formal legal instrument approved by the ICC Assembly as an aid for interpreting the crimes described in the Statute (Art. 9). The crimes are derived from other international agreements, including the Genocide Convention, the Convention Against Torture, and the Geneva Conventions. And so, with the exception of the crime of aggression, these articles repeat what are well-established international crimes. They occasioned little controversy in the nego-tiations over the Rome Statute.

The crime of aggression is different. It is listed in Article 5(1) as a crime over which the ICC will have jurisdiction, but Article 5(2) prevents it from exercising that jurisdiction while the definition of aggression is negotiated. Aggression is understood to encompass acts which at Nuremberg were called "crimes against peace" and which were outlawed in Article 2(4) of the UN Charter. However, it proved impossible in the Rome negotiations to find a definition of aggression that could win a consensus of states, and the matter was left to subsequent discussion. An agreement reached in June 2010 helped to define the language of the crime of aggression, but it includes the limit that it will not come into force until a two-thirds vote of the states parties is taken and it forbids this from taking place until 2017 at the earliest.[1] The difficulties over this issue arise from two sources: (i) concern that giving the ICC authority over aggression will impede the UN Security Council's authority over threats to international peace and security, and (ii) the essentially contested concept of aggression itself, where states see their enemies – but never themselves – acting aggressively.

The three central crimes of the Court are genocide, war crimes, and crimes against humanity. These are already encoded in international law, and the Rome Statute draws on the language of, and existing consensus around, these existing treaties. As a result the Court functions like an institutional novelty on top of a traditional foundation. The Court's focus in all three crimes is on systemic

---

[1] See Coalition for the International Criminal Court, "The Crime of Aggression," www.iccnow .org/?mod=aggression, accessed January 22, 2013.

attacks or large-scale programs of violence. It emphasizes "the most serious crimes of concern to the international community" rather than isolated acts (Art. 5(1)). One significant area of innovation is the inclusion of systematic sexual crimes among the subcategories of war crimes and crimes against humanity. These are now recognized as part of the core crimes for which international tribunals should be responsible. Their inclusion in the Rome Statute was a response to the evident ways rape, forced pregnancy, and other atrocities were used as a tactic against innocents in the Yugoslav wars and elsewhere in the 1990s.[2] These are found in Articles 6(e), 7(g), 8(2b(xxii)), and elsewhere in the Statute.

Having defined the crimes over which the Court has jurisdiction, the Rome Statute goes on to clarify two further conditions that must be met for a case to proceed: on location and citizenship, and on complementarity. Article 12 defines the necessary connection between the crime and a state party: a case can proceed if either the crime was committed on the territory of a state party or the suspect is a citizen of a state party. (These do not apply if the case was initiated at the request of the Security Council under Article 13(b).) There must therefore be a connection, either through citizenship of the perpetrator or the location of the crime, to a state that is a member of the Court. This is somewhat different than claims to jurisdiction made by many domestic courts, where cases may proceed if one can prove that citizens of the home country were harmed even if the perpetrator and the location are foreign.[3]

The last major limit on the Court's jurisdiction is in Article 17, which says inter alia that a case cannot proceed if it has been "investigated or prosecuted by a State which has jurisdiction over it." This defines the ICC as secondary to domestic courts. It has no authority in any case where the domestic courts are doing their work. This principle is known as "complementarity" and it is similar to the concept of "subsidiarity" in the European Union (described in Chapter 10). Crucial to complementarity in the ICC is the fact that the subordination to domestic courts applies only if the domestic courts are able and willing to "genuinely carry out the investigation or prosecution." In other words, if domestic courts are a sham, then the ICC can take over.

These clauses constitute the ICC as a kind of back-stop mechanism to deal with the instances where domestic courts are either not able or not permitted to

---

[2] See the diplomacy involved in this in David Scheffer, *All the Missing Souls: A Personal History of the War Crimes Tribunals*. Princeton University Press, 2012.

[3] In international law, see the Lotus Case of the Permanent Court of International Justice, 1928.

undertake genuine criminal investigations, and they show that the Court is not intended to supplant domestic authority. However, it is important to note that if there are disagreements over whether a domestic investigation has been "genuine" or not, the Statute gives the ICC itself the power to decide. Article 17(2) authorizes the Court to determine if a domestic proceeding was so seriously deficient that the Court's jurisdiction is enabled. In this light, the Court looks more like a legal superior to domestic courts than a co-equal or a complement. This has become a source of great political and legal controversy over the case of Saif Qaddafi in Libya. Qaddafi was sought by both the domestic Libyan criminal justice system and the ICC at the time he was arrested by the Libyans. A domestic prosecution is proceeding while the ICC insists that it has jurisdiction. The case is severely testing the legal and political meaning of the framework of complementarity.[4]

These sets of terms define the set of cases over which the Court has jurisdiction. A second set of rules defines how a case can arrive at the Court in the first place. Three pathways are set out in Article 13: cases can be referred to the Court by a state party (Art. 14), or by the UN Security Council (Art. 13(b)), or through the independent investigatory powers of the ICC Prosecutor's Office (Art. 15). Cases cannot come before the Court except by following one of these three paths. The Court has formal involvement in eight situations and has indicted thirty individuals in its history. All have been in Africa. Half of these situations came to the ICC by the referral of a state party (Mali, Central African Republic, Congo, and Uganda). The two investigations that originated in the UN Security Council relate to the Libyan response to its revolution in 2011 and to the Sudan/ Darfur situation. Two others arose due to the independent investigations of the ICC Prosecutor, in relation to post-election violence in Kenya (2007/08) and Côte d'Ivoire (2010/11).

The Security Council's authority to initiate proceedings (in Article 13(b)) is an extension of the Council's wide authority under the UN Charter over threats to international peace and security. Its institutional affiliation with the ICC adds to the Council's tool-kit another instrument for dealing with problems of international security. The prosecutor's independent authority to initiate investigations proprio motu (i.e. on its own initiative) was insisted on by the negotiators at Rome despite the opposition of the United States. It was seen as important that the prosecutor could gather information on his or her own and use it to

---

[4] See Kevin Jon Heller, "Libya Admits it Should Lose Its Complementarity Challenge," Opinio Juris blog, January 18, 2013, http://bit.ly/Wlk7VG. Accessed January 25, 2013.

generate a case even if no government was asking for it. The prosecutor is responsible for the investigation into cases and evidence, leading prosecutions, and in an informal sense being the lead diplomat and public face of the Court. The office is currently occupied by Fatou Bensouda, a Gambian lawyer. The power of the prosecutor to initiate cases on her own authority makes the ICC something like an independent human rights court.

The Statute is worth reading closely for its many smaller and more technical limits on its jurisdiction or authority. For instance, cases can only arise when the crimes were committed while the treaty was in effect for the relevant state, and so it is not possible for the Court to investigate behavior prior to the treaty coming into force. It also cannot prosecute people under 18 years of age (Art. 26), and cannot impose the death penalty (Art. 77). It also defines a series of rights of the accused, including the presumption of innocence, freedom from self-incrimination and from coercion, and right to fair trials, legal assistance, and transparency (Articles 55, 66, and 67). The Statute goes on to explicitly deny a priori certain claims by defendants, including a complete ban on claiming immunity from prosecution based on high government office (Art. 27(1)), and a limited ban on the defense of following the orders of superiors. For the latter issue, the Statute says that this is permissible as a defense only if the order is itself not manifestly unlawful and the person did not know the order was unlawful (orders to commit genocide or crimes against humanity are by definition unlawful). This narrows the scope of the "following orders" defense enormously (Art. 33).

Compliance

That the Court was so recently created means that there is little history on which to base an assessment of compliance or non-compliance by states. However, there are already several areas in which we can observe states carefully managing their behavior in ways that show that they are sensitive to the obligations created by the Statute. These include a relatively rapid rate of states joining the Rome Statute, and evidence that the Court's obligations enter into the internal discussions of states as they consider their policy choices. These show both that the ICC has had a significant impact in world politics in a short time, and also that this impact is not necessarily what the ICC's framers had in mind.

The Court's Statute has quickly become a widely ratified international instrument, with about two-thirds of the world's countries having joined in less than ten years. There are still many states, and some very important ones, outside the Court and in varying degrees of opposition. Significantly, the cohort of states that have not joined the Court includes three of the five permanent members of the UN Security Council (Russia, China, and the United States), as well as India, Pakistan, and Israel.

However, there are some interesting and counterintuitive patterns evident in the set of countries that have accepted the treaty. First, it is striking that many states with recent histories of human rights abuses have joined the ICC in its early years. These include Colombia, Sierra Leone, and the Democratic Republic of Congo, places where one might expect government officials, either current or from the recent past, to be sensitive to their legal liability for international crimes.[5] A lively discussion has arisen as to the motivation of these states, producing a handful of plausible explanations. Aside from the general desire to work against heinous crimes, these governments may believe that the ICC is a useful tool in response to their militarized domestic opponents, as it may help shift the balance of military power against these opponents. If one accepts the premise that atrocities are a relatively cheap instrument for producing a large political impact, then it may be that they are more useful to irregular forces than the better-funded government armies and so the government may find an advantage in binding both themselves and their enemies to an effective anti-atrocity regime. Alternately (or perhaps concurrently), there may be a reputation effect to signing the Rome Statute: states may believe that they gain status and prestige in the international community by joining the ICC. Finally, countries may have more specific signals in mind when they consider the ICC. For instance, had Iraq been an ICC member in 2003, it might have provided a useful legal path for deterring the worst abuses at Abu Ghraib and elsewhere, and it could also have provided a device for demonstrating the independence of the Iraqi authorities from the US. Interestingly, the plausibility of all of these motives rests on the fact that the Court is taken seriously as a source of either threat or reputation, and so if true they would reflect well on the success of the institution in its early years.

The rate of accession is one measure of the impact of the ICC, but it is important also to examine whether signatories take seriously its rules as they

[5] The current list of members is at: https://asp.icc-cpi.int/en_menus/asp/states%20parties/Pages/the%20states%20parties%20to%20the%20rome%20statute.aspx.

plan and carry out their actual policies. On this point, there is interesting anecdotal evidence that compliance with the ICC is entering into the internal deliberations of member states. These deliberations are often secret, and so there is good reason to believe that they reflect a serious concern on the part of policy-makers that they avoid falling under the jurisdiction of the Court. In advance of the Iraq invasion of 2003, the UK Attorney General Lord Goldsmith thought it was prudent to give his opinion to the prime minister on whether the military operation might open up British officials or military personnel to the jurisdiction of the ICC.[6] Goldsmith concluded that the decision to invade would in itself likely not qualify for investigation by the ICC (on the grounds that the crime of aggression remained non-justiciable) but he observed that the Court would have the authority to conduct independent investigations of any claims of war crimes by British troops, and that the UK government would have little capacity to stop such investigations. He also reported that some groups from domestic civil society had promised in advance that they would be monitoring British behavior in any invasion with an eye to reporting the evidence to the ICC prosecutor under the prosecutor's proprio motu authority from Article 15. The existence of this concern in a secret memo suggests that the threat of ICC prosecution (or more minimally, of investigation) is in the minds of some high government officials, in the UK at least, and that they are therefore motivated to ensure that they maintain some plausible level of compliance with the terms of the Court.

The United States as well has shown that it is alert to the legal consequences of the Rome Statute. The US has had a mixed relationship with the Court, supporting it at the Security Council with respect to Sudan and Libya but undermining it in other ways. In the 2000s the Bush administration sought to create "court-free zones" between it and countries it could influence. It interpreted the Statute's rules on the transfer of suspects to the Court in such a way that allowed it to construct an alternate legal structure which would prevent ICC members from being allowed to send Americans to the Court. This interpretive strategy centered on exploiting Article 98(2) of the Statute, which says "The Court may not proceed with a request for surrender [of a suspect by an ICC state] which would require the requested State to act inconsistently with its obligations under international agreements pursuant to which the consent of a sending State is required to surrender a person of that State to the Court, unless the Court can first obtain

[6] Memo from Lord Goldsmith, Attorney General, to Prime Minister's Office, March 7, 2003, www .ico.gov.uk/upload/documents/library/freedom_of_information/notices/annex_a_-_attorney_ generars_advice_070303.pdf. Accessed February 23, 2010.

the cooperation of the sending State for the giving of consent for the surrender." The rather inelegantly phrased article was designed to deal with cases where states held competing legal obligations with respect to a suspect that the Court was asking them to surrender. Consider, for instance, the possibility of a suspect who is a soldier from a foreign military, in the country by mutual agreement between the two states, and where a Status of Forces Agreement (SOFA) exists between the states which stipulates that soldiers suspected of crimes should be sent home. If the ICC requests that this person be surrendered to the Court, the host country would be stuck between two competing and incompatible legal obligations, one under the ICC Statute and one under its bilateral treaty. Article 98(2) says that in such cases the surrender should only happen if the country of citizenship of the individual consents to it. Otherwise, the individual should be sent home for investigation pursuant to the SOFA obligation.

The strategy of the Bush administration was to encourage ICC countries to sign new bilateral treaties that would govern Americans (and others) in those countries who might be sought by the ICC. The treaties generally require that "persons of one Party present in the territory of the other shall not, absent the express consent of the first Party, a) be surrendered or transferred by any means to the International Criminal Court."[7] The term "persons" here was defined as "current or former Government officials, employees (including contractors), or military personnel or nationals of one Party." The effect is to create an international obligation on the two sides that produces precisely the conflict that is envisioned in Article 98(2). Having created the conflict, albeit after the fact, the US argued that the bilateral agreement trumped the ICC Statute and it could be assured that no US citizens, and no US employees or contractors of whatever nationality, would be surrendered to the Court without US consent case by case. As leverage to encourage these bilateral agreements, the US Congress passed a law in 2002 ending military aid and other assistance to countries that failed to join a bilateral agreement relating to 98(2) with the United States.

These agreements with the US are generally seen among international lawyers as being legally null because they violate a more basic obligation of states not to take any actions which would defeat their obligations under an existing treaty.[8] To comply with such an agreement, a state would have to break its obligations

---

[7] This language is drawn from the US-Montenegro treaty, www.state.gov/documents/organization/100234.pdf. Accessed November 22, 2009.

[8] This is part of the Vienna Convention on the Law of Treaties (1969), which defines the rules of treaty-making between states.

under either Article 120 of the Statute (which forbids reservations to the treaty) or under Article 86 and others which require cooperation with the Court. However, these agreements are worth some attention because of the political investment that they represent by the US in reshaping the legal content of the ICC. Having failed to persuade the other states at the Rome Conference that the ICC should be subordinate to the UN Security Council, the US has tried several strategies to disempower the Court and punish its supporters, and these add to the broader politics around the institution and in the project of international criminal law more broadly. However, one consequence of the American strategy was that it helped to reinforce the idea that the terms of the Rome Statute have indeed come to be the operative legal reference for the response to international crimes and are the starting point for any discussion of contemporary rules of individual criminal responsibility. The US succeeded in generating controversy over the interpretation of some clauses of the ICC charter, but along the way it may also have accidentally invested the Court with greater legitimacy and authority. By pointing out and exploiting these loopholes, the US has contributed the unwitting effect of reinforcing the general authority of the Court in its core competencies.

On the other hand, the ICC prosecutors office has been investigating US conduct in Afghanistan and in November 2016 issued a report that found among other things that "members of US armed forces appear to have subjected at least 61 detained persons to torture, cruel treatment, [and] outrages upon personal dignity on the territory of Afghanistan between 1 May 2003 and 31 December 2014."[9] These may amount to war crimes under ICC law. It continues to investigate further in order to decide whether charges are warranted, including by asking the US government for evidence under the complementarity rules of a genuine US investigation of these possible crimes. The Court has jurisdiction because Afghanistan is a member of the ICC (since 2003), and so US citizens in Afghanistan must abide by its rules even though the US is not a state party.

Enforcement

The language of enforcement can be used in at least three ways with respect to the ICC. First, the obligations on states to cooperate with the Court can be thought of as implying the possibility of enforcement against non-compliant

---

[9] *The Guardian*, November 15, 2016.

member states. Second, because the Court is itself an instrument of enforcement of international criminal law, we can also ask about the punishments the Court can in theory impose on individuals whom it convicts. Finally, we might ask about the practice of enforcement: How has the Court conducted itself in real cases of international crimes? Because the Court is so new, the history of practical enforcement is short, and in this chapter I deal with enforcement mainly in the context of the al-Bashir indictment which forms the case study at the end of the chapter. This section therefore looks at how the Rome Statute deals with the question of enforcement against rule-breaking by states parties and against the individuals who are the subjects of its prosecutions.

States take on several legal obligations as members of the Court, described above under "Obligations." The most general of these is in Article 86: "States parties shall ... cooperate fully with the Court in its investigation and prosecution of crimes within the jurisdiction of the Court," and the more specific ones include surrendering suspects, making prison space available, and criminalizing in domestic law the international crimes described in Articles 5 through 8. There are no provisions in the Statute to respond to states parties who fail in these obligations, and it seems that any such failure would therefore fall under the general international laws on treaty obligations rather than as a matter internal to the ICC or the Rome Statute. In principle, the ICJ might be open to a case should two ICC parties find themselves in a legal dispute over the Rome Statute.

The only sanction against states parties that is anticipated in the Statute itself is for failing to pay one's share of the Court's expenses, under Articles 115, 117, and 112(8). The last of these says that a country may lose its right to vote in the Assembly of States Parties as punishment for being in arrears on its dues. Beyond this, the failure to perform as mandated by the Statute is not the subject of any formal enforcement procedure or sanction. This may become a practical question should a party to an Article 98 agreement with the US be accused of violating its obligations under the treaty. This aspect of enforcement refers to obligations owed by one state party to another, or one state party to the Court itself.

By contrast, the Court's enforcement of international criminal law takes place between the institution and an individual, and the central business of the Court lies at this intersection. International law has not traditionally focused itself on individuals as the subjects of law and enforcement, and in this respect the ICC provides an interesting case study in institutional innovation: it brings international legal responsibility directly to the citizens of states in an entirely new fashion (though pirates, hijackers, and a few others have had some direct responsibility to international law in the past). The enforcement of international law directly upon individuals puts states themselves in an odd position: they must remove themselves from their traditional position as the representatives of their citizens, and yet their assistance is required if suspects are going to be caught and transferred to the Court.

The ICC has no machinery for apprehending its suspects. For the policing function, it relies entirely on its member states, who are obligated to help under Part 9 of the Statute, and (in an ideal world) on the voluntary cooperation of non-members. The experience of the ad hoc tribunals on the former Yugoslavia and Rwanda has proved that the surrender of suspects to the tribunal is always complicated by local politics: some suspects and some witnesses are sheltered by the governments, some are eagerly handed over, and the overall fairness of the process is hardly guaranteed. However, the ICC and these tribunals have been made with a judicial model in mind and not with a military or policing model, and they rely on the help of others to make effective their investigations and their indictments.

While the ICC relies on the help of local governments in apprehending suspects, it also expects these governments to refrain from intervening substantively in their cases. This means that the Court reserves the right under Article 17 to make the ultimate decision on whether a local investigation or prosecution has been "genuine" or not. This is a significant grant of authority to the Court, and a significant concession of sovereignty by its states parties. The principle of "complementarity" in Article 17 gives the Court decisive power to interpret the workings of domestic courts, and it adds a novel aspect of hierarchy to international politics: the ICC has the legal authority to trump domestic courts. This is limited to this one aspect of the working of these institutions – namely the interpretation of whether an investigation or prosecution was "genuine" – but this is a crucial aspect of any legal regime and its implications for the model of sovereign statehood are dramatic. States parties to the ICC accept a subordinate position in a new international legal hierarchy. The practice of interpreting Article 17 will become extremely important very quickly since every case that proceeds through to trial must necessarily pass its tests. The Court is engaged from the very start in the sensitive business of second-guessing domestic courts.

CASE: The al-Bashir Indictment

The political and legal implications of the ICC are well displayed by the Court's pursuit of Omar al-Bashir, the president of Sudan. This is a long-running saga that has unfolded through the specific legal pathways of the Rome Statute, but it has also implicated the broadest conceptual problems and dilemmas associated with the Court, including on the relationship of the Court with the Security Council, with the Great Powers, and with the big issues of humanitarian disaster and international peace and security. That the case arose in the first place represents an astonishing development in world politics in at least two dimensions: first, the adamantly anti-ICC Bush administration encouraged the UN Security Council to press for the case, and second, the Court has aimed at the top of the political hierarchy in Sudan and is seeking for the first time to prosecute an incumbent head of state for international crimes. That it remains unresolved, with al-Bashir still in office in Sudan, illustrates the ambition, the power, and the limits of the ICC.

The case against al-Bashir rests on orders that he apparently gave as the president of Sudan to his military forces and the informal militias allied with them in the Darfur region of Sudan. The prosecutor maintains that the offenses against the population in Darfur, including systematic campaigns of murder, rape, and displacement (described in Chapter 4 in relation to the Security Council), were committed under orders from al-Bashir. In targeting the president, therefore, the Court is enacting the philosophy that the Court has a special obligation in international law to attack those at the leadership peaks of political and military organizations, not just those "in the field" carrying out the practices, and it is also invoking the specific legal rule in Article 25(3b) which makes no distinction between those who carry out these crimes and the person who "orders, solicits or induces" their commission.

To proceed with a case, the ICC must establish conclusively that it has jurisdiction and to do so it must fit the particulars of the case into the black-letter law of the Statute. The onus is on the Court to show that it has jurisdiction – if there is any remaining ambiguity then the presumption is that jurisdiction does not exist. The arrest warrant for al-Bashir traces the authority of the Court, beginning with the fact that Sudan is not a member of the ICC. Because it has refused to sign the Rome Statute, the ICC has no direct authority over individuals or crimes within the country and Sudan has no legal obligations under the Statute or toward the ICC. It has not consented to the terms of the Court and has not promised to cooperate with it; indeed it has vocally attacked the Court and made explicit its opposition to its powers. Under international law, a state that refuses to consent to a treaty takes on no obligations toward it. This should initially indicate that the case has no basis for proceeding. However, the case has gone forward due to the interrelationship between the ICC and the UN Security Council.

The case against al-Bashir is permissible because Article 13(b) of the Statute defines a role for the Security Council. Taken together with Article 39 of the UN Charter, Article 13(b) allows the Security Council to refer cases to the ICC prosecutor as necessary for the preservation of international peace and security. The Council can authorize the Court to claim jurisdiction over cases regardless of whether the relevant states have signed the Statute. This provision creates a pathway to jurisdiction that is separate from the membership of the Court, and one that rests on the Council's own authority to identify and respond to "threats to international peace and security" (Art. 39 UN Charter). As we saw in Chapter 4, the Security Council has exclusive authority to designate problems as threats to international peace and security, and then to enforce whatever solution it wants in response. The ICC Statute links to that authority by encouraging the Security Council to use the Court as one instrument of enforcement action. Because the Council has essentially unlimited power to require countries to comply with its demands, it is logical to presume that one such demand can be that a state cooperate with the ICC in the prosecution of a case. This is what the Council has ordered with respect to the al-Bashir case. In a resolution in 2005, the Security Council demanded that "Sudan and all other parties to the conflict in Darfur shall cooperate fully" with the ICC, including on turning over suspects and evidence (UN SC Res. 1593). This demand, made under the Council's authority in Chapter VII of the Charter, has priority over all other legal obligations and rights of states, including the right of non-intervention.

This is an intriguing mashup of international legal authorities, and its legality is something that we should expect to be challenged in the future by individuals prosecuted under this power. The Rome Statute is a treaty that is independent of the United Nations Charter, and whose list of signatories may never match exactly the membership of the UN, but one consequence of the new treaty is that the Security Council has found itself with a new power that is not in the Charter. The new treaty appears to extend the old treaty, though without requiring that the signatories of the old treaty consent to the extension. Al-Bashir provides an excellent illustration of this issue because it is he personally, as president of Sudan since 1993 (i.e. throughout the ICC era) who has made the decision that Sudan would not consent to the Court's jurisdiction and who would have presumably opposed a formal amendment to the UN Charter attaching the Court to the Council (had such an amendment been proposed). And yet, the new Court empowers the Council to act in ways that were previously impossible for it, except by creating ad hoc criminal tribunals as it did for Yugoslavia and Rwanda, and that are not escapable merely by refusing to consent to the Court. Thus, the ICC treaty enhances the powers of the existing Security Council (and at the same time the Security Council multiplies the scope and power of the ICC).

The al-Bashir case also shows that the Council can create costs for the Court which the Court's members have not consented to. As part of the 2005 resolution, the Council said "none of the expenses incurred in connection with the [case] . . . shall be borne by the United Nations," instead they "shall be borne by the parties to the Rome Statute and those States that wish to contribute voluntarily." The Council has decided that the expenses associated with the prosecution of the case are the responsibility of the ICC's members and not of the UN's members, even though it is the UN and not the ICC that has decided that the case must be investigated. The ICC has no power to refuse a referral by the Council (although it is up to the Court to decide whether there is sufficient evidence to prosecute anyone). Thus, the Council can in some degree be the master of the ICC's budget by sending it cases whether the Court wants them or not. In principle, the Council's powers could presumably be applied in this way even without Article 13(b), as the Council could direct any international organization to change its behavior as required to deal with a threat to international peace and security. Hypothetically, one could imagine the Council using its Article 39 powers to tell the World Health Organization (WHO) how to respond to a health emergency that constituted a threat to international peace and security, and the WHO, despite having no authority over peace and security, would have no legal choice but to comply. The entanglements between international organizations are often significant, and Chapter 11 examines how they might both enhance and undermine the practical powers of the organizations.

The existence of this path to jurisdiction is the result of an attempt at compromise during the ICC negotiations between the United States and the majority of pro-ICC countries. The US wanted to make all ICC cases subject to Security Council referral. This would have formally established the ICC as an extension of the Security Council and its apparatus relating to international peace and security (rather than an independent court relating to criminal law). It would also have ensured that the US, along with the other SC permanent members, had a veto over any case the ICC might pursue. The US sought via several means to increase its influence over cases so that it could protect from prosecution individuals it was interested in, but this was opposed by the bulk of the negotiating states, and thus we have a Court that stands separate from the Council. Remnants of these American efforts can be seen in the Statute today, not only in the SC path to jurisdiction but also the Council's authority under Article 16 to defer any case for twelve months at a time.

Having established ICC jurisdiction over al-Bashir through SC fiat, the Court's normal procedures then came into play, including those on prosecutorial investigation, the procedures for arrest, and the machinery of trial. The ICC prosecutor's investigation of al-Bashir led to a formal arrest warrant by the Court in March 2009 charging him with crimes against humanity and war crimes in Darfur. These included systematic campaigns of murder, rape, torture, and forcible transfer to destroy civilian populations, all designed as strategies to undermine his political opponents within Sudan.[10]

The pursuit of al-Bashir, which as of this writing has not succeeded in securing his transfer to the ICC's courtrooms in the Hague, has provoked interesting debate about the broader place of the ICC in world politics and in the field of humanitarianism. While there is little doubt that the Court has the authority and the mandate to pursue this al-Bashir in this way, there has been much discussion about the wisdom and the effects of this action. One set of issues concerns whether the charges make it more or less likely that a leader will accept a negotiated deal that removes him or her from power. It may be the case that indicted leaders will strive ever harder to remain in power by whatever means they have if they expect to be charged once they leave office. Relatedly, some observers have suggested that in striving to stay in power the individual might resort to even worse behavior against their enemies than would arise without the criminal charges, such that the net result of the Court's efforts ends up being worse rather than better for the victim populations. These are questions that are essentially empirical and must be answered with details that are specific to each particular leader and each case. For al-Bashir, it is not yet clear what effect the arrest warrant has had for the populations over whom he exercises control.

---

[10] See www.icc-cpi.int/iccdocs/doc/doc639078.pdf. Accessed November 30, 2009.

In general, there is little evidence that the Court's primary effect is in fact counterproductive in this way. The Court appears so far to have helped by further stigmatizing these crimes and by providing an institutional path for redress. Thinking more conceptually, we might in fact prefer that the Court not weigh these practical concerns as it considers the cases it pursues: should the Court refrain from pursuing a person if we expect that person to respond by massacring innocent people? On this question, the issue may come down to whether one thinks of the Court as a narrowly legal institution enacting international criminal law or as part of a broader architecture of dispute resolution or humanitarian assistance. Is the goal of the Court to pursue suspects under international law or to minimize immediate humanitarian harms? It is possible to imagine scenarios in which these two conflict (though whether they really do in practice is another question). In situations where they do conflict, Mahnoush H. Arsanjani and W. Michael Reisman have noted that this forces prosecutors and judges to decide "how to set priorities among their curial responsibilities and the inevitable political consequences of their actions."[11] In domestic law, we often expect the police to refrain from high-speed chases or storming hostage situations if the chance of further innocent casualties is high. This may be a relevant analogy to a situation in which the ICC holds back from arresting a suspect who has the capacity to inflict further harm while defying the Court. However, continuing the domestic analogy, we do not allow the police to abandon their search for the fleeing suspect – we still expect the authorities to pursue the suspect but to do it wisely; while the police may deal more carefully with a bank robber who holds hostages, once apprehended the suspect is not likely to win leniency as a function of having taken the hostages.

In this analogy, as in much of the analysis around the ICC, the appropriate domestic comparison for the Court is not clear. Is it akin to domestic courts, to domestic police, to domestic security agencies, or to something else – or is it a combination of these? The legal structure of the Court makes it clear that this is a judicial institution, not a police force and not a venue for the resolution of political disputes. The Court's self-understanding is that it fills a gap in the institutional architecture of the international system by providing a legal setting to hold accountable those accused of the worst crimes. However, keeping the ICC within this self-ascribed bubble of legalism is difficult because its cases are

---

[11] Mahnoush H. Arsanjani and W. Michael Reisman, "The Law-in-Action of the International Criminal Court," *American Journal of International Law*, 2005, **99**(2): 385–403, p. 385.

necessarily situated in conflicts with international political dimensions. Some will find it useful to use the ICC as a resource against their political opponents, and many will notice that the ICC's interventions have political consequences for local disputes. The ICC can address only a small sample of the world's worst perpetrators, and the selection of cases is necessarily influenced by the prosecutor's or the judge's political sensibilities. The investigation of cases cannot be kept entirely separate from the political context of the dispute that produced the atrocities in the first place. As a result, a strict distinction between the responsibilities of the Security Council (on peace and security) and of the ICC (on criminal law) is not possible, and the ICC itself has features that go beyond the analogy to a domestic court. This is not a reason to criticize the Court; it is instead a reflection of the different political and institutional contexts in which the Court exists as compared to the context for a domestic court.

Conclusion

The ICC represents the institutionalization of the principles established by the Nuremberg Tribunals (1945–46); that is, it provides a legal and political space for enacting the idea that individuals, regardless of their official position, should hold some personal responsibility for organizing or participating in genocide, war crimes, and crimes against humanity. This idea was largely invented at Nuremberg and it has now been put into effect across the globe (though not universally in all countries) with the ICC.

The Court requires that its members criminalize genocide, war crimes, and crimes against humanity, and that they cooperate with the Court in apprehending and prosecuting suspects when domestic Courts are unable to do so. Member states are expected to provide the police function, investigative assistance, and prison space, and the ICC provides the prosecutor, judges, and institutionalized judicial standards to carry out these cases. The jurisdiction of the Court is carefully described in the Rome Statute, with a series of limits that define when a case can proceed. Some of these are inherent in the Court's foundation in an international treaty (for instance, cases can only arise out of behavior that occurred after the treaty came into effect). Some are the result of compromises that were made during the negotiation of the treaty (for instance, cases must be delayed if the Security Council demands it). Beyond these limits, there are three fundamental sets of parameters within which the Court operates: cases can reach the ICC only when (i) the behavior fits one of the listed crimes (war crimes, genocide, and crimes against humanity), (ii) the relevant domestic courts have failed to investigate the behavior, and (iii) either the suspect is a citizen of an ICC member, the conduct happened on the territory of an ICC member, or the SC demands it.

The creation of the ICC has changed the relationship that international law has to states and to individuals. For states, the concept of "complementarity" means that the ultimate legal authority to decide matters of criminal responsibility for certain crimes has moved from states themselves to the international level. There is now an institution with the legal authority to review the behavior of domestic courts on these matters, and its judgments about the sincerity of domestic decisions is final. The Rome Statute shifts this important authority from states to the ICC. This shift comes as a result of the recognition that states frequently fail to prosecute the perpetrators of the worst crimes and that the resulting impunity is unacceptable. The relationship between international law and individuals has been changed as well. People now have a direct connection to international law and institutions to a degree that has never existed before. The direct application of international law to individuals has suddenly become the norm, rather than the very minor exception. Despite the Court's foundation in an inter-state treaty, this shift represents a step toward a model of cosmopolitanism and away from a state-centric international system: the Court treats people as individuals, as instances of a universal category of humanity, and not as elements defined by their citizenship. This is a revolutionary change for international law and institutions and its implications for individuals, for states, and for international law remain to be seen.

While formally independent and self-contained, the ICC is in practice far from being a stand-alone institution. It rests on a prior body of international criminal law that developed over the twentieth century and includes the Geneva Conventions, the Nuremberg Tribunals, the Genocide Convention, and the ad hoc international tribunals of the 1990s. It also relies heavily on its relationships with its states parties and with the UN Security Council. It is the states parties who will make meaningful its arrest warrants and its investigations – the ICC cannot accomplish these things on its own. The UN Security Council extends the authority of the ICC, as was demonstrated in the case regarding al-Bashir. It is the Security Council's authority under the UN Charter that makes it possible for the ICC to investigate cases outside the domain of its member states. These relationships with organizations and ideas outside of the ICC can increase the power and reach of the Court. They may also however be a source of weakness and frustration for the Court to the extent that these other actors may have reasons of their own not to fully cooperate with the Court. The ICC therefore illustrates a common dilemma among international organizations: they create new centers of power by pooling the resources and authorities of their members and other actors, but they thereby open themselves to failure when those players refuse to go along with the organization.

Further Reading

For overviews of the ICC's powers and structure see William A. Schabas, *An Introduction to the International Criminal Court* (Cambridge University Press, 4th edn., 2011) and Benjamin N. Schiff, *Building the International Criminal Court* (Cambridge University Press, 2008). For an account of some of its internal and external politics, see David Bosco, *Rough Justice: The International Criminal Court in a World of Power Politics* (Oxford University Press, 2014). For recent developments at the Court, including updates on ongoing cases, the ICC's own website is excellent (icc-cpi.int), as is the coverage by the Coalition for the International Criminal Court (iccnow.org).

The broader field of international criminal law is fast-changing. An excellent introduction is Antonio Cassese et al., *International Criminal Law: Cases and Commentary* (Oxford University Press, 2011). For historical developments, see Philippe Sands (ed.), *From Nuremberg to the Hague: The Future of International Criminal Justice* (Cambridge University Press, 2003). A comprehensive reference is provided by M. Cherif Bassiouni, *International Criminal Law* (Brill, 3rd edn., 2008).

The interaction of ICC rules, ideas, and power with local politics is explored in Kamari Maxine Clarke, *Fictions of Justice: The International Criminal Court and the Challenge of Legal Pluralism in Sub-Saharan Africa* (Cambridge University Press, 2009). The idea of cosmopolitanism raised in the conclusion is increasingly important for international politics and law, and is the subject of the essays in Roland Pierik and Wouter Werner (eds.), *Cosmopolitanism in Context: Perspectives from International Law and Political Theory* (Cambridge University Press, 2010), and in Daniele Archibugi, *The Global Commonwealth of Citizens: Towards Cosmopolitan Democracy* (Princeton University Press, 2009).

APPENDIX 9

Rome Statute of the International Criminal Court (1998)

Article 1: The Court

An International Criminal Court ("the Court") is hereby established. It shall be a permanent institution and shall have the power to exercise its jurisdiction over persons for the most serious crimes of international concern, as referred to in this Statute, and shall be complementary to national criminal jurisdictions. The jurisdiction and functioning of the Court shall be governed by the provisions of this Statute.

. . .

Part II Jurisdiction, admissibility and applicable law

Article 5: Crimes within the jurisdiction of the Court

1. The jurisdiction of the Court shall be limited to the most serious crimes of concern to the international community as a whole. The Court has jurisdiction in accordance with this Statute with respect to the following crimes:
   (a) The crime of genocide;
   (b) Crimes against humanity;
   (c) War crimes;
   (d) The crime of aggression.
2. The Court shall exercise jurisdiction over the crime of aggression once a provision is adopted in accordance with articles 121 and 123 defining the crime and setting out the conditions under which the Court shall exercise jurisdiction with respect to this crime. Such a provision shall be consistent with the relevant provisions of the Charter of the United Nations.

Article 6: Genocide

For the purpose of this Statute, "genocide" means any of the following acts committed with intent to destroy, in whole or in part, a national, ethnical, racial or religious group, such as:
(a) Killing members of the group;
(b) Causing serious bodily or mental harm to members of the group;
(c) Deliberately inflicting on the group conditions of life calculated to bring about its physical destruction in whole or in part;
(d) Imposing measures intended to prevent births within the group;
(e) Forcibly transferring children of the group to another group.

Article 7: Crimes against humanity

1. For the purpose of this Statute, "crime against humanity" means any of the following acts when committed as part of a widespread or systematic attack directed against any civilian population, with knowledge of the attack:

   (a) Murder;

   (b) Extermination;

   (c) Enslavement;

   (d) Deportation or forcible transfer of population;

   (e) Imprisonment or other severe deprivation of physical liberty in violation of fundamental rules of international law;

   (f) Torture;

   (g) Rape, sexual slavery, enforced prostitution, forced pregnancy, enforced sterilization, or any other form of sexual violence of comparable gravity;

   . . .

Article 8: War crimes

1. The Court shall have jurisdiction in respect of war crimes in particular when committed as part of a plan or policy or as part of a large-scale commission of such crimes.

2. For the purpose of this Statute, "war crimes" means:

   (a) Grave breaches of the Geneva Conventions of 12 August 1949, namely, any of the following acts against persons or property protected under the provisions of the relevant Geneva Convention:

      (i) Willful killing;

      (ii) Torture or inhuman treatment, including biological experiments;

      (iii) Willfully causing great suffering, or serious injury to body or health;

      (iv) Extensive destruction and appropriation of property, not justified by military necessity and carried out unlawfully and wantonly;

   . . .

Article 11: Jurisdiction ratione temporis

1. The Court has jurisdiction only with respect to crimes committed after the entry into force of this Statute.

2. If a State becomes a Party to this Statute after its entry into force, the Court may exercise its jurisdiction only with respect to crimes committed after the entry into force of this Statute for that State, unless that State has made a declaration under article 12, paragraph 3.

Article 12: Preconditions to the exercise of jurisdiction

1. A State which becomes a Party to this Statute thereby accepts the jurisdiction of the Court with respect to the crimes referred to in article 5.
2. In the case of article 13, paragraph (a) or (c), the Court may exercise its jurisdiction if one or more of the following States are Parties to this Statute or have accepted the jurisdiction of the Court in accordance with paragraph 3:
   (a) The State on the territory of which the conduct in question occurred or, if the crime was committed on board a vessel or aircraft, the State of registration of that vessel or aircraft;
   (b) The State of which the person accused of the crime is a national.

. . .

Article 13: Exercise of jurisdiction

The Court may exercise its jurisdiction with respect to a crime referred to in article 5 in accordance with the provisions of this Statute if:
(a) A situation in which one or more of such crimes appears to have been committed is referred to the Prosecutor by a State Party in accordance with article 14;
(b) A situation in which one or more of such crimes appears to have been committed is referred to the Prosecutor by the Security Council acting under Chapter VII of the Charter of the United Nations; or
(c) The Prosecutor has initiated an investigation in respect of such a crime in accordance with article 15.

Article 14: Referral of a situation by a State Party

1. A State Party may refer to the Prosecutor a situation in which one or more crimes within the jurisdiction of the Court appear to have been committed requesting the Prosecutor to investigate the situation for the purpose of determining whether one or more specific persons should be charged with the commission of such crimes.

. . .

Article 15: Prosecutor

1. The Prosecutor may initiate investigations proprio motu on the basis of information on crimes within the jurisdiction of the Court.
2. The Prosecutor shall analyse the seriousness of the information received. For this purpose, he or she may seek additional information from States, organs of the United Nations, intergovernmental or non-governmental organizations, or other reliable

sources that he or she deems appropriate, and may receive written or oral testimony at the seat of the Court.

3. If the Prosecutor concludes that there is a reasonable basis to proceed with an investigation, he or she shall submit to the Pre-Trial Chamber a request for authorization of an investigation, together with any supporting material collected. Victims may make representations to the Pre-Trial Chamber, in accordance with the Rules of Procedure and Evidence.

4. If the Pre-Trial Chamber, upon examination of the request and the supporting material, considers that there is a reasonable basis to proceed with an investigation, and that the case appears to fall within the jurisdiction of the Court, it shall authorize the commencement of the investigation, without prejudice to subsequent determinations by the Court with regard to the jurisdiction and admissibility of a case.

Article 16: Deferral of investigation or prosecution

No investigation or prosecution may be commenced or proceeded with under this Statute for a period of 12 months after the Security Council, in a resolution adopted under Chapter VII of the Charter of the United Nations, has requested the Court to that effect; that request may be renewed by the Council under the same conditions.

Article 17: Issues of admissibility

1. Having regard to paragraph 10 of the Preamble and article 1, the Court shall determine that a case is inadmissible where:
   (a) The case is being investigated or prosecuted by a State which has jurisdiction over it, unless the State is unwilling or unable genuinely to carry out the investigation or prosecution;
   (b) The case has been investigated by a State which has jurisdiction over it and the State has decided not to prosecute the person concerned, unless the decision resulted from the unwillingness or inability of the State genuinely to prosecute;

. . .

Article 20: Ne bis in idem

1. Except as provided in this Statute, no person shall be tried before the Court with respect to conduct which formed the basis of crimes for which the person has been convicted or acquitted by the Court.

2. No person shall be tried by another court for a crime referred to in article 5 for which that person has already been convicted or acquitted by the Court.

3. No person who has been tried by another court for conduct also proscribed under article 6, 7 or 8 shall be tried by the Court with respect to the same conduct unless the proceedings in the other court:

(a) Were for the purpose of shielding the person concerned from criminal responsibility for crimes within the jurisdiction of the Court; or

(b) Otherwise were not conducted independently or impartially in accordance with the norms of due process recognized by international law and were conducted in a manner which, in the circumstances, was inconsistent with an intent to bring the person concerned to justice.

Article 21: Applicable law

1. The Court shall apply:

(a) In the first place, this Statute, Elements of Crimes and its Rules of Procedure and Evidence;

(b) In the second place, where appropriate, applicable treaties and the principles and rules of international law, including the established principles of the international law of armed conflict;

(c) Failing that, general principles of law derived by the Court from national laws of legal systems of the world including, as appropriate, the national laws of States that would normally exercise jurisdiction over the crime, provided that those principles are not inconsistent with this Statute and with international law and internationally recognized norms and standards.

Article 22: Nullum crimen sine lege

1. A person shall not be criminally responsible under this Statute unless the conduct in question constitutes, at the time it takes place, a crime within the jurisdiction of the Court.

. . .

Article 24: Non-retroactivity ratione personae

1. No person shall be criminally responsible under this Statute for conduct prior to the entry into force of the Statute.

Article 26: Exclusion of jurisdiction over persons under eighteen

The Court shall have no jurisdiction over any person who was under the age of 18 at the time of the alleged commission of a crime.

Article 27: Irrelevance of official capacity

1. This Statute shall apply equally to all persons without any distinction based on official capacity. In particular, official capacity as a Head of State or Government, a member of a Government or parliament, an elected representative or a government official shall in no case exempt a person from criminal responsibility under this Statute, nor shall it, in and of itself, constitute a ground for reduction of sentence.

2. Immunities or special procedural rules which may attach to the official capacity of a person, whether under national or international law, shall not bar the Court from exercising its jurisdiction over such a person.

Article 28: Responsibility of commanders and other superiors

In addition to other grounds of criminal responsibility under this Statute for crimes within the jurisdiction of the Court:

(a) A military commander or person effectively acting as a military commander shall be criminally responsible for crimes within the jurisdiction of the Court committed by forces under his or her effective command and control, or effective authority and control as the case may be, as a result of his or her failure to exercise control properly over such forces, where:

  (i) That military commander or person either knew or, owing to the circumstances at the time, should have known that the forces were committing or about to commit such crimes; and

  (ii) That military commander or person failed to take all necessary and reasonable measures within his or her power to prevent or repress their commission or to submit the matter to the competent authorities for investigation and prosecution.

. . .

Article 29: Non-applicability of statute of limitations

The crimes within the jurisdiction of the Court shall not be subject to any statute of limitations.

Article 30: Mental element

1. Unless otherwise provided, a person shall be criminally responsible and liable for punishment for a crime within the jurisdiction of the Court only if the material elements are committed with intent and knowledge.

. . .

Article 33: Superior orders and prescription of law

1. The fact that a crime within the jurisdiction of the Court has been committed by a person pursuant to an order of a Government or of a superior, whether military or civilian, shall not relieve that person of criminal responsibility unless:
   (a) The person was under a legal obligation to obey orders of the Government or the superior in question;
   (b) The person did not know that the order was unlawful; and
   (c) The order was not manifestly unlawful.

2. For the purposes of this article, orders to commit genocide or crimes against humanity are manifestly unlawful.

Article 86: General obligation to cooperate

States parties shall, in accordance with the provisions of this Statute, cooperate fully with the Court in its investigations and prosecutions of crimes within the jurisdiction of the Court.

Article 120: Reservations

No reservations may be made to this treaty.

10 The European Union and Regional Organizations

The European Union is a vast collection of international institutions, laws, and political arrangements. At its heart, it is a regional international organization that integrates the economies of its twenty-eight member states. This has grown, in scope and in territory, out of the European Coal and Steel Community of 1951 to encompass a customs union, a monetary union, a single labor market, and more. These new areas and competencies have been added through additional treaties negotiated among its states, and not all these treaties have been accepted by all members – as a result, the obligations of member states to the EU can vary widely. For instance, the Euro currency is used in nineteen countries while the Schengen borderless-travel area comprises twenty-two EU countries and four non-EU countries, and the customs union encompasses all EU members and several non-members. This chapter examines the legal and political structures of the European Union and places the EU in the context of other regional international organizations. It introduces several other regional organizations, including the African Union, ASEAN, and the Organization of American States, for the sake of comparison. These are much less comprehensive in their integration than the EU though and often use "EU-like" language to describe their aspirations.

The distinctive features of regional organizations arise from the fact that while they strive to integrate a smaller set of countries they also aim to reach across a wider range of substantive issues than the other international organizations in this book. The regional organizations in this chapter are vastly different from each other but they face the same challenge of integrating members on an almost limitless range of policies. They deal with this challenge very differently: the EU has created powerful central authorities, including a bureaucracy and a legal hierarchy between the center and the member states; in contrast, the AU, ASEAN, and the OAS leave most powers of decision in the hands of meetings of their heads of government. These are more typical of regional international organizations in that they could in theory make forceful collective decisions but in practice their main contribution is as a forum in which inter-governmental negotiation takes place.

They also all show the strains of striving for political/legal integration: member governments often disagree with each other on what should be integrated and how, and on how general rules and ideas of integration should be applied to particular cases. There are winners and losers in these processes, and gains and losses are unevenly spread both among member-states and within them. The political forces that produced the "leave" vote in Britain in 2016 were startling for people who see EU integration as a natural solution to problems of interdependence, but they were not unusual – controversy over the *politics* of regional integration are present throughout the EU members and in all other regional organizations.

The Association of Southeast Asian Nations (ASEAN) has all the institutional architecture of a formal international organization but is virtually empty of actor-like properties, and its influence comes when it is pressed into service as a legitimating device for the interests of its strongest members. The European Union (EU) has taken on an enormous share of the sovereign powers of its member states, to the point that it challenges the very categories of "inter-national organization" and "sovereign state." The African Union (AU) follows the tradition of the old Organization of African Unity from which it grew (OAU). The OAU had little organizational autonomy from its most powerful members. The AU has added an intriguing peacekeeping capacity that may make it a consequential military and political actor in Africa.

These organizations are all expressions of a more general belief that prosperity, or peace, or some other important value in a region, depends on certain kinds of inter-state coordination. All of them purport a faith that regional integration has a pacifying effect on inter-state interaction and that reducing barriers to economic activity leads to greater wealth. In practice, however, they achieve these integrationist goals to very different degrees, and they are dramatically different in the kinds of obligations they impose on their members. They are therefore very different in the kinds of compliance and enforcement that they induce, and they manifest very differently as actors, fora, and resources in the wider world of international politics.

With their breadth, regional organizations are generally faced with a choice between making either extraordinarily deep commitments of sovereignty, in which members give up a lot of autonomy, or very shallow ones, where they give up very little. The EU takes the former route toward complex integration, while the AU and ASEAN take the latter path wherein virtually no powers are taken away from the member states. The middle ground appears to be hard to sustain for regional organizations and they therefore tend toward the poles, though the OAS is particularly instructive on this point. In addition, these broad organizations provide many opportunities for a dramatic gap between the stated intentions of the organization and their actual practice. The grand scale of their integrationist ambitions means that there is a large potential for dead letters and insincere promises in their charters, and it takes some work to parse out in the legal charters what is meaningful and important from what is not.

Given the nature of these organizations, the separate themes of obligation, compliance, and enforcement are not distinguishable in the ways that organized the previous chapters. The AU and ASEAN create few formal obligations on members and therefore their impact cannot be understood through a framework that focuses on compliance and enforcement. The EU, by contrast, creates so many obligations that the category boundary between the member state and its EU obligations has blurred – its member states are in part constituted by their existence in the EU, at least for many issues. The EU cannot be understood in terms of sovereign states making choices about compliance with the organization's rules because the distinction between the EU and its member states is blurred. None of these organizations fits the framework applied in this book to the universal institutions, and so the presentation in this chapter aims to describe the organizations through their powers and their impacts, rather than through the three guiding questions of previous chapters.

The European Union

key facts

Headquarters:
- the Commission and its main bureaucracy are in Brussels, Belgium
- the European Parliament is in Strasbourg, France
- the Court of Justice of the EU is in Luxembourg
- the European Central Bank is in Frankfurt, Germany

Members: 28 member countries

Website: www.europa.eu

Key structures:

European Commission

- executive organ and bureaucracy of the EU
- represents the common EU interest
- has direct regulatory power within member states on many issues

European Parliament

- directly elected by EU citizens
- represents the people of Europe
- has authority of "co-decision" with the Council

Council of the European Union

- comprised of ministers from all EU members, representing their governments
- represents the national governments
- the EU's main decision-making body

Court of Justice

- judicial authority of the EU
- hears cases on whether member states and the European institutions are acting properly within EU law

Key legal texts of the European Union:

Treaty of Lisbon (2009): reframed the relationships among EU institutions and between these institutions and EU citizens.

Treaty on European Union (Maastricht, 1992): changed the EEC into the European Union.

Treaty on the Functioning of the European Union (Rome, 1957): established the European Economic Community.

Treaty Establishing the European Coal and Steel Community (1952): created the ECSC.

The European Union presents many faces to the world. It is at once a set of linked inter-state institutions, an idea about the meaning of "Europe," a collection over overlapping treaties, and a system of distributed authority among local, national, and supranational levels. Its nature looks very different depending on which of the perspectives from Chapter 2 is used to study it. It can be seen as a new kind of state, a new kind of nation, a "postnational" constitutional order, or merely a set of deals among sovereign states.[1] Scholarship on the EU is organized in part around disagreements about how the thing itself should be interpreted. My goal in this section is not to review the literature on the EU – for that, excellent book-length treatments of the EU exist.[2] Instead my goal is to see how the EU illuminates the broader study of international organizations as set out in this book by showing a set of ways that the tensions between state sovereignty and international commitment can be managed which is very different than the other organizations in this book.

The EU begins from the familiar premise of an inter-state treaty that defines the obligations that states owe to each other and to the central body. Like other organizations in this book, it is both constituted and delimited by the authority that its member states assigned to it when they consented to its treaties. The content of that assignment is substantially more than any other international organization, and so the EU has the greatest claim to being a truly supranational institution. The broad investiture of legal authority in the central organization represents the EU's attempt to solve the compliance problem by removing the right to autonomous policy-making from member states. This does not displace self-interest and political disagreement among the members, and indeed within them; instead it molds disagreement by forcing much of it through the institutions and procedures of the organization.

In the EU, the central institutions are empowered on many topics of policy (though not all) to make rules that are directly enforceable in the member states. Where the AU, ASEAN, and the OAS tread lightly around the authority of their member states (as we will see later in this chapter) and leave all important powers to meetings of their heads of government, the EU does the opposite by removing the state from the decision chain (again, on some but not all issues). Very different in practice and in their effect, these two approaches should both be seen as responses to the same simple challenge: how to manage inter-state commitments in a community of sovereign states. The EU is also bound by the general principle of "subsidiarity," which says "in areas which do not fall within its exclusive competence, the Union shall act only if and in so far as the

---

[1] For an excellent discussion, see Nico Krisch, *Beyond Constitutionalism: The Pluralist Structure of Postnational Law*. Oxford University Press, 2010.

[2] See for instance, John McCormick, *Understanding the European Union: A Concise Introduction*, 5th edn. Palgrave Macmillan, 2011; Herman Lelieveldt and Sebastiaan Princen, *The Politics of the European Union*. Cambridge University Press, 2011.

objectives of the proposed action cannot be sufficiently achieved by the Member States" (Art. 5(3), Treaty of Lisbon).

At the core of the EU is a common market for goods, services, people, and money – that is, a shared space in which the borders among the member states are more or less irrelevant and a common external border separates this space from the outside world. This has largely been accomplished for the movement of goods and services around the territory of the EU's members, and in a more limited fashion for money and people. For goods and services, the EU represents a single economic market, unified in the sense of having no internal barriers to movement and a single external tariff (and no internal tariffs).

These changes in what borders mean are a kind of grand experiment in society. They move the locus of authority for decisions in society and so alter the relationship between people and governments and private firms. The hypothesis behind the EU is that freeing market actors from some border restrictions will improve overall welfare by allowing firms to find ways to reduce inefficiencies in production and distribution. It is a social experiment in the sense that the complexity of economy and society make it impossible to know what will come from this. Changing the nature of the state in this way has profound and unpredictable political and social effects, as Karl Polanyi showed in *The Great Transformation* around the first experiments with "market society" in Britain as the common lands became enclosed and labor was commodified in the eighteenth century. Polanyi charted the backlash in England as (as he says) society tried to protect itself from these new forces, and the tensions and accommodation that followed. On a smaller scale the history of the EU has been marked by frequent resistance that has sometimes surprised those who see the EU in technical rather than political/social terms.

The British referendum on the EU in 2016 may be one of those moments. It produced a narrow majority in favor of exit – 51.9 percent of voters opted for Brexit – but the campaigns ahead of the vote showed that the "stay" side worked from the assumption that people appreciated the stability that came from further integration while the "leave" side saw an opportunity to draw out people's sense of political disempowerment. This is the first time a country has opted to leave the EU and also the most complicated withdrawal from an international organization ever. The procedure for withdrawal is set out in the Treaty on the European Union and until this is satisfied Britain remains a full and regular member of the organization. Article 50 of the Treaty governs withdrawals. It requires that a member notify the European Council of its intent to withdraw and then sets up a two-year window for negotiating the terms of the divorce.

As this has never been done before it is not clear what those terms should include, but presumably they will decide the key aspects of the post-Brexit relationship: how people, goods, money, and services will move across the Britain–EU border. It is also not clear what happens if the parties cannot agree on new terms within the two-year window or how many EU countries need to approve them. The Council can extend the negotiating period but if it does not then it appears that at the two-year mark EU law simply stops applying to Britain regardless of whether new agreements are in place. Much of the confusion over Brexit reflects the fact that the referendum itself was promised by Prime Minister David Cameron in 2012 without much thought as to its domestic constitutional implications or its international legal consequences. He believed the referendum would support staying in the EU and the entire experience would neutralize his anti-EU rivals in the Conservative Party. His quick idea, apparently hatched in a pizza restaurant at O'Hare airport in Chicago, has produced a constitutional crisis in the UK among Parliament, the government, and the constituent regions, that may well unravel the country itself. It remains to be seen what effects this process has on the UK and on the EU, and whether it comes to be seen as the first move in a chain of disintegration that undoes what the EU has become.

The European integration "project" has generally operated on the "bicycle theory," which suggests that "just like a bicycle has to keep going to avoid falling over... [so too] European integration has to progress in order to avoid backtracking."[3] The European Coal and Steel Community (1957) set the thing in motion by creating a single market for the heavy industries of the six original member states (France, West Germany, Italy, Belgium, Netherlands, and Luxembourg), and to this were gradually added more countries and more kinds of goods and services, until there was essentially a free-trade area for all products across essentially the entire continent and its 500 million citizens. Together this entity is the largest economy in the world by GDP. But a free-trade area can be undone if the parties resort to non-tariff barriers or other policy instruments to disadvantage imported goods or services relative to domestic products and so a common market was seen as not enough. The issue of NTBs arose also with respect to the WTO in Chapter 5 and it motivated the WTO's policies on non-discrimination and national treatment, and its dispute-settlement procedure and rules against non-tariff barriers. The EU dealt with this issue by demanding that

---

[3] Christian Noyer, "How to Combine a Deepening and Widening of the European Union," speech to the Oxford University European Affairs Society, November 22, 2000, http://bit.ly/W8Lkgt, accessed January 25, 2013.

its members adopt standardized policies on a wide range of issues including labeling, taxation, health standards, agricultural subsidies, and more. Coordination across member governments on these and other issues is understood to be necessary in order to avoid government interference with the common market. Much of the architecture of the European Commission, the bureaucracy in Brussels, is designed to ensure the consistent implementation of these common standards across the countries of Europe. This is a much more centralized and authoritative form of international organization than the WTO.

Thus, once the free-trade area was essentially completed in the 1970s European leaders turned to integration and coordination on new issues, notably in political and monetary affairs. From these efforts came significant integration on monetary policy including a common currency, and much talk but less action on coordinating foreign policy and military affairs. This ideology of the inevitability of further integration may be partly to blame for the populist backlash against the EU project in many countries, shown most notably in the Brexit vote, as it presumes that integration is its own justification and does not need to be explained to anybody.

The European Economic and Monetary Union (EMU) is the set of EU treaties that govern monetary policy and the common currency. Its goal is to reduce frictions in trade and investment that are associated with the discrepant monetary policies across EU members, such as shifting exchange rates, divergent interest rates and rates of inflation, and differences among governments regarding budget deficits and money supply. The current EMU system grew out of the various attempts into the 1980s to keep exchange rates relatively stable across the major European currencies. The present system dates to the mid-1990s when a series of major decisions were taken by the leading governments. These included to create a common currency across the EU, to limit governments' discretion on budget deficits and the money supply, to create a European Central Bank, and to include a set of opt-out provisions that permit EU members to decline to participate in some of these arrangements. This last decision has allowed a subset of EU states (the Eurozone 17) to go ahead with a full monetary union including the common Euro currency, while the others remain outside the system. This is an example of the bifurcation that the EU has sometimes engineered to allow developments opposed by some members to go ahead without them.

On military affairs and national defense, the EU has aimed to integrate its members into a common foreign policy and defense structure, but this has largely foundered in the face of the unwillingness of the main states in Europe to pool their foreign policy decisions. Looking to protect what are seen as vital national interests, the EU members have placed defense matters under a unanimity decision rule so that no member can be forced to go along with something to which they fundamentally object. With such a strict process, relatively few decisions get made. Compared with other parts of the EU architecture described above, the EU's statements on defense are notable for the way that they are expressed in aspirational, future-oriented terms, rather than as existing obligations on members. Among the most prominent examples of successful EU military policy are several peace operations, modeled on UN peacekeeping (rather than peace-enforcement), including a naval operation to prevent piracy off the coast of Somalia (known as EU NAVFOR).

The existence of NATO (the North Atlantic Treaty Organization) has also played a role in diminishing the defense integration of the European Union. Much of what a united EU defense policy might accomplish could be said to be already being done by NATO, and the US has long made clear that it does not want a joint EU military that takes the place of NATO.[4] NATO's membership includes twenty-eight states, twenty-one of which are also EU members. The central obligation in the NATO Charter (known as the North Atlantic Treaty of 1949) is that "the parties agree that an armed attack against one or more of them in Europe or North America shall be considered an armed attack against them all" (Article 5). This leads to the obligation that all members are justified in invoking the rule on self-defense in the UN Charter to respond to the attack. This trigger mechanism makes NATO the quintessential expression of "collective security" in the international system, and it is entirely different than anything currently in place for the EU. However, the integration of military and defense policies in Europe is likely held back by the twin forces of the existence of NATO and the desire by the strong European states to maintain their freedom of action with respect to foreign policy.

Institutions and Legal Framework

The basic framework of the EU follows the traditional form of an inter-state organization as the model has been examined in this book, in the sense that the EU institutions exist by virtue of a grant of authority from the organization's

---

[4] For instance, Congressional Research Service, "The European Union: Foreign and Security Policy," August 15, 2011, 7–5700.

member states. The rules and institutions of the EU have their legal authority as a result of the explicit and consensual delegation of power to them by sovereign states in the Treaties of Rome, Maastricht, Lisbon, and beyond. These treaties form the "primary" legislation of the EU. This maintains the traditional form that we have seen in the United Nations, the World Trade Organizations, and other international organizations.

The core legal document of the EU is the Lisbon Treaty which, as of 2009, amended the formal framework of the EU set out by the Maastricht Treaty of 1992 and the Rome Treaty of 1957, along with other more minor agreements (this is known generically as the Treaty of the European Union). The project of European integration has proceeded through a series of such treaties, with each new agreement extending the previous, so that the obligations of the member states and the powers of the central institutions have grown by layering the new atop the old. The content of those obligations has therefore also changed enormously from one period to another. The Lisbon Treaty takes the existing institutions of the EU and modifies their powers and their inter-relations. For instance, it reduces the need for unanimity in some settings, making it easier to pass decisions but guaranteeing more conflict over compliance; it promotes the European Parliament relative to the Council of Ministers, in the interest of increasing democratic oversight, though at the cost of requiring both bodies to consent to the same legislation. It also attaches a Charter of Fundamental Rights of the European Union, which defines a set of individual rights for EU citizens and protects them from the decisions of the EU itself. Many of these changes address the legal and conceptual relationships between individual people and the institutions of the European Union, and represent a move away from the EU's inter-state origins – and therefore even further away from its original status as a conventional international organization.

The key institutions of the EU include the European Commission, the European Parliament, the European Council, and the Court of Justice of the European Union. These are arranged in and around a basic framework of legal and political commitments by the states whose broad outlines are simple to chart but whose practical application depends on many exceptions, exemptions, and special cases. These institutions can create directives, regulations, decisions, and other products which are binding on EU members (these are known as the "secondary" legislation of the EU). The complexities of the EU arise in large part because these institutions and their products have different powers over different areas of policy and in relation to different EU members.

The combinations and permutations multiply rapidly and these motivate the debates over whether the EU is a super-state or a traditional international organization or some entirely novel form of political governance.

The European Commission encompasses the administrative apparatus of the EU. It is the EU's executive branch, headed by twenty-eight "commissioners." Serving under them are the administrative employees of the EU, about 23,000 European civil servants who implement the laws and decisions of the EU. The Commission and the Commissioners represent the interests of the EU itself, rather than their home governments. The Commission is responsible to the European Parliament in something like the way that the British Cabinet is responsible to its parliament: a motion by the EU Parliament to dissolve the Commission would require all the Commissioners to resign.

The Council of the EU is comprised of ministers from each government. This is also known as the Council of Ministers (though not the Council of Europe, which is a separate international organization, nor the European Council, which is an EU institution discussed below). The Council of Ministers represents the governments of the EU and makes the major policy decisions for the EU. It operates mostly by qualified majority vote in a system in which countries have a number of votes proportional to their size.[5] The composition of the Council depends on the issue being discussed, so that it sometimes meets as a gathering of foreign ministers, sometimes as agriculture ministers, sometimes as transport ministers, and so on. Many Council decisions must now be approved by the European Parliament as well, through a system known as "co-decision."

The European Council is the gathering of heads of government. It meets quarterly and at this high political level it is the direction-setting and conflict-resolving body set atop the Council of Ministers. The European Parliament is a body of representatives elected directly by the populations of EU members. Its purpose is to integrate democratic accountability into the EU legislative process, and so has some authority to review the acts of the Commission and to cooperate in the development of legislation by the Council.

Together these institutions make up a system that can be roughly summarized as follows. The governments of the EU set the major policy directions and treaty initiatives at meetings of the European Council. Disparities in political influence among the governments matter a great deal in these negotiations. Agreements

---

[5] The formula for assigning votes to countries combines mathematics and politics, and the distribution is in the end a negotiated settlement among them rather than the product of a clear formula.

reached in the European Council are developed into legislation by the Council of Ministers and the European Parliament. Once approved, they are implemented by the Commission. The Commission's work may require that member states change their laws or practices and this can be contentious. The Court of Justice of the EU provides judicial review for non-compliance by governments.

However, this sketch leaves out much of what makes the EU conceptually interesting, including the influence of political power, the different treatment of different policy areas, the degree of autonomy for these institutions, and the increasingly complex legal arrangements among European courts, governments, and citizens. I explore the last of these briefly next, before turning to the more conventional regional international organizations.

A key test of any international organization arises when its rules or decisions conflict with the laws or preferences of a member state. As we have seen, these moments of conflict help illuminate both the legal and the political arrangements at the heart of the organization. For the EU, the issue is especially interesting because the members have granted the organization very deep powers to make laws that are effective across the Union, as opposed to making recommendations or other decisions that do not have the status of "law" as in the ILO or the UN General Assembly. It is therefore common for the EU to find itself in a condition where its decisions contradict national policies and these two bodies of law must then somehow be reconciled.

For many EU decisions, the reconciliation principle is simple: EU law takes precedence over a contradictory national law. This is the rule known as the "supremacy" of EU law and it developed over time largely through the decisions of the European Court of Justice.[6] It has now been codified in the Lisbon Treaty of 2009. The supremacy of European law gives in principle a clear answer to contradictions between national and EU law: EU law prevails. For instance, national labor laws have frequently been struck down for being inconsistent with EU rules on employment and industrial relations.[7] However, its scope and its application to particular cases are highly contested, and the embrace of the doctrine varies across EU member states. As a constitutional arrangement, however, supremacy establishes the fact that EU law is hierarchically superior to competing national laws that might govern the same substantive question.

---

[6] Karen Alter, *Establishing the Supremacy of European Law: The Making of an International Rule of Law in Europe*. Oxford University Press, 2003.

[7] Andrea Eriksson, "European Court of Justice: Broadening the Scope of European Nondiscrimination Law," *International Journal of Constitutional Law*, 2009 **7**(4): 731–753.

The consequences of legal supremacy are compounded by the fact that many EU regulations and articles have "direct effect" in national law. That is, they create rights which an EU citizen can use in the domestic courts against a contrary claim of the national government. This empowers citizens to use their domestic courts to challenge EU-contradicting national laws, and requires those courts in turn to enforce the doctrine of supremacy. It therefore enlists national courts in the task of enforcing EU regulations at the demand of local citizens, and fills the institutional void that often exists where rights may be claimed but there is no legal body available to enforce them (as is often the case with international human rights norms). While there are many important limits to direct effect, the principle itself is well established in EU law and creates a legal relationship between citizens and the EU that may be unmediated by, or perhaps even antagonistic to, the national government.

The legal relations between the EU, its governments, and its citizens are vastly complicated by the fact that the EU takes many kinds of decisions and these vary in their legal status, and there are competing institutions of the EU and beyond it which may find themselves interpreting those rules in relation to competing claims. Supremacy and direct effect exist alongside subsidiarity and national constitutions, as well as in the context of the human rights norms and laws and the European Court of Human Rights. These complexities give rise to EU Studies as an interdisciplinary field of scholarship that combines political theory, law, political science, and international relations.

In its simplest form, we can conclude by saying that the central accomplishment of the project of European integration has been the creation of a single economic market and a common external tariff policy. Together these represent the fulfillment of the original goals of the integration movement and put the EU at the head of a growing list of regional free-trade areas, including NAFTA, Mercosur in South America, and perhaps one day ASEAN. Much of the EU's regulatory authority and activity can be seen as an elaboration of the institutional underpinnings of the single market and external tariff: to ensure that the single internal market is not de facto fragmented by divergent national policies, the European institutions have broad authority to harmonize national regulations regarding product labeling, marketing, manufacturing, investment policy, competition policy, and many other areas of government authority. Creating common policies in these areas, in turn, has led to a demand for a range of further institutions to manage their implications. Thus, the increasing authority of the European Parliament is a response to the fact that these central institutions of the EU are exercising their powers without democratic accountability – they expressly bypass domestic institutions, and as a result they are not included in the democratic processes that have developed in the states.

There is nothing inevitable about the EU's advance toward greater integration. The overarching teleology of its history since the 1950s shows an arc toward integration, but there have also been many failures along the way and we should remain open to the possibility that it will sometimes reverse itself. Among the failures, it is worth noting that major new treaties are frequently defeated in popular referenda after being negotiated among the states, and this occurred in Ireland in 2008 and France and the Netherlands in 2005. The EU has also divided itself into multiple tracks so that the opposition of some members to new provisions does not stop their application for the rest, with the result that the EU cannot be described as a single set of rules that cover the entire community.

This is evidence of both success and failure, in that it advances the project of integration but it admits that the integrationists were unable to convince all members to come along. The Euro as common currency is a major innovation in integration but it is far from clear that the rules that underpin it (on, for example, budget deficits) are sustainable. The Greek financial crisis in early 2010 showed not only that governments find it very difficult to keep themselves within the allowable deficit range of less than 3 percent of GDP, but also that governments will behave strategically and even deceitfully in constructing their spending and borrowing decisions to mask violations of the rule.[8] For Greece, the other Euro-zone members were willing to make an exception from the rules, but the long-term stability of the rules is brought into some doubt.

---

[8] See for instance Charles Forelle and Stephen Fidler, "Europe's Original Sin," *Wall Street Journal*, March 3, 2010, p. A1.

African Union

key facts

Headquarters: Addis Ababa, Ethiopia

Members: 54 countries

Website: www.africa-union.org

Mandate: to "achieve greater unity and solidarity between the African countries and the peoples of Africa" (Art. 3(a)), and to "defend the sovereignty, territorial integrity and independence of its Member States" (Art. 3(b)).

key facts

Key structures: annual meeting of heads of governments (the "Assembly") to set common policies, more frequent meetings of ministers (the "Executive Council"), and a smaller "Peace and Security Council" to manage the AU's peace operations.

Key obligations: to pay dues to the organization (Art. 23(1)) and "to comply with the decisions and policies of the Union" (Art. 23(2)).

Enforcement: the Assembly can impose sanctions for violations under Article 23 but not use military force; the Peace and Security Council can authorize "peace support" operations to resolve conflicts but does not enforce the policies of the Union.

Key clauses of the Constitutive Act:
Article 3: The Union shall function in accordance with the following principles:
a) sovereign equality and interdependence among members;
b) respect of borders existing on achievement of independence; . . .
e) peaceful resolution of conflicts among Member States; . . .
g) non-interference by any Member State in the internal affairs of another
    Article 7(1): The Assembly shall take its decisions by consensus or, failing which, by a two-thirds majority of the Member States of the Union.
Article 9(1)a: The Functions of the Assembly shall be to determine the common policies of the Union.

Key clauses of the Protocol on the Peace and Security Council:
Article 7(1): In conjunction with the Chairperson of the Commission, the Peace and Security Council shall:
a) anticipate and prevent disputes and conflicts . . .;
b) undertake peace-making and peace-building functions to resolve conflicts where they have occurred;
c) authorize the mounting and deployment of peace support missions.

The African Union was formally incorporated in 2002, making it among the newest of the world's high-profile international organizations. It arose out of the Organization of African Unity (OAU) which ran from 1963 to 2002 and which is formally its precursor. The AU aims for "unity, solidarity, cohesion and cooperation among the peoples of Africa and African States" (Preamble, Constitutive Act). It includes all countries in Africa except Morocco (Morocco refuses to join as a response to the inclusion of Western Sahara as a member, under the name Sahrawi Arab Democratic Republic).

The AU's predecessor, the OAU, was a product of the decolonization movement in the 1950s and 1960s as independent countries emerged from the collapsed European empires of Africa. These new countries, and some of their older supporters, formed the OAU to consolidate the anti-colonial process in Africa, and its structure and early efforts were largely oriented toward ending what remained of white-minority rule on the continent. The post-colonial countries existed in an ideological context that included both independence and pan-Africanism, and this dual ideology greatly shaped the OAU.[9] During the liberation struggle, these two ideas supported each other in the sense that independence movements across the continent could appeal to both African unity and anti-colonialism to strengthen and explain their goals. After independence, however, the two themes made for an uneasy combination since the winners of local anti-colonial wars did not wish to see their newly achieved independence dissipated by pan-African unification. Unity and "national" independence became contradictory, and the OAU was in many ways a manifestation of that contradiction: it represented the myth of post-colonial pan-African unity but the reality of sovereign statehood within existing (i.e. colonial) territorial boundaries. The Charter of the OAU reflected this tension in that it included pan-Africanist rhetoric but a strict state-centric legal form. The AU perpetuates this dualism while also continuing the clear dominance of state-centrism over pan-African integration. The legal arrangements of the AU are founded on the principles of non-intervention, inviolable borders, and the equality of its members.

The African Union replaced the OAU when the AU's Constitutive Act came into effect in 2002. It has formal corporate personality as an organization under international law and contains within it a series of institutions, such as a central bank, a court of justice, and a "peace and security council" to develop or manage common policies on substantive questions. Many of these institutions are advertised by the Constitutive Act but have not yet been instantiated, and their powers and structure relative to member states have yet to be negotiated. The actually existing AU is therefore much more limited than the potential AU described in the Act.

---

[9] See Samuel M. Makinda and F. Wafula Okumu, *The African Union: Challenges of Globalization, Security, and Governance*. Routledge, 2008.

The Constitutive Act follows the pattern established by the UN Charter in that it defines the goals of the organization, then the legal principles that frame it, and then the structures and institutions that it brings into being. The first set the normative context for the organization, the second its legal framework, and the third its operational structures.

The objectives of the organization, listed in Article 3, include "to: achieve greater unity and solidarity between the African countries and the peoples of Africa; defend the sovereignty ... and independence of its Member States; ... respect and promote human and peoples' rights ...; promote sustainable development ..." These are presented as goals and aspirations rather than as legally binding commitments. They are therefore not of legal consequence in assessing the powers of the organization, though they are set up nicely to become the site of contestation in the future.

Article 4 sets out the "principles" under which the AU is to function. The overall effect of the principles is to reinforce the inviolability of members' borders, and so (somewhat paradoxically for an international organization) the AU entrenches rather than transcends state sovereignty – with one important exception in Article 4(h). The key provisions of Article 4 say that "The Union shall function in accordance with the following principles: a) the sovereign equality and interdependence among Member States ...; b) respect of borders existing on achievement of independence ... e) peaceful resolution of conflicts among Member States ...; g) non-interference by any Member State in the internal affairs of another ..." These restate the norms and laws of state sovereignty, and layer on top of the universal rules on non-intervention contained in the UN Charter.

Article 4(h), however, says that there exists a "right of the Union to intervene in a Member State pursuant to a decision of the Assembly in respect of grave circumstances, namely: war crimes, genocide, and crimes against humanity." This opens state sovereignty to a form of limited regional authority. It has not been enacted yet and so its practical shape remains unknown, but it is a clear legal statement that sovereignty is to some degree subordinate to the authority of the AU. Notice that the combination of Articles 4(h) and 4(g) makes it explicit that the right to intervene is a right of the AU and not of individual member states. Article 4(g) expressly forbids interference by another member state, while Article 4(h) permits it by the AU. To make an intervention, the Assembly of the AU must decide that it is necessary and that the situation qualifies as one of the forms of "grave circumstance" defined in

Article 4(h). The Assembly, as we will see below, is governed by a decision rule that requires two-thirds majority for a decision to pass. An AU intervention in a member state could therefore be mandated in response to war crimes, genocide, or crimes against humanity, if two-thirds of its members voted for it. This is a potentially important legal and military power, and provides an interesting contrast to the interventionary capacity of both the UN Security Council and the AU's own Peace and Security Council.

The Constitutive Act defines the legal structures of the individual bodies of the AU. The most important of these are the Assembly, the Executive Council, and the Parliament, supported by the Authority of the AU (its bureaucracy, known in the Act as the Commission), as well as the Peace and Security Council. (The other bodies of the AU, including the central bank, parliament, and court of justice, are listed in the Act but their composition and everything about their work is left for future development in protocols that will be appended to the Act.)

The Assembly and the Executive Council both comprise representatives of all of the AU members. The Assembly is a meeting of the heads of state or heads of government of the AU countries, and the Executive Council is a body at the ministerial level, usually of foreign ministers. The Assembly is meant to meet once per year to set general policies for the organization, to manage military conflicts, to set the budget, and to admit new members, as well as to meet in emergency session as needed for special problems (as with Article 4(h) above). Its power is to "determine the common policies of the Union" (Article 9(1)a. It also decides on what penalties should follow for members that fail in their obligations to the Union, though including only "measures of a political and economic nature," prominently leaving out military enforcement (Article 23(1)). The Executive Council, by contrast, meets more often and is authorized under Article 13 to "take decisions on policies in areas of common interest to the Member States" which might include any of the issues typically associated with line departments of a domestic government. The Executive Council has no authority over foreign policy, and can deal in dispute settlement or military affairs only at the direction of the Assembly.

The important question for the AU is how the decisions of these bodies relate to the authority of the member states, and on this issue two facts are revealing: first, the most important decision-making powers are reserved for the Assembly, which is made up of the leaders of the member countries; second, the Act contains no statement that the organization in general takes decisions on behalf of its members. Taken together, these two points suggest that the organization is both legally and politically secondary to its members. Its decision apparatus is dominated by the heads of government, making it much more like a forum for inter-state negotiations than an actor with independent capacity. In addition, these leaders can set "common policies" for the organization but these fall short of a legally binding obligation on members to comply. In practice so far, the AU has been dominated by the leaders of its most powerful countries, in large part by making the Authority of the AU, which was to have been its bureaucracy, into a substantive executive organ.[10]

The Peace and Security Council (PSC) is an addition to the AU since the Constitutive Act was signed. It is formally governed by a protocol appended to the Act in 2004, using the authority of the Assembly to establish new organs for the Union (under Article 5(2)). One of the objectives of the organization in Article 3 is to "promote peace, security, and stability on the continent" (Art. 3(f)), and the new PSC is therefore a product of Articles 5(2) and 3(f) together. The PSC is roughly modeled on the UN Security Council. It is composed of fifteen members elected from the AU Assembly who have the authority to send "peace support" missions in response to conflicts (Article 7(1)c of the PSC Protocol), drawn from a standing force of military units provided by AU members (Article 13 of the PSC Protocol). It also has the authority to enforce the "grave circumstances" provisions of Article 4(h) of the AU Act. In taking its decisions, the PSC requires a two-thirds majority vote of its members and has no veto members, and so in principle it could provide a centralized military capacity that is legally superior to AU members. This remains to be seen, but at present it seems doubtful on at least two grounds: the surrounding laws of the AU create a framework that is highly deferential to state sovereignty, and the AU's approach toward military and humanitarian crises so far (in Darfur, in the Democratic Republic of Congo, and elsewhere) has reinforced that relationship. The presumption must be that the PSC will not be as activist as the Protocol suggests is possible, though the legal possibility for AU authority remains and is intriguing.

[10] See the discussions in Samuel M. Makinda and F. Wafula Okumu, *The African Union: Challengers of Globalization, Security, and Governance.* Routledge, 2008, pp. 50–52, and Rodrigo Tavares, *Regional Security: The Capacity of International Organizations.* Routledge, 2009.

ASEAN

key facts

Headquarters: Jakarta, Indonesia

Members: 10 countries and 2 observer countries

Website: www.aseansec.org

Mandate: to "maintain and enhance peace, security and stability and further strengthen peace-oriented values in the region" (Art. 1(1)), to "ensure that the peoples and Member States of ASEAN live ... in a just, democratic and harmonious environment" (Art. 1(4)) and to "create a single market and production base which is prosperous" (Art. 1(5)).

Key structures: periodic meetings of the heads of governments (the ASEAN Summit) and of the "Coordinating Council" composed of ministers from all members.

Key obligations: Member States shall take all necessary measures, including the enactment of appropriate domestic legislation, to effectively implement the provisions of this Charter and to comply with all obligations of membership (Art. 5(2)).

Enforcement: the ASEAN Summit can consider measures in response to "a serious breach of the Charter or non-compliance" by a member state (Art. 20(4)).

Key clauses of the ASEAN Charter:

Article 2(2): ASEAN and its members shall act in accordance with the following principles:

a. respect for the independence, sovereignty, equality, territorial integrity and national identity of all ASEAN Member States; ...

g. enhanced consultation on matters seriously affecting the common interest of ASEAN;

h. adherence to the rule of law, good governance, the principle of democracy and constitutional government.

Article 20:

1. As a basic principle, decision-making in ASEAN shall be based on consultation and consensus.

2. Where consensus cannot be achieved, the ASEAN Summit shall decide how a specific decision can be made ....

4. In the case of a serious breach of the Charter or non-compliance, the matter shall be referred to the ASEAN Summit for decision.

ASEAN has long been seen as operating mainly in the realm of symbolic politics rather than of concrete obligations and policies, yet it is worth examining because it is often mentioned as a potential source of regional governance for Asia. Its legal structure, like that of the AU, reserves all the important decision-making for the plenary meetings of heads of government, and thus the entire organization is overwhelmingly dominated by the member governments. It is in practice almost entirely a forum for ad hoc negotiations among the governments rather than an actor in its own right. It imposes no substantive obligations on its members and therefore has little need for compliance or enforcement. Despite these features, it is perpetually in the process of negotiating substantive components, such as on a regional free-trade area, and so there remains the possibility that its future will be significantly different than its past.

As with all international organizations, the legal structures of ASEAN are helpful in revealing the political arrangements that are its core. The founding instrument for the group was a declaration among the five original governments in 1967. This declaration did not create a free-standing legal organization, but rather was comprised of statements of shared principles, chief among them "to accelerate economic growth," "to promote regional peace," and to "promote active collaboration and mutual assistance on matters of common interest" among the signatory governments.[11] The institution that resulted had neither a secretariat nor legal corporate personality. These aspirations were attached to a schedule of meetings of the countries' foreign ministers and assorted committees of specialists, but not to any legally binding commitments or rules. The group gave itself a Secretary-General and related staff only in 1976, and even after that the Secretary-General remained subordinate to officials sent to ASEAN by the national governments.[12]

The current version of ASEAN rests on the 1967 declaration but it adds to it a formal treaty, the ASEAN Charter of 2008, which re-established the group as a concrete international organization with legal personality and a corporate existence. The document of the ASEAN Charter has a structure familiar from the UN Charter and the AU Constitutive Act. It lists the principles and aspirations of the body (in terms borrowed from the 1967

---

[11] The Bangkok Declaration, 1967, www.asean.org/1212.htm. Accessed February 9, 2010.

[12] Philippe Sands and Pierre Klein, *Bowett's Law of International Institutions*, 5th edn. Sweet & Maxwell, 2001, pp. 230–231.

Declaration), but contains no substantive obligations that bind members in any way. The clauses of the Charter that are written in the strongest language are also the most trivial: for instance, Article 40 reads in full "ASEAN shall have an anthem." The original five members (Indonesia, Malaysia, the Philippines, Singapore, and Thailand) were joined by Brunei in 1984, Vietnam in 1995, Laos and Myanmar in 1997, and Cambodia in 1999. These ten members have committed to pursuing economic integration in the form of free trade, openness to intra-ASEAN foreign investment, a security community, and social and cultural integration. These commitments together are promised to create a web of commitments and institutions which will be known as the "ASEAN Community" but the actual commitments and institutions remain to be agreed upon. Sharp disagreements among its members over the details have made it impossible to implement, for instance, the long-talked-about free-trade area. Moving forward with integration may be made easier by recent emphasis on something less than consensus in the group, allowing a subset to go ahead with something that a few refused to do. This would follow an institutional example set by the EU for how to deal with internal disagreement. However, in the case of ASEAN, the "10 minus X" formula for "flexible consensus"[13] may do more to hasten the splintering of the group rather than its integration.

There is a substantive emptiness behind ASEAN as an international organization that is remarkable. It is a framework for possible future cooperation but not much more than that, which is to say that it is an excellent example of the "forum" function for an international organization. The existence of the organization may say more about the value that states attach today to the practices and rituals of international organization than it does about any shared interests of the Southeast Asian countries. It is an example of the importance that states see in being members of formalized and long-running inter-state cooperation, even where the cooperation is limited to the declaration of cooperation itself.

There has been an interesting controversy within the group over the presence of Myanmar as a member. It was admitted in 1997, in a mini-wave of expansion that the group hoped would solidify its standing as the primary

---

[13] Alice D. Ba describes these terms in *(Re) Negotiating East and Southeast Asia: Region, Regionalism, and the Association of Southeast Asian Nations.* Stanford University Press, 2009, pp. 154–155.

international organization representing the region. However, as the Myanmar regime moved itself from outcast to pariah in the 2000s, ASEAN found itself struggling to deal with both the internal and external politics that its presence in the organization created. The internal problem cannot be traced to Myanmar's failure to comply with any rules of the ASEAN Declaration or its Charter since, as we have seen, there are no such formal obligations to violate – though it may well be in violation of the vaguely worded provisions on the norms of the "ASEAN way." It is rather a problem of how to embrace as a member a country with such an appalling human rights record. This controversy was in full boil even before Myanmar became a member and it was responsible for delaying its admission into the late 1990s. The aspiration to integrate the economies of the ASEAN 10 is challenged by the presence of Myanmar among them. The internal discomfort at having Myanmar as a member has been exacerbated by the external pressure the group has felt to deal more forcefully with Rangoon. Foreign governments have expected ASEAN to have some leverage over Myanmar, or to use what leverage it has more convincingly, and the failure to have much impact has been interpreted as a failure of the organization more generally.[14] Many voices inside and outside ASEAN believe it should expel Myanmar rather than continue to tolerate its malpractices.

The ASEAN framework presents few formal commitments or obligations for its members. It provides a means for negotiating future steps toward integration but it gives few clues as to what these might be or how it will overcome its internal disagreements. The African Union Constitutive Act at least spells out what its future institutions might be, and the states of the AU have succeeded in agreeing on the required protocol to bring one of these, the Peace and Security Council, into existence. This has made the AU into an actor in the inter-state affairs of Africa to a degree (limited though it is) that the ASEAN organization has never managed to be. Both, of course, follow in the shadow of the European Union, which has come to define the archetypal model for projects of regional integration. While it is often said that the EU is sui generis, it is also true that the AU and ASEAN have borrowed heavily from the language and structures that describe the European Union.

---

[14] See for instance "ASEAN's Mid-Life Crisis," *The Economist*, August 2, 2007, and Lee Hudson Teslik, "The ASEAN Bloc's Myanmar Dilemma," Council on Foreign Relations Analysis Brief, October 2, 2007.

Organization of American States

key facts

Headquarters: Washington, DC

Members: 35 countries

Website: www.oas.org

Mandate: to promote "democracy for peace, security, and development" in the Americas.

Key structures: General Assembly of all members, Meeting of Consultation of Ministers of Foreign Affairs, Permanent Council (of ambassadors), various councils and committees.

Key obligations: to settle disputes by peaceful means, to respond collectively to acts of aggression, to refuse to recognize non-democratic changes of government among the members.

Enforcement: the Meeting of Consultation can impose sanctions or use force against a member that violates terms of the Rio Treaty (1947).

Key clauses of the OAS Charter:

Article 2: The OAS, in order to put into practice the principles on which it is founded . . . proclaims the following essential purposes:
a) to strengthen the peace and security of the continent;
b) to promote and consolidate representative democracy . . .;
c) . . . to ensure the pacific settlement of disputes . . .;
d) to provide for common action on the part of those States in the event of aggression;
Article 3: The American States reaffirm the following principles:
a) international law is the standard of conduct of States in their reciprocal relations; . . .
b) every state has the right to choose, without external interference, its political, economic, and social system . . .;
c) the elimination of extreme poverty is an essential part of the promotion . . . of representative democracy . . .;
d) the American States condemn wars of aggression: victory does not give rights;
Article 9
A Member of the Organization whose democratically constituted government has been overthrown by force may be suspended from the exercise of the right to participate in the sessions of the General Assembly, the Meeting of Consultation, the Councils of the Organization and Specialized Conferences as well as in the commissions, working groups and any other bodies established.

The Organization of American States links thirty-five countries of North, South, and Central America. It is founded on the Charter of the Organization of American States (1948), which itself followed after decades of intergovernmental cooperation agreements and conferences dating to the late nineteenth century, most notably the Pan-American Union (1890) and the Act of Chapultepec (1945, a collective security commitment). Like the AU and ASEAN, the OAS has few substantive powers and it is best seen as a framework or a shell. It is heavily influenced by the priorities of the US, by far its strongest member, and it was historically mainly used to promote an anti-Soviet agenda in the Americas. More recently, it has taken on a role in policing democratic governance, notably by declaring all non-constitutional changes of government in its members to be illegal and illegitimate.

The goals and principles set out in the OAS Charter will be familiar to readers of the UN Charter as much of the language is similar. It preserves the sovereignty of its member states and limits the authority of the institution in Article 1, which says that the OAS "has no powers other than those expressly conferred upon it by this Charter, none of whose provisions authorizes it to intervene in matters that are within the internal jurisdiction of the Member States." This echoes the domestic jurisdiction clause in Article 2(7) of the UN Charter, discussed in Chapter 3. (As we shall see below, the definition of an "internal matter" has been controversial for the OAS, though on different terms than at the UN.) OAS members also commit to "the fundamental rights of the individual without distinction as to race, nationality, creed, or sex" (Art. 31) – though interestingly when referring to Foreign Ministers and other officials, the English version of the Charter uses the pronoun "he" exclusively.

The OAS Charter asserts the independence of the member states (Art. 3b, Art. 10, and more) as well as their commitment to peaceful dispute settlement (Chapter V), collective security of the members (Chapter VI), development (Chapter VII), and democratic governance. It also creates a number of organs and institutions, including the OAS General Assembly, a Juridical Committee (to promote codification of international law), the Inter-American Commission on Human Rights (to report on human rights in each state), and a forum of states' foreign ministers known as the Meeting of Consultation.

The General Assembly is the collection of member states of the organization, analogous to the Assembly of States Parties in the ICC or the UN General Assembly. It meets once per year and is the main policy-making organ of the OAS, and decides the budget of the organization and apportions dues among members, as well as deciding on "general action and policy of the Organization" (Art. 54).

In practice, much of the energy in the OAS comes from decisions taken at the Meeting of Consultation of Ministers of Foreign Affairs. These are the settings where the political initiatives of states enter into the framework of the OAS, and where big conflicts take place. It was this body that suspended Cuba from participation in 1962 after the Cuban revolution, and which suspended Honduras after the coup d'état of 2009.

These two crises help to show the legal and political role that the OAS has developed for itself in the Americas. Both Cuba and Honduras lost their privileges in the OAS due to changes in government which were seen as unacceptable to a powerful section of the membership. Their offenses were different, but in both cases the governments were not seen to be protected by key clauses in the Charter regarding sovereignty, autonomy, or self-government (see Ch. IV of the Charter). How this came to pass is therefore interesting for considering the place of the OAS in international politics.

For Cuba, the OAS made strong statements to the effect that its communist form of government was in itself reason enough to bar it from participating. The Consultation of Ministers said that "adherence … to Marxism-Leninism is incompatible with the Inter-American system and the alignment of such a government with the communist bloc breaks the unity and solidarity of the continent."[15] It declared more generally that "the principles of communism are incompatible with the principles of the inter-American system."

There was no discussion of how this conclusion fit with the legal prohibition in the OAS Charter against interfering in the domestic affairs of member states. Indeed, Article 3e would seem precisely to protect the domestic sovereignty of member states: it says "Every State has the right to choose, without external interference, its political, economic, and social system and to organize itself in the way best suited to it, and has the duty to abstain from intervening in the affairs of another State."

It is apparent from the 1962 debate that the OAS at the time understood communist government as ipso facto external interference within the legal meaning of Article 3e. This is clear from the language used elsewhere in the Consultation of Ministers' report that explained the decision. Among other classic artifacts of Cold War language, it said "The Ministers have been able to verify that the subversive offensive of communist governments… has intensified," and "In order to achieve their subversive purposes and hide their true

---

[15] OAS Eighth Meeting of Consultation of Ministers of Foreign Affairs, 1962, p.14. www.oas.org/columbus/docs/OEASerCII.8Eng.pdf. Accessed January 28, 2013.

intentions, the communist governments and their agents exploit the legitimate needs of the less-favored sectors of the population." The tension between the OAS Charter's rule of non-interference and the expulsion of Cuba was resolved to the satisfaction of the US and its allies by the finding that "The subversive methods of communist governments and their agents constitute one of the most subtle and dangerous forms of intervention in the internal affairs of other states." By defining a communist government as in itself a form of foreign intervention, the OAS in 1962 reconciled the fact that it was passing judgment against the domestic organization of a sovereign member state.

It was episodes such as this that earned the OAS the reputation throughout the Cold War of being an instrument of American foreign policy, and indeed of being an extension of the Monroe Doctrine by which the US claimed the right to oversee and perhaps overthrow governments throughout the hemisphere. In the OAS the US found a useful tool with which to continue this influence, with the added benefit of being a multilateral institution founded on the consent of the members. This illustrates the "resource" view of international organizations presented in Chapter 2 of this book. It is interesting to consider how and why the OAS was useful in both mitigating and perhaps limiting US power in Latin America. Cuba was allowed to return to the OAS only in 2009, but has not yet chosen to actively participate in the organization.

The Honduras crisis of 2009 shares some similarity with the Cuban episode as far as the OAS is concerned. Both involved governments being overthrown from within, and both led to the country being suspended from the OAS. In Honduras, President Manuel Zelaya was removed from office by the military, backed by the Supreme Court, in response to his plans for a referendum on constitutional reforms. His ouster was, depending on one's reading of the constitution, either an emergency measure to protect the constitution or an unconstitutional coup d'état. The US and many other states saw it as the latter, and they invoked Article 9 of the OAS Charter (a member "whose democratically constituted government has been overthrown by force may be suspended from the exercise of the right to participate"). This was widely seen as a successful exercise of a new norm in the Americas, by which countries refuse to recognize non-democratic changes in government. After the coup, President Zelaya fled the country, snuck back in, semi-reconciled with the new government, changed his mind, fled again, and finally returned to Honduras in 2011 though he never regained his post. The OAS restored the country's privilege of participation in 2011.

These cases help to show one version of an inherent problem in all international organizations: where do the sovereign rights of the state end and its answerability to the collective begin? With its Article 9, the OAS has taken on a relatively broad right to pass judgment on domestic governance structures of its members. The application of this rule will depend on how the strongest OAS members interpret both the rule and developments in other countries, and so one can expect it to be both uneven and politically motivated. Still, it represents an interesting innovation in the history of international organizations.

Conclusion

Regional organizations represent an intriguing category of international organizations. They exist as mechanisms for coordinating the policies of a regional group of states, and as such they begin in concept as empty vessels into which substantive obligations may be added. The EU contains such enormous obligations that it confounds the concept of "inter-state organization." The African Union and ASEAN rest at the other end of the spectrum, demonstrating that it is possible for an international organization to exist as a forum without substantive content. The substantive obligations of members await decisions by the plenary bodies regarding what the common policies of the organizations shall be, and these might never come. The OAS has had two substantive projects in its history, first anti-communism and later pro-democracy, and its relationship to the internal sovereignty of its members depends on seeing these as something other than internal choices made by governments.

These regional organizations take upon themselves the project of integrating the economies and polities of their member states. They therefore have a different central purpose than do all of the other organizations in this book, whose authority is always bounded by the terms of a single substantive issue area (such as trade for the WTO, balance of payments for the IMF, and international security for the UN Security Council) or to commitments whose limits are known in advance (as with the UN Charter). They also therefore have a different kind of political problem at their core: as regional integration has come to be perceived as a cause worth proclaiming, they encourage governments to make grand statements in favor of integration while perhaps remaining in practice committed to their own national autonomy. They are arguably therefore more likely to be empty promises, where there is no reasonable expectation that the integrationist sentiments in their Charters will be implemented. The accomplishments of the EU come alongside a good deal of this kind of hypocrisy (or hopefulness), as evidenced by the gap between statements and reality regarding common defense and military policies.

The striking difference between these regional organizations and the other international organizations in this book is that the former prioritize cooperation ahead of the substantive problems for which cooperation might be a solution, while the latter address a particular problem for which international organization is a solution. In other words, these regional organizations were originally motivated by the general desire to integrate their members, and the substantive policy questions which might become integrated were identified later. Thus, the African Union Constitutive Act establishes a structure of meetings for the heads of government (in the Assembly of the Union) and a decision rule, and leaves it entirely up to the Assembly to identify problems and solutions which could be discussed through this procedure. The ASEAN Charter makes a similar move. The implications of this have already been addressed but the reasons for it are puzzling and highly suggestive.

What explains the appeal of regional organizations, and why now? And what explains their appeal in situations (such as ASEAN) where the countries have little reason to believe that they will be able to agree on common policies of significance with their partners? Do countries believe that by creating the architecture of a regional forum they may be moving themselves closer to an agreement on the substance of (for instance) a customs union? Do strong states see an advantage in institutionalizing their regional dominance through an international organization, and if so do the weaker partners recognize this, or do they believe they are increasing their leverage by means of the institution?

All of these questions suggest that the practice of regional integration contains interesting features that may be inextricable from the political and economic environment in which they arrive. The OAS was a relatively unmasked extension of American anti-communist foreign policy in Central and South America. Ultimately, the explanation for ASEAN and the AU may have more to do with their placement relative to other powerful actors in international politics than it does with their contribution to the economic integration of the members. This contrasts with the EU, where the original motivation to pool coal, steel, and then trade policies seems clearly driven by internal motives – even though the desire to keep the EU a perpetual-motion machine toward ever-more integration has an air of insecurity about it, as the 2016 Brexit referendum demonstrated.

Further Reading

The EU's website (www.europa.eu) is elaborate and informative on the structures and history of the organization. It tends toward the self-serving, and so for information on the controversies and trade-offs that make the organization interesting one could look at high-quality media sources (in English, the *Guardian* and the *Financial Times* provide excellent coverage of current developments) and at scholarly networks and journals (such as the *Journal of Common Market Studies*, the *European Law Journal*, and the European Union Studies Association and its publications). There are many good books on the EU but the frequent changes in EU structure mean that they quickly become dated. See Eric Jones, Anand Menon, and Stephen Wetherill (eds.), *The Oxford Handbook on the European Union* (Oxford University Press, 2012), Michelle Cini and Nieves Perez-Solorzano Borragan (eds.), *European Union Politics* (Oxford University Press, 2010), and Andreas Staab, *The European Union Explained: Institutions, Actors, Global Impact* (Indiana University Press, 2nd edn., 2011). On the African Union, see Samuel M. Makinda and F. Wafula Okumu, *The African Union: Challenges of Globalization, Security, and Governance* (Routledge, 2007), and sections of Rodrigo Tavares, *Regional Security: The Capacity of International Organizations* (Routledge, 2009). For a longer history, see the excellent book by Christopher Clapham, *Africa and the International System* (Cambridge University Press, 1996). The Tavares book is also useful for thinking about ASEAN's potential role in security affairs and that subject is also treated in depth by Alice D. Ba, *(Re) Negotiating East and Southeast Asia* (Stanford University Press, 2009). On ASEAN more generally, see Mark Beeson, *Institutions of the Asia-Pacific: ASEAN, APEC and Beyond* (Routledge, 2008). The AU and ASEAN websites can be useful as a starting point but they provide little beyond the basic details.

11 Conclusion

The legal hierarchy between international organizations and their member states is interestingly unclear. The organizations are clearly the products of state decisions but the particular legal commitments that states make to international organizations mean that states by definition will find themselves legally subordinated to the rules, decisions, or procedures of the organizations. And while international organizations have few coercive tools of enforcement, it is not costless to states to violate these rules. The costs to violation come in many currencies, both internal and external, both explicit and subtle. The practical power of an international organization may therefore be either more or less than is revealed in its legal charter, and indeed it may be both more and less. To study the impact of international organizations in world politics today requires looking closely at individual cases and crises rather than aiming for generalizations.

All international organizations face the same fundamental problem: how to influence their members to comply with the commitments they made upon joining the organization. These are institutions that exist by virtue of authority delegated to them by states and yet their purpose is to constrain or otherwise shape those same states. The success of an international organization can be judged by the metric of whether its members carry out their obligations, and it is generally considered a glaring failure when a member is blatant in its non-compliance. Filling the interstices between sovereign states, international organizations are the results of inter-state agreements but their functions and their utility in the world depend on changing how those states behave or think. This book has been organized around the investigation of how and whether countries fulfill their commitments to the organizations that they have created.

Each organization in this book tells a different version of this common story. They display various techniques that induce state compliance. Some, like the UN Security Council, are given decisive powers of enforcement with which to encourage compliance and to punish non-compliance. Others strive to maximize compliance by making the obligations as easy as possible to satisfy, as the ILO does by allowing states to choose which of its labor conventions they will adopt. Others, such as the World Trade Organization, incorporate disciplining powers by which the members themselves may retaliate directly against violators, and these powers are encoded in legal procedures managed by the organization. The organization retains its position as legally superior to states and delegates the practical enforcement powers back down to them.

The two lending organizations, the IMF and the World Bank, follow a different strategy, taking advantage of the long-term interests that their members have in maintaining the ability to borrow at low interest rates. This leverage over their members reflects the organizations' particular power as lenders – as well as members' interest in being able to continue to borrow – and it is not a tool that is available to other international organizations. Thus, the different ways the organizations are structured to induce compliance reflect differences in their historical origins and in the political contexts in which they operate. None of these techniques is foolproof, and the practical life of each organization involves constant negotiation between the organization, its members, and outside players over compliance, contestation, and enforcement.

Each organization is also characterized by a complex relationship with its environment. Most of them are highly dependent on the cooperation of other actors for their success. As a result, most of them are also destined for failure if they cannot gain the collaboration of these key outsiders. This is perhaps most stark in the case of United Nations peace operations, for which the UN Security Council has the legal capacity but none of the material resources that make them real. Chapter 4 described how each peace operation rests on two pillars: a legal mandate from the Council and a set of contributions of personnel and resources from states. The first is entirely under the control of the Council, in the sense that the Council decides for itself what constitutes a threat to international peace and security and what kind of peace mission should be sent to deal with it. The second is almost entirely *not* under the control of the Council. Resources come from voluntary contributions made by UN member states. These states are obligated in a general way to assist the Council (by Articles 43, 45, and 49 among others) but in practice each operation presents a discrete case for which new contributions must be sought. If the Council and the Secretary-General are unable to arrange for sufficient material contributions, the Council's authority to create legal mandates becomes irrelevant, and so the Council can be held hostage by its troop-contributing countries. If the Council fails to take effective action on a case, it could be because of a failure of the Council or a failure of the UN members to contribute to it.

Most international organizations find themselves in a condition of dependence on other actors. In some cases these others are powerful states, and sometimes they might be other international organizations or even private actors. The World Trade Organization is highly dependent on both private firms and on government tariff choices, both of which are outside its scope of authority. The WTO is, in effect, a set of rules about how government policy is allowed to influence trade patterns. It has nothing to say about what actual tariffs those governments should charge on imports; that is up to the governments to decide for themselves, and to negotiate among themselves. It also relies on the self-interest of the member governments to police violations of the rules, both in pressing a complaint at the Dispute Settlement Body and in imposing retaliatory tariffs if the case is supported. Moreover, its ultimate objective is to influence the behavior of the private firms that conduct international trade, and yet it has no authority to set any policy or pass any judgment relating to firms directly. It seeks to influence firms by influencing the states that influence them. There are many important steps that intervene between the WTO's rules and the practical decisions of international trade. The same could be said of the distance between the International Labor Organization and the practical working standards in any ILO member country.

The International Criminal Court exists in a dramatically dependent condition. It relies on its members (and perhaps even non-members) to capture suspected criminals and help gain the information about their conduct that will form the basis of its cases. It also asks its members to contribute prison space to hold those who are sentenced to jail. These forms of assistance are all legally required of ICC members under the Rome Statute, and so at the level of legal formalism there is no doubt that they are compelling obligations. Their practical application in relation to particular cases is of course another matter, and one that is subject to myriad cross-cutting influences. The enforcement challenges faced by the Court are a product of this dependence on others.

Dependency does not mean powerlessness. These organizations that rely on the cooperation of others may still be enormously powerful, even over apparently strong states. Recognizing the diverse ways that international organizations might exercise power over states is important in getting a realistic picture of the effects and consequences of international organizations. Michael Barnett and Raymond Duvall have described four components of social power which are useful in understanding the different kinds of influence that international organizations can have.[1] These are the compulsory, institutional, structural, and productive aspects of power. Where an international organization directly controls a state and causes it to change its policy we see the "compulsory" form of power. This was on display when, for instance, the United Nations inserted itself into the domestic governance of Cambodia in the 1990s, and when the US changed its trade and environmental policies after losing the Shrimp-Turtles case at the WTO. But not all influence comes in such a direct form, and to focus only on those moments where a state is directly challenged by an international organization would understate the influence of the latter. The International Labor Organization is exercising its power when it requires that states give consideration to adopting its conventions. This is a form of "institutional" power in the language of Barnett and Duvall. It may not in itself produce much by way of improved labor conditions, but the capacity to insert an item on the legislative agenda of domestic institutions is a form of power – it causes the institutions of the state to consider an issue they would not otherwise have considered – and the results of that power are impossible to know in advance. There may be instances where this sets in motion a process that leads to a substantive result.

The IMF displays a form of power different than both of these examples. States approach the IMF with a request for a loan, and the two parties negotiate a set of policy changes upon which the loan is conditional. The Fund's conditions are built from its pre-existing conceptual framework that explains how markets and societies operate and its structural adjustment programs contribute to institutionalizing these ideas in the political economy of the borrower. The state remains formally free to accept the loans or walk away, and so it is not under the influence of direct coercion or institutional power (both of which are premised on the absence of choice for the actor). But the state also knows that accepting the policy changes is a precondition for access to the loan, and the unbreakable connection between the two appears to the state as a structural reality of the world in which it exists. The IMF can cause changes in the policies of sovereign states without deploying threats or coercion; the changes are made by choice by the states themselves as they strive to navigate the international

---

[1] Michael Barnett and Raymond Duvall, "Power in International Politics," *International Organization*, 2005, **59**: 39–75.

institutional environment as best they can. This is "structural" power. The Fund's position in the structure of international power makes it an actor with influence over others, and its operation propagates an ideology of private-market capitalism further into the international system.

The final category of power ("productive" power) has been neatly described by Martha Finnemore in her history of humanitarian intervention.[2] She describes two hundred years of changes in the ideas held by people about when it is appropriate for states to use force. At the end of the nineteenth century, it was considered entirely reasonable for the US to forcefully seize the customs houses of countries that owed it money and collect revenue from them until the debt was repaid. This idea has gone away – if a state behaved this way today it would likely be met with outrage and disbelief. After World War II, the idea that military force could be used to defend innocent citizens from the depredations of their own governments gradually became common currency. The details of such interventions remain controversial, and likely always will be, but Finnemore's point is that this development opened a new way to justify military intervention in other states. In a general sense, the idea of humanitarian intervention has become legitimate, and the consequences for international law and politics are significant. The parameters of humanitarian intervention have largely been developed in the United Nations, and the UN Security Council is the primary actor with the power to legitimate any particular instance of the concept. The UN has had a productive role in defining this category of behavior for states, and in legitimating it. This is a powerful thing, though it does not fit any of the previous three conceptions of power. The ability to define the categories and ideas of society, and to define them as normal or legitimate, or as taken for granted, is a potentially transformative kind of power (thus, Barnett and Duvall's "productive" form of power). International organizations sometimes find themselves with this capacity. Aside from humanitarian intervention, other examples might be the ideas of the Washington consensus in the IMF and World Bank, the ideas of state sovereignty in the UN Charter, and perhaps the ideas of regional affinity that are put into practice by the AU, ASEAN, and the EU, as well as in the WTO rules on regional customs unions.

These different ways that international organizations can exercise power over states are important also when we attempt to assess the success or failure of an international organization. How do we know if an international organization is

[2] Martha Finnemore, *The Purpose of Intervention: Changing Beliefs about the Use of Force.* Cornell University Press, 2004.

a success? The question of success is multifaceted, as are the goals and capacities of the organizations, and there is probably no single measure that can aggregate all aspects of the organization into a metric of success. Still, it is instructive to examine some of the most common ways of assessing it in order to see both where they might be most useful and also what they reveal about our expectations regarding international organizations.

For a new organization such as the International Criminal Court, we might measure success by the growth in its membership. The very quick addition of members to the ICC is a sign that something about the organization has great appeal for many states, and this is undoubtedly evidence of success of some kind. The converse would presumably hold as well: had the Rome Statute not attracted signatories, it would have been considered a failure. By this metric, more popular organizations are more successful, and those with fewer members are less successful. The African Union often cites its near-universal membership (based on its target audience of African countries) as a sign of its importance and its success. This approach to success leaves open many questions, of course, since it does not address why countries are joining (or not joining), or what they are doing (or not doing) as a result of membership, or how to interpret the absence of certain countries. For the ICC, its fast growth in membership leaves out the United States, China, Russia, India, and Pakistan, among others. Their absence does not in itself mean the Court cannot be a success, but it does show the complexity of using membership numbers as a proxy for success – more members may or may not mean a more successful organization – and so we need further information to judge the organization.

A second approach to success suggests that the longevity or persistence of the international organization is a useful metric. This can make sense in some cases – for instance, the UN Security Council managed to survive the Cold War despite having within it as permanent members the Soviet Union, China, and the United States. The Council's ability to avoid collapse is in part a function of its designers' foresight in including the veto for the permanent members. The veto allowed each of the most powerful players to remain in the organization with the full confidence that the Council could never be used directly against their interests. Had the Council been built on a majority-voting scheme without the veto, no doubt it would have imploded at some point in the Cold War. The Council persisted, and this is a success of some kind. The trade-off is that the Council went into a kind of vegetative state on important questions, unable to take action, in order to avoid inciting its members to rebel against each other and against the institution.

The ILO has a long history as well, the longest of any organization in this book (though the PCIJ adds to the ICJ's score on this scale), and it could perhaps be given credit for persistence in a complex and politicized field. However, the ILO's technique for survival has been from the start to set low expectations and avoid controversial issues. It has never had, nor has it sought, the power to confront states that accept terrible working conditions; it allows its members to choose for themselves what rules will apply to them; it does not even insist that all members accept what it considers to be the eight "core" labor standards. It has persisted for almost a century by taking the least controversial path through a very controversial topic. The Myanmar case discussed in Chapter 7 represents perhaps the most controversy-seeking moment in the organization's history, and it remains to be seen whether its confrontational approach in this instance will lead to a better or worse outcome, or a stronger or weaker organization.

Finally, perhaps the ideal measure of success should be "effectiveness" – that is, to what degree does the organization succeed in bringing about the effects for which it was established? By this standard, we could ask that the ILO be measured against the conditions of labor in its member countries. We would expect the UN to be held accountable if the rate of inter-state war among its members rose rather than fell after it came into being. The ICC could be assessed on the number of successful prosecutions for international crimes, or perhaps on the number of serious crimes that were deterred by its presence. These are after all the goals for which the organizations were invented. The ICC example, however, begins to show the difficulty with this approach: it requires that we have a clear sense of what the goals of the organization really are (or were), and in many cases this is not as clear as it seems. Was the ICC established to deter crimes, or to prosecute criminals, or both – or something else? If the purpose of the ICC was in fact to express the outrage felt by much of the world in response to the existence of genocide, war crimes, and crimes against humanity, or to express a common humanity among those who work against these atrocities, then its success begins to be seen differently. If it had an expressive and symbolic purpose to begin with, then it may have already succeeded, even without its first conviction. The ambiguity in the goals of the organizations afflicts all of these international bodies. The ILO, after all, sets for itself the goal of encouraging its members to consider adopting its labor standards. It does not include the goal of forcing them to actually adopt them. Is its effectiveness then measured by the rate of adoption of conventions, or the rate at which conventions are considered by states, or by the actual working conditions in the countries? There is a wide range of effects in the world that might be a sign of power, influence, or effectiveness for an international organization (domestic influence, making new norms, setting voluntary standards, and on and on).

Assessing the effectiveness of an international organization presumes that we know a great deal about its goals. For that, we need to return to the original charters and treaties that establish the organizations and examine what legal obligations they really create for their members. It is only by looking at what the organizations actually require of members that we can begin to judge whether they have succeeded in their goals or not. Organizations are empty vessels until we provide them with substantive goals. This turns attention back to the formal obligations of members, those written in the texts of their legal documents, and with this we return to the premise set out at the start of this book.

Index